Secure Health

In today's interconnected world, healthcare systems are increasingly turning to digital technologies to enhance patient care and optimize operations. However, this digital transformation presents significant challenges in guaranteeing the security and privacy of sensitive healthcare data. *Secure Health: A Guide to Cybersecurity for Healthcare Managers* confronts these challenges head-on, offering a comprehensive exploration of the latest advancements and best practices in securing digital health systems.

From examining the convergence of Internet of Things (IoT) applications with healthcare privacy and security to investigating ethical hacking frameworks and biometric access management, each chapter delves into valuable insights for safeguarding healthcare data in an ever-more digitized landscape. What sets this book apart is its holistic perspective, encompassing not only technical aspects but also governance standards, the unique cybersecurity challenges of telehealth, and the optimization of healthcare supply chain management.

KEY FEATURES:

- Explores the integration of IoT devices into healthcare and the associated privacy and security risks.
- Examines security frameworks and best practices for e-health information governance.
- Introduces a novel framework for ethical hacking in digital health.
- Analyzes the effectiveness of different artificial intelligence (AI) models for botnet traffic classification.
- Delves into the unique challenges of securing telehealth and remote monitoring systems.
- Offers practical guidance on securing the future of e-health through smart sensor network management.

Secure Health

A Guide to Cybersecurity for Healthcare Managers

Edited by
Mohamed Hammad, Gauhar Ali, Mohammed A. El-Affendi, Yassine Maleh, and Ahmed A. Abd El-Latif

CRC Press
Taylor & Francis Group
Boca Raton London New York

CRC Press is an imprint of the
Taylor & Francis Group, an **informa** business

Designed cover image: © Shutterstock

First edition published 2025
by CRC Press
2385 NW Executive Center Drive, Suite 320, Boca Raton FL 33431

and by CRC Press
4 Park Square, Milton Park, Abingdon, Oxon, OX14 4RN

CRC Press is an imprint of Taylor & Francis Group, LLC

ISBN: 978-1-032-74265-6 (hbk)
ISBN: 978-1-032-74601-2 (pbk)
ISBN: 978-1-003-47003-8 (ebk)

DOI: 10.1201/9781003470038

Typeset in Sabon
by Apex CoVantage, LLC

Contents

About the Editors

Mohamed Hammad received his Ph.D. degree in 2019 from the School of Computer Science and Technology, Harbin Institute of Technology, Harbin, China. He is an assistant professor at the Faculty of Computers and Information, Menoufia University, Egypt. He is currently a researcher at the Emerging Intelligent Autonomous Systems (EIAS) Data Science Lab, College of Computer and Information Sciences, Prince Sultan University. His research interests include biomedical imaging, bioinformatics, cybersecurity, Internet of Things (IoT), computer vision, machine learning, deep learning, pattern recognition, and biometrics. He has published more than 50 papers in international Science Impact Factor (SCI-IF) journals. Furthermore, he has served as an editorial board member in *PLOS ONE* journal, an editorial board member in *BMC Bioinformatics* journal, an associate editor in *IJISP*, a topics board editor in *Forensic Sciences* journal, a guest editor in many international journals such as *IJDCF*, *Sensors* journal, and *Information* journal. He has reviewed more than 500 papers for many prestigious journals and is listed in the top 2% of scientists worldwide (according to the recently released list by Stanford University, USA, in 2022 and 2023).

Gauhar Ali received his M.S. degree in computer science from the Institute of Management Sciences, Peshawar, Pakistan, in 2012, and Ph.D. degree in computer science from the University of Peshawar, Peshawar, since 2019. He is currently a postdoctoral researcher with the *Emerging Intelligent Autonomous Systems EIAS* Data Science and Blockchain Laboratory, College of Computer and Information Sciences, Prince Sultan University, Riyadh, Saudi Arabia. His research interests include the Internet of Things, access control, blockchain, machine learning, wireless sensor networks, intelligent transportation systems, formal verification, and model checking.

Mohammed A. El-Affendi is currently a professor of computer science with the Department of Computer Science, Prince Sultan University. He is the former Dean of College of Computer and Information Sciences (CCIS), AIDE; the Rector, Founder, and Director of the Data Science Laboratory

(EIAS); and the Founder and Director of the Center of Excellence in CyberSecurity. His current research interests include data science, intelligent and cognitive systems, machine learning, and natural language processing.

Yassine Maleh received his Ph.D. degree in computer science from Hassan 1st University in Morocco, in 2017. He is currently a professor of cybersecurity and a practitioner with industry and academic experience. Since 2019, he worked as a professor in cybersecurity with Sultan Moulay Slimane University, Beni Mellal, Morocco. From 2012 to 2019, he was the Chief Security Officer with the National Ports Agency in Morocco. He is the Founding President of the African Research Center of Information Technology & Cybersecurity. He is a member of the International Association of Engineers and Machine Intelligence Research Labs. He has made contributions in the fields of information security and privacy, the IoT security, and wireless and constrained networks security. His research interests include information security and privacy, Internet of Things, networks security, information system, and IT governance. He has authored or coauthored more than 200 papers (book chapters, international journals, and conferences/workshops), 40 edited books, and 6 authored books. He is currently the Editor-in-Chief of the *International Journal of Information Security and Privacy* and *International Journal of Smart Security Technologies*. He also holds editorial positions, including Series Editor of *Advances in Cybersecurity Management* (CRC Press). Additionally, he serves as an academic editor or associate editor for many indexed journals in the Web of Science (WoS) and Scopus, covering various quartiles.

Ahmed A. Abd El-Latif graduated with distinction from the Harbin Institute of Technology, China, in 2013, earning his Ph.D. Since then, he has led and participated in several successful research projects and secured grants in Egypt, the Russian Federation, Saudi Arabia, China, Malaysia, and Tunisia. Currently, he holds staff positions at Menoufia University, Egypt, and Prince Sultan University, Saudi Arabia. With over 18 years of professional experience, he has published approximately 300 papers in journals and conference proceedings, including 12 books, with over 10,000 citations. Since 2022, he has served as a Head of the MEGANET 6G Lab Research in the Russian Federation. He holds several leadership positions, including Vice Chair of the EIAS Research Lab and Founder and Deputy Director of the Center of Excellence in Quantum & Intelligent Computing (Prince Sultan University, Saudi Arabia). He has received several awards, including the State Encouragement Award in Engineering Sciences from the Arab Republic of Egypt in 2016; the Best Ph.D. Student Award from the Harbin Institute of Technology, China, in 2013; and the Young Scientist Award from Menoufia University, Egypt, in 2014. He actively participates in the scientific community, serving as the Chair/Co-chair of several Scopus/EI conferences. He also holds editorial positions, including Editor-in-Chief of the *International Journal of Information Security and Privacy*, Series Editor of *Quantum Information Processing and Computing*, and Series Editor of *Advances in Cybersecurity Management* (CRC Press). Additionally, he serves as an academic editor or associate editor for many indexed journals in the Web of Science (WoS) and Scopus, covering various quartiles. His research interests span quantum communications and cryptography, cybersecurity, artificial intelligence of things (AioT), AI-based image processing, information hiding, and applications of dynamical systems (discrete-time models: chaotic systems and quantum walks) in cybersecurity.

Contributors

Gauhar Ali
EIAS: Data Science and Blockchain Lab
College of Computer and Information Sciences
Prince Sultan University
Riyadh, Saudi Arabia

Abdelhamied A. Ateya
EIAS: Data Science and Blockchain Lab
College of Computer and Information Sciences
Prince Sultan University
Saudi Arabia
And
Department of Electronics and Communications Engineering
Zagazig University
Zagazig, Egypt

Nur Syafika bin Bahrudin
Department of Computer Science
Kuliyyah of Information Communication Technology
International Islamic University Malaysia
Kuala Lumpur, Malaysia

Phuc Hao Do
The Bonch-Bruevich Saint-Petersburg State University of Telecommunications
Saint-Petersburg, Russian Federation
And
Danang Architecture University
Danang, Vietnam

Mohammed A. El-Affendi
EIAS: Data Science and Blockchain Lab
College of Computer and Information Sciences
Prince Sultan University
Riyadh, Saudi Arabia

Ahmed A. Abd El-Latif
EIAS: Data Science and Blockchain Lab
College of Computer and Information Sciences
Prince Sultan University
Riyadh, Saudi Arabia
and
Department of Mathematics and Computer Science
Faculty of Science
Menoufia University
Menoufia, Egypt

Muhammad Falikh Fikri bin Mohd Fauzi
Department of Computer Science
Kuliyyah of Information Communication Technology
International Islamic University Malaysia
Kuala Lumpur, Malaysia

Muhammad Hazrin Fahmi bin Abd Halim
Department of Computer Science
Kuliyyah of Information Communication Technology
International Islamic University Malaysia
Kuala Lumpur, Malaysia

Mohamed Hammad
EIAS: Data Science and Blockchain Lab
College of Computer and Information Sciences
Prince Sultan University
Riyadh, Saudi Arabia
and
Department of Information Technology
Faculty of Computers and Information
Menoufia University
Shibin El Kom, Egypt

Hafiz Adnan Hussain
Fakulti Teknologi dan Sains Maklumat (FTSM)
Universiti Kebangsaan Malaysia (UKM)
Kuala Lumpur, Malaysia

Uzma Jafar
Fakulti Teknologi dan Sains Maklumat (FTSM)
Universiti Kebangsaan Malaysia (UKM)
Bangi, Malaysia

Rohit Gupta Kunala
SASTRA University
Thanjavur, India

Tran Duc Le
Faculty of Information Technology, University of Science and Technology—University of Danang
Danang, Vietnam

Yassine Maleh
LaSTI Laboratory
Sultan Moulay Slimane University
Beni Mellal, Morocco

Nik Muhammd Faris Firdaus bin Norazman
Department of Computer Science
Kuliyyah of Information Communication Technology
International Islamic University Malaysia
Kuala Lumpur, Malaysia

Van Dai Pham
Department of Information Technology
Swinburne Vietnam, FPT University
Hà Nội, Vietnam

Padmapriya Pravinkumar
SASTRA University
Thanjavur, India

Kartheek Pusala
SASTRA University
Thanjavur, India

Amirtharjan R
SASTRA University
Thanjavur, India

Vijay Ramasamy
SASTRA University
Thanjavur, India

Abdelkebir Sahid
ENCG Settat, Hassan
1st University
Settat, Morocco

Lokesh Sakamuri
SASTRA University
Thanjavur, India

Aida bin Shahiedun
Department of Computer Science
Kuliyyah of Information
Communication Technology
International Islamic
University Malaysia
Kuala Lumpur, Malaysia

Issam Taqafi
Hassan 1st University
Settat, Morocco

Sai Chandana Thiruvuru
SASTRA University
Thanjavur, India

Thanh Liem Tran
IT Network Department
The University of Danang
Danang, Vietnam

Siva Swetha Vennapusa
SASTRA University
Thanjavur, India

Ahmad Anwar Bin Zainuddin
Department of Computer Science
Kuliyyah of Information
Communication Technology
International Islamic
University Malaysia
Kuala Lumpur, Malaysia

Chapter 1

Introduction

Mohamed Hammad, Gauhar Ali, Mohammed A. El-Affendi, Yassine Maleh, and Ahmed A. Abd El-Latif

Secure Health: A Guide to Cybersecurity for Healthcare Managers is a scholarly exploration of the intricate interplay between technology and healthcare security. In this introductory chapter, we embark on an academic journey through the dynamic landscape of digital transformation within the healthcare sector, emphasizing the paramount importance of cybersecurity in safeguarding patient data and ensuring operational resilience. The advent of the Internet of Things (IoT) has heralded a new epoch of possibilities, fundamentally altering the landscape of patient care, monitoring, and management. As healthcare managers grapple with the complexities of this technological paradigm, a nuanced understanding of the transformative potential of IoT applications becomes imperative. This compendium serves as a scholarly beacon, illuminating critical considerations and methodological best practices for harnessing the transformative power of IoT while concurrently mitigating associated risks. In our book, we present a cohesive narrative spanning seven chapters, each offering valuable insights and strategies for navigating the complex landscape of cybersecurity within the healthcare sector.

Starting with Chapter 2, "IoT Application, Privacy and Security in Healthcare: A Review," readers delve into the transformative impact of IoT on healthcare delivery. This chapter meticulously examines the multifaceted applications of IoT, highlighting its potential in chronic disease management, real-time monitoring, and personalized treatment modalities. Amidst the promises of IoT, the chapter addresses privacy and security concerns, offering insights into fortifying systems against cyber threats while ensuring patient confidentiality.

Chapter 3, "Securing Future of E-health: Challenges and Key Management Strategies in Smart Healthcare Sensor Networks," investigates how the Internet of Things (IoT) is revolutionizing embedded systems and communication technologies. Moreover, this study explores the revolutionary role of sensor networks in modern healthcare through real-time health evaluations and remote patient monitoring, with a specific focus on Wireless Body Area Networks (WBANs).

DOI: 10.1201/9781003470038-1

Moving forward, Chapter 4, "Securing Digital Health: A Comprehensive Ethical Hacking Framework and Comparative Analysis Using a Novel Hybrid Quality Evaluation Model," shifts the focus to cybersecurity methodologies. Here, readers are introduced to a novel ethical hacking framework designed specifically for healthcare cybersecurity. Through comparative analysis and a novel evaluation model, the chapter provides actionable strategies for enhancing technical specificity and adaptability in combating evolving cyber threats.

In Chapter 5, "Biometric Security and Access Management in E-health Services," the narrative pivots to explore the role of biometric technologies in safeguarding sensitive medical data. Readers gain insights into various biometric modalities such as fingerprint recognition and iris scanning, along with considerations for privacy, interoperability, and regulatory compliance.

Chapter 6, "Investigating the Effectiveness of Different GNN Models for IoT-Healthcare Systems Botnet Traffic Classification," delves into the burgeoning threat landscape of botnet attacks in IoT-enabled healthcare systems. Through a comprehensive investigation, readers explore the efficacy of GNN models in classifying and mitigating botnet traffic, thereby bolstering cybersecurity defenses.

The narrative continues in Chapter 7, "Addressing Unique Cybersecurity Challenges in Telehealth and Remote Physiologic Monitoring," where the focus shifts to the cybersecurity implications of telehealth and remote monitoring technologies. Here, readers gain insights into the multifaceted challenges facing healthcare providers, along with strategies for mitigating cyber risks and fostering a culture of cybersecurity resilience.

Chapter 8, "Optimum Transportation Scheme for Healthcare Supply Chain Management," delves into the critical importance of efficient supply chain management in healthcare delivery. Through a scholarly examination of transportation logistics optimization, readers explore strategies for enhancing the responsiveness and resilience of healthcare supply chains, ensuring the timely delivery of life-saving resources.

Finally, Chapter 9, "Securing Healthcare: A Comprehensive Examination of Information Security Governance Standards and Frameworks," explores healthcare information security governance standards and frameworks, addressing the need for robust protection amid evolving cyber threats and regulatory demands. It discusses the role of Health Information Systems (HIS) in healthcare delivery and their vulnerability to security threats. The chapter examines key information security standards like COBIT, ISO/IEC 27001:2005, and HITRUST CSF, alongside IT governance frameworks such as COBIT and ITIL. By synthesizing industry best practices, it provides actionable insights for healthcare IT professionals to enhance security, protect patient data, and ensure regulatory compliance in the digital healthcare landscape.

Throughout our book, *Secure Health: A Guide to Cybersecurity for Healthcare Managers*, readers are presented with a comprehensive narrative that synthesizes scholarly insights with practical imperatives. By embracing innovative solutions and strategic foresight, healthcare managers are empowered to navigate the complexities of cybersecurity, safeguarding patient welfare and organizational integrity in the digital age. Figure 1.1 shows a diagram outlining the chapters in this book.

Chapter 2: IoT Application, Privacy and Security in Healthcare: A Review
Authors: Ahmad Anwar Zainuddin, Muhammad Hazrin Fahmi bin Abd Halim, Nur Syafika Bahrudin, Aida Shahiedun, Nik Muhammd Faris Firdaus bin Norazman, and Muhammad Falikh Fikri Mohd Fauzi

Chapter 3: Securing Future of E-health: Challenges and Key Management Strategies in Smart Healthcare Sensor Networks
Author: Yassine Maleh and Issam Taqafi

Chapter 4: Securing Digital Health: A Comprehensive Ethical Hacking Framework and Comparative Analysis using a Novel Hybrid Quality Evaluation Model
Authors: Gauhar Ali, Mohammed El-Affendi, and Ahmed A. Abd El-Latif

Chapter 5: Biometric Security and Access Management in E-health Services
Author: Mohamed Hammad

Chapter 6: Investigating the Effectiveness of Different GNN Models for IoT-Healthcare Systems Botnet Traffic Classification
Authors: Phuc Hao Do, Thanh Liem Tran, Van Dai Pham, Abdelhamied A. Ateya, and Tran Duc Le

Chapter 7: Addressing Unique Cybersecurity Challenges in Telehealth and Remote Physiologic Monitoring
Authors: Uzma Jafar and Hafiz Adnan Hussain

Chapter 8: Optimum Transportation Scheme for Healthcare Supply Chain Management
Authors: Lokesh Sakamuri, Sai Chandana Thiruvuru, Rohit Gupta Kunala, Siva Swetha Vennapusa, Kartheek Pusala, Vijay Ramasamy, Amirtharjan R, and Padmapriya Pravinkumar

Chapter 9: Securing Healthcare: A Comprehensive Examination of Information Security Governance Standards and Frameworks
Author: Abdelkebir Sahid

Figure 1.1 Book outline.

Chapter 2

IoT Application, Privacy, and Security in Healthcare

A Review

Ahmad Anwar Zainuddin, Muhammad Hazrin Fahmi bin Abd Halim, Nur Syafika Bahrudin, Aida Shahiedun, Nik Muhammd Faris Firdaus bin Norazman, and Muhammad Falikh Fikri Mohd Fauzi

2.1 INTRODUCTION

Internet of Things (IoT) has been defined as a collection of networks that have many connections between devices and technologies. IoT is built to make sure the operation in this world runs smoothly and gives the value of services to better decision-making [1]. Healthcare is the treatment or services to take care of health and maintain it from damage to personal well-being. Healthcare can be delivered in various settings.

IoT integration entails incorporating various medical devices and applications that seamlessly connect with healthcare information technology. The concept of IoT in healthcare is to create a smart hospital environment where it can connect to healthcare IT systems over the Internet to improve patient care. Unfortunately, IoT in healthcare poses several issues in data security and privacy that may result in the release of private patient data, system disruptions, and patient safety risks [1].

This chapter consists of six sections describing IoT in healthcare. Section 2.1 covers the introduction. Section 2.2 outlines the methodology. Section 2.3 addresses the challenges and implementation, benefits and impact, application of IoT, impact, and privacy and security roles. Section 2.4 highlights the literature review. Section 2.5 discusses the crucial role in transforming education and healthcare.

2.2 METHODOLOGY

The methodology adopted for this study on IoT in healthcare encompasses a comprehensive approach that covers various aspects. The selection criteria for the literature review prioritize scholarly papers and articles published from 2018 onward, focusing on peer-reviewed journals, conference papers, and reputable sources. The search strategy involves utilizing academic databases such as IEEE Xplore, IJHPM, ScienceDirect, and Springer, employing relevant

DOI: 10.1201/9781003470038-2

keywords and filtering search results to ensure relevance and currency. Inclusion criteria encompass studies providing insights into the application of IoT in healthcare, implementation strategies, benefits and challenges, and privacy and security concerns. Exclusion criteria involve studies outside the specified domain or published before 2018, as well as non-peer-reviewed sources and duplicates. Data extraction and analysis entail systematic extraction of relevant data and thematic analysis to identify common themes such as application areas, implementation, benefits, and challenges of IoT in healthcare. Recommendations are formulated on the basis of identified gaps, challenges, and opportunities, with conclusions drawn regarding the significance of IoT in improving hospital operations, treatment outcomes, and patient care, while considering security aspects and emerging technologies.

2.3 IoT IN HEALTHCARE

2.3.1 Previous Challenges and IoT Implementation in Healthcare

Previously, medical records were recorded on a paper that lead to human error limited accessibility, privacy issues, security, and insufficient storage [2]. Medical records provide valuable data for studies to expand and advance the medical field [3]. Medical records can be stolen from healthcare facilities. Natural disasters such as floods are a concern while taking care of medical records. Recognizing the privacy and security risk associated with paper records led the society to prioritize protecting patient information.

There was an increase in the usage of IoT in the medical field during the outbreak of COVID-19 pandemic. Moreover, the rising prevalence of chronic disease has made the incorporation of IoT in healthcare. Increasing chronic contributes toward the implementation of IoT in healthcare. IoT can manage large volumes of patient data, including treatment histories, genetic information, and biometric data [4]. The process of transmitting data can provide data security and privacy that can be achieved through encryption and secure communication protocols. Implementing end-to-end security, regular updates, and compliance with regulations further strengthen the protection of sensitive health information. By applying IoT, it can help reduce human errors and cybersecurity risks. IoT provides real-time feedback on user performance, helping them identify and correct errors as they occur.

2.3.2 Benefits of IoT in Healthcare and Its Impact on Emerging Technology

Implementing IoT in healthcare benefits both patients and providers. IoT devices enable simultaneous reporting and monitoring, enhancing treatment outcomes and care. Remote patient monitoring reduces hospital visits and readmissions, enabling personalized care. Cost-effective interactions are facilitated through secure, real-time communication between patients, clinics, and healthcare institutions [5]. Patient data security is ensured through robust security measures, safeguarding sensitive information, and ensuring compliance with regulations [6].

The potential impact of emerging technologies on IoT in healthcare is important to give the opportunities to change the medical treatment of patients. Improvement of the technologies can lead to efficiency of the system including enabling accurate data collection, distributed computing, and data filtering [7]. Emerging technologies can give profit because they produce better technologies. IoT can manage large volumes of patient data, including treatment histories, genetic information, and biometric data [8].

2.3.3 IoT Applications in Healthcare

2.3.3.1 *Depression and monitoring mood*

Depression is a severe mental illness characterized by persistent sadness and a loss of interest. It is non-communicable and not contagious. IoT devices help monitor depression by providing discrete, real-time patient assessments, as well as gathering and examining physiological data about mental health [9]. Depression and mood monitoring can be done using various methods that are shown in Figure 2.1. The use of fitness trackers and smartwatches makes

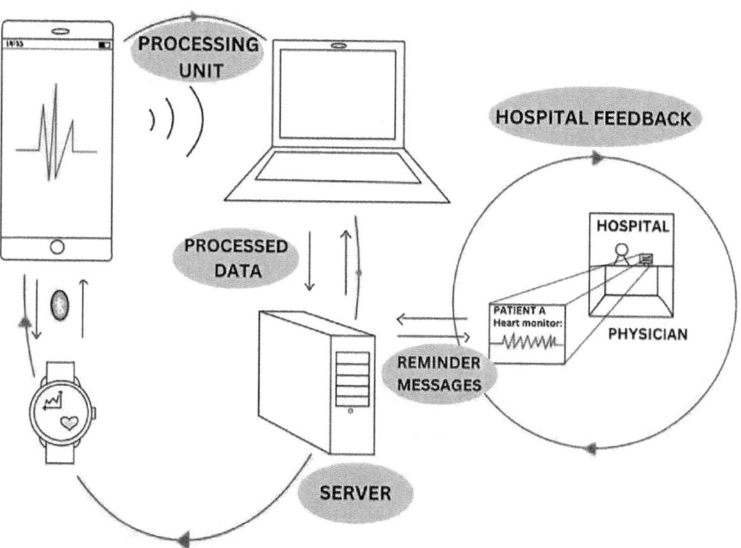

Figure 2.1 The process of transmitting patient data.

it possible to seamlessly collect physiological data related to mental health. These gadgets allow for real-time monitoring and offer vital information about a person's general well-being [10]. Machine learning models provide an advanced method through the analysis of digital data that is passive [11]. Furthermore, IoT platforms enable remote mood monitoring making it possible to track a person's mood from a distance, offering early intervention and support from medical professionals [12]. One benefit of depression monitoring is its ability to personalize treatment for patients [13].

2.3.3.2 Remote patient monitoring

Remote patient monitoring (RPM) is an innovation that offers opportunities to enhance health outcomes and provide cost-effective care. RPM technology allows the patient to be evaluated in a different way instead of the typical healthcare setting [14]. This data will be sent to the healthcare practitioner to identify the condition of the patient and provide the best care. RPM allows patient data to be forwarded and stored until reviewed by providers, enabling non-synchronous monitoring. Figure 2.2 illustrates RPM's process. Patients are given medical devices with sensors during check-up sessions to transmit to devices for remote monitoring by clinicians. RPM was reported to have reduced the use of acute care in approximately 45% of studies, and some reported to increase while the remaining reported no change [15]. RPM represents a significant yet relatively unexplored area for improving patient safety, achieving operational efficiencies, and decreasing the cost [16]. Introducing an RPM platform would have to be managed carefully to avoid corrupting records [17].

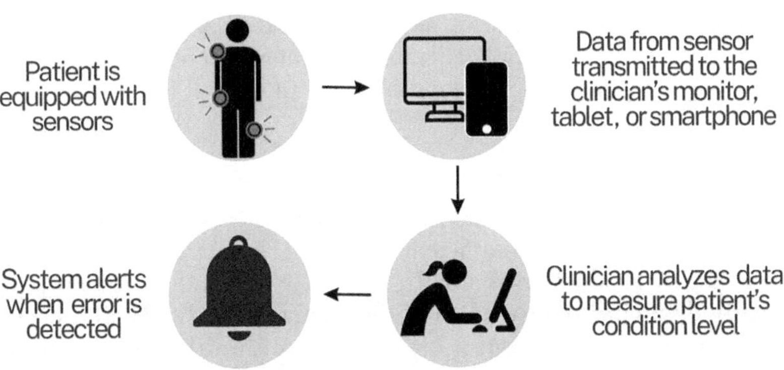

Figure 2.2 Remote patient monitoring.

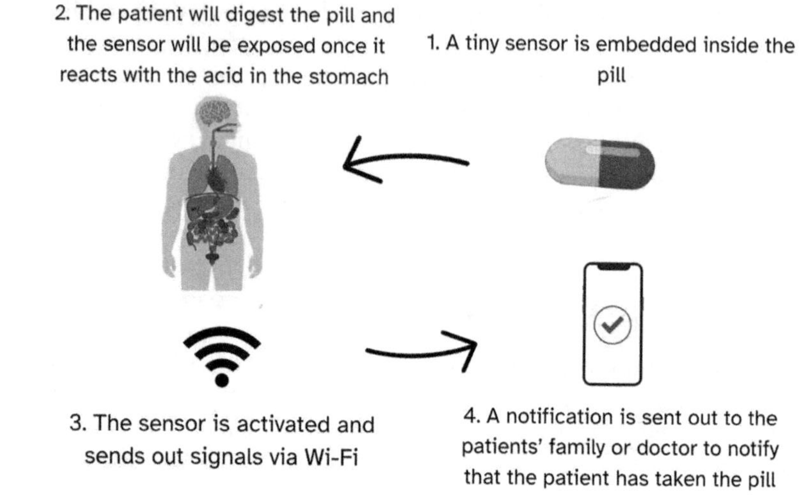

Figure 2.3 How ingestible sensors work.

2.3.3.3 Ingestible sensor

Ingestible sensors are small and non-invasive means of monitoring and collecting vital health data. Figure 2.3 shows that devices are integrated with wireless sensor systems and encapsulated in a pill. Then, they wirelessly transmit data to external devices for analysis. These sensors are equipped with various monitoring capabilities that allow them to track parameters within the body [18]. The data collected by these sensors can help doctors diagnose gastrointestinal difficulties and monitor various health parameters in real time. Ingestible sensors offer several benefits such as reducing the need for physical check-ups as patients can easily know through their health indicators such as calorie intake [19]. Moreover, these sensors enable continuous real-time monitoring of health parameters [20]. These sensors can improve disease diagnostics, monitoring, and management by providing detailed information on gut health and nutrient absorption. Moreover, these sensors have potential applications in sports and fitness monitoring.

2.3.3.4 Glucose monitoring

Type 1 diabetes happens when blood glucose level is too high because the body cannot produce sufficient insulin [21]. Type 2 diabetes happens when insulin production is not enough to withstand the glucose levels in the body due to the pancreas not working properly [21]. Blood sugar levels that go up and down a lot might harm health in ways including hyperglycemia and hypoglycemia [22]. Continuous Glucose Monitoring (CGM) is a tool that measures and estimates glucose level every minute and keeps track of it over time when you are wearing the device [23, 24]. Figure 2.4 displays how continuous glucose monitoring works. First, a

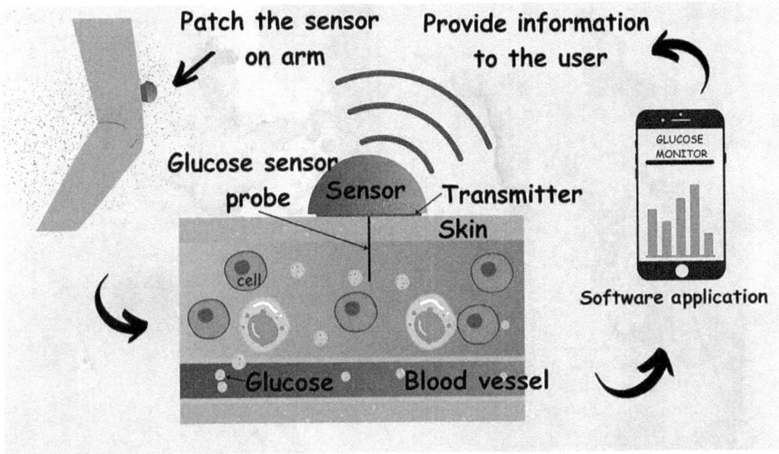

Figure 2.4 Continuous glucose monitoring.

sensor is inserted beneath your skin [25]. These sensors are called disposable sensors, and they are intended for short-term and rapid measurement [22]. Second, they transmit information without using any wire [25]. Lastly, the software application is stored on your smartphone and via it you can monitor your glucose levels [23, 24].

2.3.3.5 *IoT in percutaneous transluminal coronary angioplasty (PTCA)*

Coronary artery angioplasty also known as percutaneous transluminal coronary angioplasty (PTCA) is the procedure to make sure the artery widens because of plaque for blood can be transferred normally to the heart [26]. Figure 2.5 shows the steps in PTCA that is placing the needle into the artery for the sheath to go through the artery to find the clogged vessel. A catheter will be advanced over the wire into the artery to remove the sheath. The clogged vessel later inflates with the balloon to expand it and make sure the stent stays in the vessel so that blood can run normally in the vessels [27]. These procedures can gather data, do research for developing the technique to give a better performance, and improve the outcomes of the patient's records [28]. There are many benefits of healthcare that collaborates with IoT, which gives the facility to the healthcare authorities to monitor the patient remotely [29]. So, any emergency cases from the patient's status will be known quickly. IoT can be connected to many healthcare equipment such as in the PTCA to show the real-data transmission for consultation from professionals [30]. Implementation of IoT in PTCA involves the integration of various sensors, devices, and equipment to collect and transmit the data. Smart stents with pressure sensors allow the monitoring of intravascular pressure [31]. RPM is used before, during, and after the PTCA to ensure that decision-making can be adjusted by the healthcare professional [29].

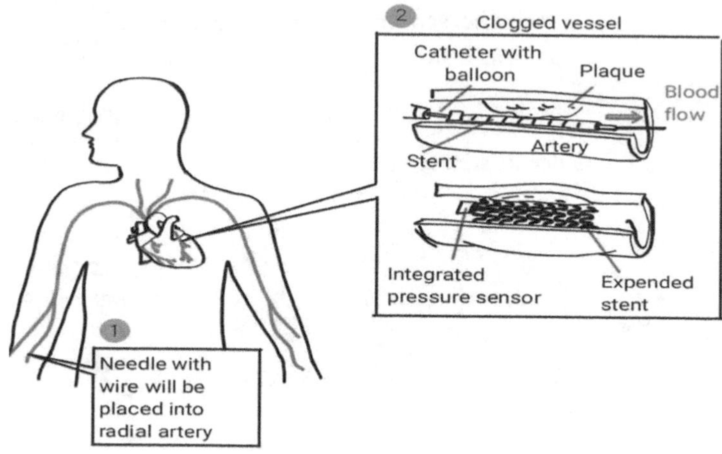

Figure 2.5 Coronary artery angioplasty.

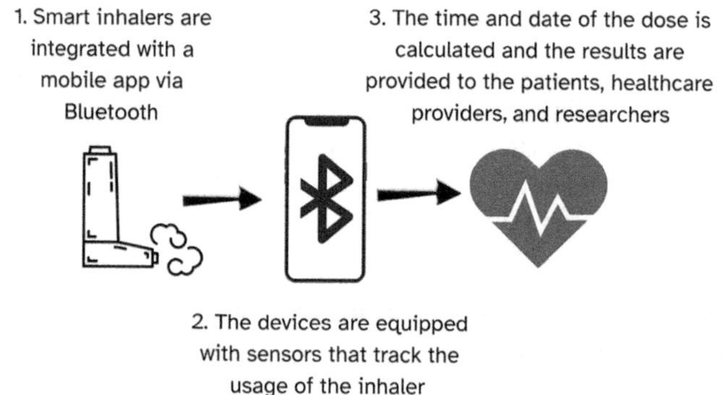

Figure 2.6 Smart inhalers.

2.3.3.6 *Smart inhalers*

Smart inhalers are inhalers that can track the usage of the inhaler and provide feedback to the patient and healthcare provider. They can also remind patients to take their medication and monitor the medication. Smart inhalers can be used in conjunction with SMART (Single Maintenance and Reliever Therapy), which allows patients to use a single inhaler for both maintenance and reliever therapy. The budesonide/formoterol combination is the first treatment recommended for moderate to severe asthma [32].

As shown in Figure 2.6, smart inhalers work by integrating connectivity with a mobile app, typically via Bluetooth. These devices are equipped with sensors that track the usage of the inhaler and send this information to a mobile application [33]. The data collected by smart inhalers includes comprehensive information about each use, such as the time and date of the dose. This approach simplifies asthma management and can improve patient adherence to medication regimens.

2.3.4 Privacy and Security of IoT in Healthcare

Healthcare should have confidentiality to protect patients' data from any irresponsible or unauthorized authorities because it consists of sensitive health information [34]. The privacy and security rules are significant in terms of technical safeguards and access controls. Confidentiality in IoT implementation should have encryption, access authorization, and monitoring to preserve confidentiality during storage and transmission [29, 30]. Integrity in healthcare is the assurance that the patients' data can be protected from illegal data alteration including human error [35]. It is dangerous because it will lead to wrong treatment procedure [34]. Implementation of robust measures is required to secure electronic health records, medical data, and any sensitive data [36]. Cloud computer is a delivery of computing service that covers servers, storage, databases, networking, software, and intelligence over the Internet [37]. Implementing cloud computing in the industry of healthcare, hospitals do not have to maintain their own databases and computing equipment. Instead, they can rent cloud service provider to access everything from storage to application [37].

Regulatory and compliance issues related to healthcare data and IoT are important to ensure patient safety, data security, and legal adherence. IoT adoption in healthcare has led to plenty of regulatory considerations that require mindful attention to data privacy, security, and healthcare regulations. It relates close with Health Insurance Portability and Accountability Act (HIPAA) and General Data Protection Regulation (GDPR), which established the regulations to protect patient data and strictly controls over personal data, with significant consequences for violations [38]. By making regulatory compliance a top concern, conducting regular audits and putting in safe places to monitor compliance efforts, healthcare authorities can play a role of dedicative authorities to protect patient data and reduce risks. Additionally, proper discovery, classification, and securing of all IoT devices on a healthcare provider's network are important to ensure the privacy and security of patients' data [39].

2.3.5 Technological Limitations and Potential Scalability Issues of IoT in Healthcare

One of the technological limitations of IoT in healthcare is data security and privacy. It is a significant challenge that prevents users from fully adopting IoT technology in medical settings [40]. Healthcare monitoring solutions have the potential to be compromised or hacked. For example, tampering with sensor data can lead to information disclosure of patient's health and location. It can have serious consequences that undermine the benefits of IoT [41]. Data security and privacy are major challenges for IoT in healthcare. While many Internet of Medical Things (IoMT) devices lack proper data protocols and security measures, many still collect and transmit data in real-time. Data ownerships regulation is unclear, which makes things difficult. Data about patients and doctors is exposed by their vulnerability, making it vulnerable to cyberattacks. Hackers may use personally identifiable information to commit fraud, such as faking identification to purchase medical supplies or submit insurance claims [42]. Additionally, there may be scalability problems with IoT in healthcare due to data overload and accuracy [42]. Scalability may be impacted by the challenges posed by the massive amount of data produced by IoT devices. In terms of data aggregation, accuracy, and seamless information flow between connected devices, it is challenging for doctors to identify relevant information from the overwhelming volume of data. Although, it's a great resource for gaining insights.

2.3.6 Ethical Consideration in IoT and Healthcare

The everyday use of IoT gadgets, like continuous glucose monitoring and RPM, is making our life easier [43]. Ethical consideration must be taken before developing these types of gadgets. Important areas of attention have been identified by the Federal Trade Commission (FTC) that has outlined keys that companies need to take care of before promoting their applications and software to the public [44]. One of them is a concept known as "security by design" where employees and owners need to prioritize security when developing an application or a device [44]. Therefore, patients or consumers don't need to worry about the security of their personal information.

Patient ownership in IoT healthcare has a complex issue. The concept of electronic health record (EHR) and personal health record (PHR) was created to handle this issue. EHR is a digital health record for patients that contains all patients' medical history including their medication and treatments [45]. EHR is designed to be shared across different locations such as hospitals and laboratories. Next, PHR is an electronic application used by patients to manage their health information privately [45]. This includes information such as patients' medication, medical history, and body condition. PHR is controlled by the patient, and hence all the decisions are based on the patients. It is designed to not be shared among healthcare providers [46].

2.4 LITERATURE OVERVIEW

Literature overview provides the summary of 15 papers published from 2018 onward of the key sources on IoT in healthcare including the application of IoT in healthcare. Table 2.1 shows several articles and papers related to the paper's title.

Table 2.1 Survey IoT in Healthcare: Applications, Privacy, and Security

Article	*Key Findings/Arguments*	*Supporting Evidence/Sample Characteristics/Methods*	*Strength/Limitations*	*Significance/Implications*
		Research Question: IoT in Healthcare: Applications, Privacy, and Security		
[37]	The article discusses about cloud computing	Core elements such as infrastructure as service, platform as a service, and software as a service	Differentiate between existing cloud providers	Relates cloud computing with security, relevancies, cost, and companies
[28]	The article discusses IoT application in coronary artery angioplasty	Procedures to make the artery widen because of plaque	IoT used in helping people who have problems with cholesterol and any related diseases	It is important in monitoring health remotely and know the trends of the data
[12]	The article investigates the application of remote patient monitoring	Vital monitoring and disease diagnosis monitoring	Equipment is large and expensive and allows one person at a time	The disease can be detected remotely and provide real-time data
[34]	IoT has the integrity that it will not go to any unauthorized people	Analysis of data integrity in healthcare from many threats	Encryption, and monitor the performance and network	IoT should have blockchain method for data integrity techniques
[31]	IoT has confidentiality, integrity, and availability that are needed in preserving healthcare data	Designed to guide policies for securing information	Medical devices are used to strengthen information security and cybersecurity	Ensure the equipment of the medical device is safe from cyberattacks
[4]	The rise of COVID-19 correlates with increasing use of IoT	The existence of smart hospitals and smart beds	Accurate decision-making based on data gathering	Store and analyze data of COVID-19 patients and can check the status recovery
[22]	Continuous glucose monitoring device is a commercialized tool	The article lists the risk and benefits of using the device	Glucose monitoring is costly and cannot cure diabetes	It provides a platform to monitor blood glucose remotely and quickly

(Continued)

Table 2.1 (Continued) Survey IoT in Healthcare: Applications, Privacy, and Security

Article	*Key Findings/Arguments*	*Supporting Evidence/Sample Characteristics/Methods*	*Strength/Limitations*	*Significance/Implications*
[47]	Benefit of using IoT in healthcare	Analyzing the advantages of using healthcare in many aspects	The number of patient visits to the hospital decreases	IoT provides a better experience to the patient
[6]	This article provides the overview of the trends in technologies for healthcare industries	Addresses challenges for increasing decision-making	Identify the current IoT used in healthcare	Comprehensive writing of IoT applications, patterns, and techniques in healthcare management
[10]	The article discusses depression monitoring using wearable sensors	Wearable IoT can connect to various sensors	Physicians can access medical information from data locations	Potential to improve healthcare through early illness identification
[12]	This article talks about how to investigate IoT-based smart health monitoring devices	Statistical data analysis to generate the necessary signals	Early detection of health issues in implementing the required emergency procedures	Remotely monitored and necessary measures
[3]	Usage between paper and electronic medical records	Proper explanation regarding medical records	Advantage and disadvantage of both methods	Recommending the best method
[9]	Depression detection with wireless sensor networks (WSN)	Model the gathering of basic health data to monitor stress level	Gather information and insights about their heart rate	Make use of two detectors, non-intrusive and non-invasive
[13]	Digital technology that can track mood and behavior	Wearable and smartphone sensors for heart rate, motion, and physiological variables	Improving clinical care and advancing the study of depression	Generate features to explain the behaviors
[5]	Proactive treatment, healthcare delivery, and streamline potential	Fitness, system monitoring, patient safety, and potential benefit of IoT in healthcare	Overview of the current state of IoT in healthcare	Highlight the transformative potential of IoT

2.5 CRUCIAL ROLE OF TECHNOLOGY IN EDUCATION AND HEALTHCARE

Education is an important industry that plays a crucial role in shaping individuals, societies, and economies. It serves as the foundation for personal and intellectual development, skills, and necessary values for success in many aspects of life. Integrating IoT technology into healthcare education may transform education in a good term. Project Polaris is a project that has been developed by a team from NUS Medicine and Microsoft Industry Solutions. The project introduces 3D mixed reality technology and holographic technology to train medical and nursing students in clinical procedural skills. It covers various tasks including inserting cannulas and catheters in male and female urinary tracts with three difficulty levels [48]. The purpose of this project is to train and provide sufficient direction to allow students to achieve the highest standard of clinical practice [48].

2.6 CONCLUSION

IoT connects devices in healthcare to improve treatment management and outcomes, though cost remains a challenge. Its benefits include real-time monitoring, remote medical assistance, and secure communication. To address concerns, strong security measures and compliance are essential. Overall, IoT has the potential to revolutionize healthcare by overcoming obstacles for a secure and effective environment. The integration of IoT with machine learning is one area of future research interest for IoT in healthcare.

REFERENCES

[1] J. M. Tien, "Internet of Things, real-time decision making, and artificial intelligence," *Annals of Data Science*, vol. 4, no. 2, pp. 149–178, Jun. 2017, doi: 10.1007/s40745-017-0112-5.

[2] A. Witt, "The pros and cons of paper medical records," Record Nations. Accessed: Jan. 01, 2024. [Online]. Available: https://www.recordnations.com/blog/pros-and-cons-of-paper-medical-records/

[3] J. Kay, "The pros & cons of paper and electronic medical records," Pimsy Electronic Health Records Software. Accessed: Jan. 01, 2024. [Online]. Available: https://pimsyehr.com/battle-of-the-records-pros-cons-everything-you-need-to-know-about-paper-vs-electronic-medical-records/

[4] M. Javaid and I. H. Khan, "Internet of Things (IoT) enabled healthcare helps to take the challenges of COVID-19 pandemic," *Journal of Oral Biology and Craniofacial Research*, vol. 11, no. 2, pp. 209–214, 2021, doi: 10.1016/j.jobcr.2021.01.015.

[5] A. Rejeb *et al.*, "The Internet of Things (IoT) in healthcare: Taking stock and moving forward," *Internet of Things*, vol. 22, p. 100721, Jul. 2023, doi: 10.1016/j.iot.2023.100721.

[6] M. Haghi Kashani, M. Madanipour, M. Nikravan, P. Asghari, and E. Mahdipour, "A systematic review of IoT in healthcare: Applications, techniques, and trends," *Journal of Network and Computer Applications*, vol. 192, p. 103164, Oct. 2021, doi: 10.1016/j.jnca.2021.103164.

[7] "Using IoT & AI in healthcare—the future of medical data," Arrow.com. Accessed: Feb. 10, 2024. [Online]. Available: https://www.arrow.com/en/research-and-events/articles/healthcare-driven-by-ai-and-iot

[8] T. Joseph, "7 Major impacts of technology in healthcare," Fingent. Accessed: Feb. 10, 2024. [Online]. Available: https://www.fingent.com/blog/7-major-impacts-of-technology-in-healthcare/

[9] G. Gupta, S. Joshi, and S. Kulkarni, "IoT based depression detection," in *2022 IEEE 3rd Global Conference for Advancement in Technology (GCAT)*, Bangalore, India: IEEE, Oct. 2022, pp. 1–7. doi: 10.1109/GCAT55367.2022.9971845.

[10] M. V. Ranaware and K. Joshi, "Depression monitoring using wearable sensors," vol. 7, no. 3, 2020.

[11] J. Goltermann *et al.*, "Smartphone-based self-reports of depressive symptoms using the remote monitoring application in psychiatry (ReMAP): Interformat validation study," *JMIR Mental Health*, vol. 8, no. 1, p. e24333, Jan. 2021, doi: 10.2196/24333.

[12] A. Rahaman, Md. Islam, Md. Islam, M. Sadi, and S. Nooruddin, "Developing IoT based smart health monitoring systems: A review," *Revue d intelligence artificielle*, vol. 33, no. 6, pp. 435–440, Dec. 2019, doi: 10.18280/ria.330605.

[13] V. De Angel *et al.*, "Digital health tools for the passive monitoring of depression: A systematic review of methods," *npj Digital Medicine*, vol. 5, no. 1, p. 3, Jan. 2022, doi: 10.1038/s41746-021-00548-8.

[14] E. E. Thomas *et al.*, "Factors influencing the effectiveness of remote patient monitoring interventions: A realist review," *BMJ Open*, vol. 11, no. 8, p. e051844, Aug. 2021, doi: 10.1136/bmjopen-2021-051844.

[15] K. Boikanyo, A. M. Zungeru, B. Sigweni, A. Yahya, and C. Lebekwe, "Remote patient monitoring systems: Applications, architecture, and challenges," *Scientific African*, vol. 20, p. e01638, Jul. 2023, doi: 10.1016/j.sciaf.2023.e01638.

[16] D. Whitehead and J. Conley, "The Next frontier of remote patient monitoring: Hospital at home," *Journal of Medical Internet Research*, vol. 25, no. 1, p. e42335, Mar. 2023, doi: 10.2196/42335.

[17] M. Harvey and A. Seiler, "Challenges in managing a remote monitoring device clinic," *Heart Rhythm O2*, vol. 3, no. 1, pp. 3–7, Feb. 2022, doi: 10.1016/j.hroo.2021.12.002.

[18] Copperpod, "Ingestible Electronic Sensor (IES)—A new dimension of digital healthcare industry," Copperpod IP. Accessed: Jan. 01, 2024. [Online]. Available: https://www.copperpodip.com/post/ingestible-electronic-sensor-ies-a-new-dimension-of-digital-healthcare-industry

[19] L. A. Beardslee *et al.*, "Ingestible sensors and sensing systems for minimally invasive diagnosis and monitoring: The next frontier in minimally invasive screening," *ACS Sensors*, vol. 5, no. 4, pp. 891–910, Apr. 2020, doi: 10.1021/acssensors.9b02263.

[20] H. Liu *et al.*, "Ingestible sensor system for measuring, monitoring and enhancing adherence to antiretroviral therapy: An open-label, usual care-controlled, randomised trial," Dec. 2022, doi: 10.1016/j.ebiom.2022.104330.

[21] S. Watson, "What is glucose?" WebMD. Accessed: Jan. 01, 2024. [Online]. Available: https://www.webmd.com/diabetes/glucose-diabetes
[22] "Continuous Glucose Monitoring (CGM): What is it & how does it work," Cleveland Clinic. Accessed: Jan. 01, 2024. [Online]. Available: https://my.clevelandclinic.org/health/treatments/11444-glucose-continuous-glucose-monitoring
[23] C. Wang, T. He, H. Zhou, Z. Zhang, and C. Lee, "Artificial intelligence enhanced sensors—enabling technologies to next-generation healthcare and biomedical platform," *Bioelectron Medicine*, vol. 9, no. 1, p. 17, Aug. 2023, doi: 10.1186/s42234-023-00118-1.
[24] "Ingestible IoT sensors | Perle News," Perle Systems. Accessed: Jan. 01, 2024. [Online]. Available: https://www.perle.com/articles/ingestible-iot-sensors-40193889.shtml
[25] "Continuous glucose monitoring—NIDDK," National Institute of Diabetes and Digestive and Kidney Diseases. Accessed: Jan. 01, 2024. [Online]. Available: https://www.niddk.nih.gov/health-information/diabetes/overview/managing-diabetes/continuous-glucose-monitoring
[26] "Coronary angioplasty and stent insertion," nhs.uk. Accessed: Jan. 01, 2024. [Online]. Available: https://www.nhs.uk/conditions/coronary-angioplasty/
[27] "Coronary angioplasty and stents—Mayo Clinic." Accessed: Jan. 01, 2024. [Online]. Available: https://www.mayoclinic.org/tests-procedures/coronary-angioplasty/about/pac-20384761
[28] L. Chhabra, M. A. Zain, and W. J. Siddiqui, "Angioplasty," in *StatPearls*, Treasure Island (FL): StatPearls Publishing, 2023. Accessed: Jan. 01, 2024. [Online]. Available: http://www.ncbi.nlm.nih.gov/books/NBK499894/
[29] S. Dami, "Internet of Things-based health monitoring system for early detection of cardiovascular events during COVID-19 pandemic," *World Journal of Clinical Cases*, vol. 10, no. 26, pp. 9207–9218, Sep. 2022, doi: 10.12998/wjcc.v10.i26.9207.
[30] M. Alghrairi, N. Sulaiman, and S. Mutashar, "Health care monitoring and treatment for coronary artery diseases: Challenges and issues," *Sensors*, vol. 20, no. 15, Art. no. 15, Jan. 2020, doi: 10.3390/s20154303.
[31] U. Umar, S. Nayab, R. Irfan, M. A. Khan, and A. Umer, "E-Cardiac care: A comprehensive systematic literature review," *Sensors (Basel)*, vol. 22, no. 20, p. 8073, Oct. 2022, doi: 10.3390/s22208073.
[32] "A practical guide to implementing SMART in asthma management—PubMed." Accessed: Feb. 10, 2024. [Online]. Available: https://pubmed.ncbi.nlm.nih.gov/34666208/
[33] "Medical news | Medical articles," News-Medical. Accessed: Feb. 10, 2024. [Online]. Available: https://www.news-medical.net/
[34] A. Finnegan, "CIA triad for medical devices—Strengthening information security," Nova Leah. Accessed: Jan. 01, 2024. [Online]. Available: https://www.novaleah.com/the-cia-triad-of-cybersecurity-for-medical-devices/
[35] M. Zarour *et al.*, "Ensuring data integrity of healthcare information in the era of digital health," *Healthcare Technology Letters*, vol. 8, no. 3, pp. 66–77, Apr. 2021, doi: 10.1049/htl2.12008.
[36] J. George and T. Bhila, "Security, confidentiality and privacy in health of healthcare data," *International Journal of Trend in Scientific Research and Development*, vol. 3, Jun. 2019, doi: 10.31142/ijtsrd23780.

[37] "What is cloud computing? Everything you need to know about the cloud explained," ZDNET. Accessed: Jan. 01, 2024. [Online]. Available: https://www.zdnet.com/article/what-is-cloud-computing-everything-you-need-to-know-about-the-cloud/
[38] "Top Challenges of IoT in healthcare and ways to overcome them," Relevant Software. Accessed: Feb. 10, 2024. [Online]. Available: https://relevant.software/blog/challenges-of-iot-in-healthcare/
[39] R. Herold, "IoT devices and HIPAA compliance: 6 things healthcare orgs must know." Accessed: Feb. 10, 2024. [Online]. Available: https://www.secureworld.io/industry-news/iot-devices-and-hipaa-compliance-6-things-healthcare-orgs-must-know
[40] "(13) Advantages and disadvantages of implementing IoT in healthcare | LinkedIn." Accessed: Feb. 10, 2024. [Online]. Available: https://www.linkedin.com/pulse/advantages-disadvantages-implementing-iot-healthcare-iot-for-all/
[41] A. Cooper, "IoT in healthcare: Benefits, challenges and applications," ValueCoders | Unlocking the Power of Technology: Discover the Latest Insights and Trends. Accessed: Feb. 10, 2024. [Online]. Available: https://www.valuecoders.com/blog/technology-and-apps/iot-in-healthcare-benefits-challenges-and-applications/
[42] C. Studies *et al.*, "IoT in healthcare: Applications, benefits, and challenges in 2023," Stfalcon. Accessed: Feb. 10, 2024. [Online]. Available: https://stfalcon.com/en/blog/post/iot-in-healthcare-benefits-challenges
[43] "Health data ownership in IoT and the cloud," Ebrary. Accessed: Feb. 10, 2024. [Online]. Available: https://ebrary.net/206092/computer_science/health_data_ownership_cloud
[44] R. Singh *et al.*, "Ownership of healthcare data in the Internet of Things era, Part 3." Accessed: Feb. 10, 2024. [Online]. Available: https://compliancecosmos.org/ownership-healthcare-data-internet-things-era-part-3
[45] "I vs EHR vs PHR (differences, advantages & disadvantages)," CRM.org. Accessed: Feb. 10, 2024. [Online]. Available: https://crm.org/news/emr-vs-ehr-vs-phr
[46] Admin, "What is the difference between EHR, EMR and PHR?" Peloton College. Accessed: Feb. 10, 2024. [Online]. Available: http://pelotoncollege.edu/what-is-the-difference-between-ehr-emr-and-phr/
[47] B. Al-Shargabi and S. Abuarqoub, "IoT-enabled healthcare: Benefits, issues and challenges," Nov. 2020, doi: 10.1145/3440749.3442596.
[48] A. Raj, "Microsoft redefines healthcare education with mixed reality," Tech Wire Asia. Accessed: Jan. 01, 2024. [Online]. Available: https://techwireasia.com/01/2022/microsoft-redefines-healthcare-education-with-mixed-reality/

Chapter 3

Securing the Future of E-health

Challenges and Key Management Strategies in Smart Healthcare Sensor Networks

Yassine Maleh and Issam Taqafi

3.1 INTRODUCTION

A major turning point has been reached in the dynamic field of embedded systems and communication technologies with the advent of the Internet of Things (IoT). Not only does this revolutionary change herald a move towards a more linked technology ecology, but it also ushers in many new complications. The Internet has expanded beyond a network of computers to include a vast array of devices, such as radio-frequency identification (RFID) tags, sensor networks, automotive networks, and more (Maleh, Sahid, Ezzati, and Belaissaoui 2018). IoT is at the heart of this paradigm change; it involves the networking of numerous entities and suitable wireless devices, such as mobile phones and sensors, made possible by various communication protocols. This level of interconnection applies to items that have practical consequences. Hence, a strong security architecture is needed to reduce hazards. Consequently, protocols should be revised to incorporate new limitations, focusing on strengthening security mechanisms (Maleh, Ezzati, and Belaissaoui 2018).

Additionally, wireless body area networks (WBANs) have exploded in popularity because of their great potential for remote patient health monitoring via wireless sensor nodes worn by patients. WBANs can measure various physiological indicators, including temperature, heart rate, blood sugar, and blood pressure. They are a great choice for patients since they may be worn or implanted. With the help of physiological data collected by wearable sensors, medical servers can assess a patient's health state, which is the main goal of WBANs (Xu, Wu, Daneshmand, and Liu 2015).

By tracking people's vitals and detecting when diseases manifest, sensor networks are changing the face of modern healthcare. All through treatment, these networks can lessen expenses and hazards. To monitor patients' vital signs, medication schedules, and doctor–patient interactions, state-of-the-art medical institutions now use simple sensor technologies. In some instances, it is feasible to remotely monitor patients' health by integrating sensor networks. As technology advances and the Internet becomes more

DOI: 10.1201/9781003470038-3

widely used, remote monitoring systems can properly determine a person's physical status, even if they are still in the early phases of development. The care of the elderly is one crucial area where sensor networks show their worth in healthcare. Muscle movements, falls, unconsciousness, vital signs, food habits, and activity levels may all be detected by a complex network of sensor cameras. This technology's real-time health evaluations can make up for delays in recognizing, degenerative illnesses, which might save lives and lower healthcare costs. Surveillance sensors equipped with ultrawideband technology can communicate massive volumes of data, improving medical services, healthcare results, treatment costs, and sickness prevention—all while being small.

Wireless body sensor networks (WBSNs) are an exciting new development in healthcare technology. In addition to paving the way for novel medical procedures and treatments, they improve the ease, adaptability, and precision with which people may track their health. As this field progresses, we should expect much more inventive and groundbreaking uses of WBSNs in healthcare and other fields. Worries regarding the safety of the data acquired are on the rise, in tandem with the widespread usage of WBANs. Protecting patients' health data from unauthorized access is critical because of how sensitive it is. Encryption, secure communication protocols, and access control methods are essential for data protection. Such safeguards prevent unauthorized parties from gaining access to the data and maintaining its secrecy and security. The major goal of this chapter is to examine various security techniques for protecting smart healthcare sensor networks (SHSNs) against unauthorized access and to identify security concerns in these networks. Particularly, WBANs' unique characteristics, including their star topology design with an internal sinkhole for data collection from nodes, pose one-of-a-kind security risks, such as unauthorized access to the sinkhole. The data's availability, integrity, and secrecy depend on resolving these issues. We believe this contribution would help identify future research directions in this domain. This chapter mainly aims to make the following contributions:

- It defines various requirements of a good threat and mitigations classification.
- It analyses the SHSNs security threats.
- It studies and analyses in-depth the SHSNs key management protocols.

The structure of this chapter is as follows. Section 3.2 describes the research methodology. Section 3.3 reviews the related SHSNs requirements and threats. Section 3.4 discusses security threats. Section 3.5 presents the most important key managements schemes for SHSNs. Finally, this chapter concludes with Section 3.6.

3.2 RESEARCH METHODOLOGY

We delve into pivotal aspects of SHSNs, focusing on security requirements, threats, and key management schemes. By addressing fundamental questions, this inquiry aims to illuminate critical elements necessary for ensuring the integrity, confidentiality, and privacy of patient data within SHSNs while evaluating key management strategies vital for maintaining robust security measures. Understanding the security landscape of SHSNs is paramount to safeguarding sensitive patient information. We analyze the main security requirements, including data integrity, confidentiality, and privacy, essential for maintaining trust and compliance within healthcare environments. Additionally, we identify prevalent threats such as unauthorized access, data breaches, and network intrusions that pose significant risks to SHSNs, highlighting the importance of implementing robust security measures to mitigate these threats effectively. Effective key management is pivotal for maintaining the security and integrity of healthcare sensor networks. We explore the key management schemes deployed in SHSNs, focusing on secure key generation, distribution, and utilization strategies. By evaluating existing protocols and schemes, we aim to provide insights into best practices and challenges associated with key management in healthcare sensor networks, offering recommendations for enhancing the security posture of SHSNs. Through a comprehensive analysis of security requirements, threats, and key management strategies, this section contributes valuable insights into the overarching security framework of SHSNs, paving the way for the development of robust security solutions tailored to the unique challenges of healthcare environments (Maleh et al. 2022).

Here we detail the procedures that were followed to conduct this survey. We depend on the process of systematic literature reviews (SLRs) to enhance our understanding of related categories. SLR supposedly differentiates itself from conventional common reviews by pursuing a reproducible, scientific, and transparent procedure. Initially implemented in the medical profession, SLRs offer a reproducible research approach and should yield enough data for other researchers to duplicate. Several researchers in the field of computer security have recently begun employing the SLR technique. With the emergence of high-quality research on Software-Defined Network (SDN) security, SLR can help classify these studies, which are still in their early phases.

The research topics were defined initially to organize the SLR. The potential benefits of SHSN security had to be considered for this. This established three foundational subject categories: exposures, assaults, and critical management processes. To emphasize the need to conduct a current and comprehensive assessment of SHSNs risks and important management strategies, we have posed two research questions that we shall endeavor to answer in this chapter:

RQ1: What are the main security requirements and threats in SHSNs?
RQ2: What are the main key management schemes in SHSNs?

We use a three-stage selection approach to select the articles pertaining to these research issues: (1) defining search keywords, (2) selecting sources, and (3) determining and applying inclusion/exclusion criteria for chosen papers. Figure 3.1. shows the selection methodology of our paper.

(1) **Search terms:** Choosing the best keywords to use in our evaluation is the goal of this step. To locate pertinent articles, we have also included synonyms, which are other spellings of the key terms in the field of risks and mitigations within the framework of the letter S. Therefore, such keywords are "SHSN security threats," "WSN security threats," "Smart healthcare sensor network vulnerabilities," "SHSN attacks," "Security in healthcare sensor networks," "SHSN security issues," "Key management in healthcare sensor networks," "SHSN security measures," and "Key management in WBANs."
(2) To define the search string, the Boolean operations "OR" was used to select optional words and synonyms and "AND" to select the terms related to population, intervention, and effect, resulting in the search string (("Smart Healthcare Sensor Networks" OR "Wireless Body Area Network" OR "WBAN" OR "SHSNs") AND ("security" OR

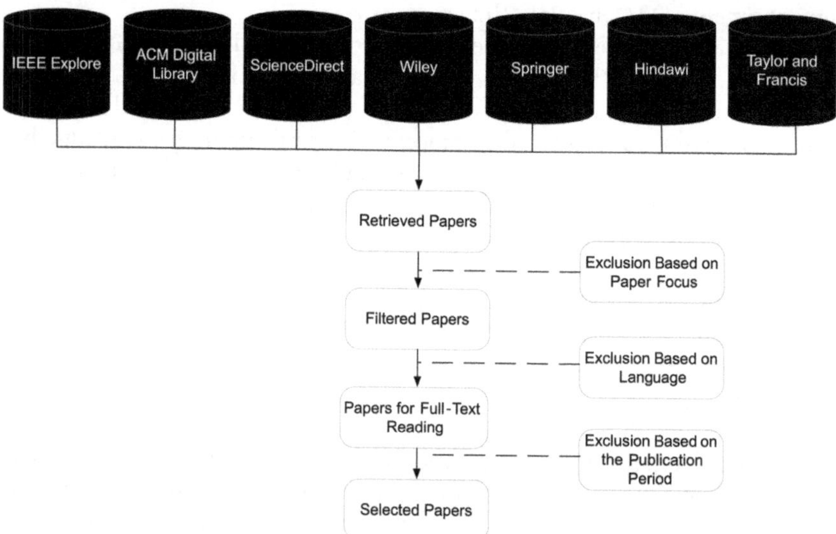

Figure 3.1 The proposed papers selection methodology.

"secure" OR "attack" OR "vulnerability" OR "threats" OR "key management" OR "key protocols")).

(3) **Selection of sources:** For this search phase, we have chosen to use the popular digital academic databases listed in Table 3.1. For this review, we looked at both journal publications and conference proceedings. Some of the papers that were downloaded had their references checked, and we also added publications that were relevant to the subject. For various reasons, such as the difficulty or infeasibility of instantiating the search string, the high index of duplicate articles with IEEE and ScienceDirect databases, or the fact that the databases (like Google Scholar) only performed one indexing, other databases were not utilized.

(4) **Inclusion/exclusion criteria:** Table 3.2 summarizes the inclusion–exclusion criteria for the SLR.

3.3 SECURITY REQUIREMENT IN SHSNs

To protect the authenticity, privacy, and secrecy of patient information, it is essential to fulfill the following fundamental security needs:

- **Data originality**: Must be met by SHSNs to guarantee the security and reliability of transmitted data. To do this, services related to licensing and verification are required (Yassine and Ezzati 2015). Each sensor and base station (BS) in an SHSN must use its authentication technique to ensure genuine data. This ensures the data is trustworthy and accurate, which helps avoid wrong diagnosis and treatments. Another important goal of authentication techniques is ensuring that patient data remains discreet and private throughout transmission (Maleh, Ezzati, and Belaissaoui 2016a).
- **Data privacy:** Attackers can eavesdrop on sensitive data being shared between nodes in SHSNs because of the wireless channel. The end consequence can be the unauthorized disclosure of private patient

Table 3.1 Digital Databases Used in the SLR

Online Databases #	*Online Database*	*URL*
1	IEEE	http://ieeexplore.ieee.org/
2	ScienceDirect	http://www.sciencedirect.com/
3	ACM	http://www.acm.org/
4	Wiley	http://www.wiley.com/
5	SpringerLink	http://link.springer.com/
6	Hindawi	https://www.hindawi.com/
7	Taylor & Francis	http://taylorandfrancis.com/

Table 3.2. Summary of the Inclusion–Exclusion Criteria for Selection Papers

Criterion	*Rational*
Inclusion 1	Early stage studies proposing key management schemes specific to smart healthcare sensor networks (SHSNs) are considered. These solutions are pivotal for addressing the unique security challenges within SHSNs.
Inclusion 2	Studies detailing security requirements and attacks within SHSNs include academic and industrial perspectives to ensure a comprehensive understanding of the security landscape.
Inclusion 3	Studies engaging in discussions surrounding security issues pertinent to SHSNs are incorporated, providing valuable insights into the complexities of safeguarding healthcare data in sensor network environments.
Exclusion 1	Studies that do not center on security issues within SHSNs are excluded, as this research focuses solely on taxonomies addressing security challenges specific to healthcare sensor networks.
Exclusion 2	Non-English papers are excluded from consideration, as the primary language for inclusion in this study is English to ensure accessibility and consistency in reviewing the literature.
Exclusion 3	Studies not published between 2010 and 2023 are excluded, with further exclusionary criteria applied during full-text reading to ensure relevance to SHSNs threats and key management protocols.

information. One solution to this problem is to encrypt data before transferring it. Only approved users will be able to decipher this encrypted material. Employing encryption methods is crucial in ensuring that sensitive patient information remains secure from unauthorized parties. The data will be protected during transmission because of this.

- **Data integrity:** Important for protecting sensitive patient information during transmission. System failures and patient harm can result from intruders intercepting and altering data. This highlights the need for safeguards to avoid data manipulation while in transit. Data integrity checks, which ensure the data received at the destination is real, are one approach to doing this. These verifications examine if the data that has been received has been altered or changed in any way by comparing it to the data that was originally transmitted. Healthcare professionals may make better decisions regarding patient care when they have access to accurate and trustworthy patient data, which is why data integrity measures are so important.
- **Data availability:** Medical sensor nodes must be readily available to guarantee that health data is always available for medical treatment. Data loss may occur if an unauthorized person were to seize a sensor

node, making it very difficult to provide medical treatment. As a result, keeping medical care software accessible is crucial for ensuring that doctors and other medical staff have constant access to vital patient records.

- **Updated data:** A freshness method prevents attackers from reusing old data by implementing protections that prevent the attacker node from recording, replaying, and publishing data. Because SHSNs ensure the data is new and undamaged, they assure its accuracy and reliability, leading to better patient care outcomes. Accurate and current data is essential in healthcare apps so clinicians can swiftly make excellent patient treatment decisions.
- **Data authentication:** Every node may identify and confirm the identity of the nodes that supply it with data using an authentication mechanism, ensuring the data is genuine and unaltered. Data authentication allows SHSNs to guarantee that only authorized nodes may access and share sensitive patient data, which improves patient privacy and security.
- **Secure management:** The coordinator has a number of options for safely distributing keys, including encrypted communication channels, secure authentication mechanisms, and other similar measures. In addition, the coordinator can take the required steps to revoke the keys to stop unauthorized individuals from accessing the network and its data. Using a coordinator and secure key management procedures allows WBANs to better safeguard sensitive data during transmission and reception on the network, preventing unauthorized access.
- **Reliability:** For the receiver to be able to identify and fix any transmission problems, error coding is a method that includes adding redundant data to the sent data. If the data being communicated is susceptible to noise or interference from the wireless channel, this method can be very effective in SHSNs. Regarding applications like medical monitoring, where data mistakes might have life-altering effects, SHSNs' error coding feature is invaluable for ensuring the data supplied and received by the network is accurate and reliable. Further, by decreasing the possibility of data corruption or loss caused by transmission mistakes, error coding can assist in making the network more reliable.
- **Safe positioning:** Intruders can compromise patient privacy and security by entering fraudulent signals and information into the location registration system through patient movements and updates. Avoiding this problem is possible with the use of secure authentication and encryption techniques, which limit the ability to update the patient's location information to authorized devices only. In addition, the location registration system may be set up with frequent monitoring and detection systems to catch suspicious activities or attempts at unauthorized access. To protect the confidentiality of patient information and stop unauthorized people from accessing or tampering with their location data, patients must be securely positioned in WBANs. With the right safeguards in place, WBANs can ensure that patient location data is tracked safely and reliably.

- **Accountability:** All healthcare team members, including administrators, should be aware of the gravity of the situation and act accordingly to keep patients' personal information secure. Someone must be held accountable if they are responsible for the unauthorized use or disclosure of patient information, because it can have catastrophic implications. Consequently, it is critical to set up transparent protocols for handling and securing patient information and to check in on these steps often to ensure they're working.
- **Flexibility:** Patients may need a second party or hospital to access their information in the event of an emergency. To guarantee the privacy and accuracy of the data, the system should offer a safe and effective way for authorized parties to access and share this information. The collection of patient permission and the regulation of data access are two of the most important components of an effective policy and procedural framework for sharing patient information.
- **Privacy and compliance:** Ensuring the security of patients' private information is the highest priority. Worldwide standards and legislation, such as the US Health Insurance Portability and Accountability Act (HIPAA), have been implemented to guarantee this. Penalties, both criminal and civil, such as fines and jail time, await those who disobey these rules. Healthcare providers must follow these rules and protect their patients' personal information.
- **Data authenticity:** Data must be legitimate and originate from reliable sources for wireless medical sensor networks to function properly. One can employ authentication methods such as public and private keys to do this. The data is encrypted using public keys and decrypted using private keys. This ensures that no unauthorized parties may access the data and that it hasn't been altered. The trustworthiness and precision of patient records, which are essential for their care and treatment, depend on data authentication.
- **Data authorization:** The authorization technique controls user access to network resources and services. Access policies and access control lists (ACLs) work together to provide fine-grained management of who has access to what on a network. In healthcare settings, where unauthorized access to sensitive patient data is a major concern, this is of the utmost importance.

3.4 SECURITY THREATS IN SHSNs

The monitoring and tracking of vital signs in body sensor networks raise serious concerns about patient privacy. The unauthorized exposure of sensitive patient information might occur if attackers eavesdrop on communication lines. An adversary with access to a powerful enough receiver antenna can intercept a patient's network connections and steal sensitive information such as their position, time stamps, message IDs, and source and destination addresses. Malicious actors can utilize this data to inflict bodily harm.

Patients' right to privacy and security are gravely endangered by these kinds of eavesdropping operations (Butt et al. 2019). Medical IoT sensor systems often employ wireless networks for communication, which have vulnerabilities during transmission and are not intrinsically restricted in communication range. This might lead to possible dangers to sensitive data. The information that medical IoT sensors communicate to the doctor's and hospital's server may be tampered with if an attacker were to intercept and alter the data. An extremely dangerous situation may arise if this unauthorized data tampering included changing the patient's physiological data and sending it to a server. It is crucial to prioritize implementing strong security measures to safeguard patients' data during transmission, ensuring its confidentiality, integrity, validity, and privacy (Abouzakhar, Jones, and Angelopoulou 2017).

3.4.1 Different Types of Attacks

3.4.1.1 Interception

The wireless communication route that carries the patient's vital signs data from their device to their healthcare practitioner becomes compromised when an attacker obtains access. Once intercepted, this data might contain sensitive information including a patient's location, medical history, or other personal details.

3.4.1.2 Message change

This attack occurs when someone or something other than the intended receiver can intercept a communication and change its contents before sending it. In healthcare settings, this kind of assault is especially problematic since it might cause the transmission of false medical instructions or information, which can have a negative impact on the patient's health. An attacker may, for example, tamper with a patient's prescription, causing them to experience unwanted side effects. Hence, methods like digital signatures and encryption are crucial for healthcare communication to guarantee the authenticity and integrity of messages.

3.4.1.3 Wireless sensor routing threats

In the context of wireless sensor networks (WSNs), these terms describe harmful actions taken at the network layer. False alerts might be caused by these threat activities, which include stealing or altering packets and sending them to the remote-control centre. Another way attackers might cause network disruption is by tampering with the address fields of captured packets. This can lead to routing loops or even complete network disruption. Transmitted data may lose its integrity and confidentiality due to these assaults. As a result, protecting WSNs against routing attacks requires strong security measures.

3.4.2 Active Attacks on SHSNs

Because they can jeopardize the data's validity, integrity, and secrecy, active assaults pose a major threat to WBSNs and other WSNs. To cause confusion and damage, the attacker can alter the data, insert bogus data, or play back previously recorded data. Moreover, the attacker can take over the network without anyone's knowledge by masquerading as a valid node and stealing important data.

3.4.2.1 DoS attack

The goal of a denial-of-service (DoS) assault is to block access to a system or network by many legitimate users by flooding it with traffic or other harmful activities. Specifically, DoS attacks can interrupt the regular operation of WBANs, which hinders the transmission of medical data and might put the patient at risk. The "jamming" attack is a common DoS technique against WBANs. This kind of attack involves the perpetrator overwhelming the wireless spectrum with excessive noise or interference, impeding or blocking the transmission of valid data. Serious health complications may arise if the medical personnel overseeing a patient did not get vital signs or other data collected by the patient's sensors. A further DoS attack in WBANs is known as a "sleep deprivation" assault. This kind of assault involves the perpetrator repeatedly sending wake-up signals to the patient's battery-powered sensors, stopping them from going into power-saving low-power sleep modes. This can rapidly deplete the battery life of the sensors, making them unable to transmit critical medical data. Medical monitoring systems are generally quite vulnerable to DoS assaults in WBANs (Sikder et al. 2021).

3.4.2.1.1 Physical Attacks

Because they are dispersed and vulnerable, physical attacks pose a significant risk to outdoor wireless networks. Compared to wired networks, they are more prone to these types of assaults. Physical attacks on sensor nodes are common and often result in permanent damage. Attackers can steal sensitive information or alter software code to do more damage if they gain physical access.

3.4.2.1.2 Deceptive Routing Information

This attack hopes to cause performance degradation by rerouting network traffic by forming routing loops or less-than-ideal pathways. An adversary can alter data packet header information during transmission to provide erroneous routing information. One can play about with routing metrics such as hop counts, source or destination addresses, and so on to achieve this. This attack can spread throughout the network if additional nodes get this erroneous routing information and utilize it to route their packets.

3.4.2.1.3 Blackhole Attack

Here, a bad actor in the network makes an exaggerated claim about the quickest route to the sink node—the final destination of the network's gathered data. The malicious actor will start ignoring or discarding any data packets

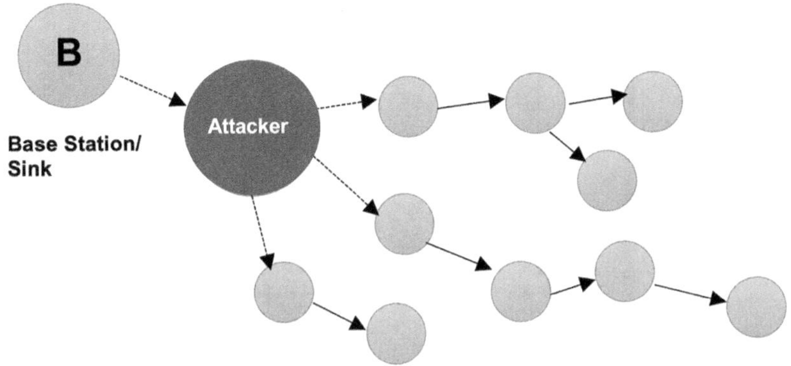

Figure 3.2 Blackhole attack.

sent to it after convincing other network nodes that it has the shortest path (Mucchi et al. 2019). Consequently, the network is severely compromised since all packets destined for the sink node are lost. There are a number of strategies at the blackhole attacker's disposal for making other nodes believe it has the shortest path. For instance, it can impersonate routing messages, alter the hop count or sequence the number of routing messages, or take advantage of network protocol vulnerabilities, as shown in Figure 3.2.

3.4.2.1.4 Sybil Attack

A security risk in WSN is the Sybil attack, which happens when an attacker uses a rogue node to mimic other nodes in the network. The hacker takes control of the network by establishing a number of false identities, or Sybil nodes, and then manipulates the data and processes therein. A DoS assault, a routing information flood, or both are possible outcomes of these Sybil nodes' malicious actions. Due to the attacker's ability to assume several false identities in a Sybil attack, the WSN's security and functioning are at risk. An attacker can intercept and alter network traffic by manipulating other nodes to route communication through Sybil nodes. Additionally, an attacker can trick genuine nodes into making the wrong routing decisions by manipulating Sybil nodes to provide an inaccurate picture of the network structure, as shown in Figure 3.3.

3.4.2.1.5 Wormhole Attack

In WSNs, an attacker can launch a wormhole attack by stealing packets and rerouting them to another location in the network. To avoid detection by standard network routing algorithms, an attacker can launch this kind of assault by establishing a tunnel, also known as a virtual connection, between two network parts. This gives the hacker access to the network and allows them to breach it by interfering with data transfer, causing data loss, or even introducing harmful material, as shown in Figure 3.4.

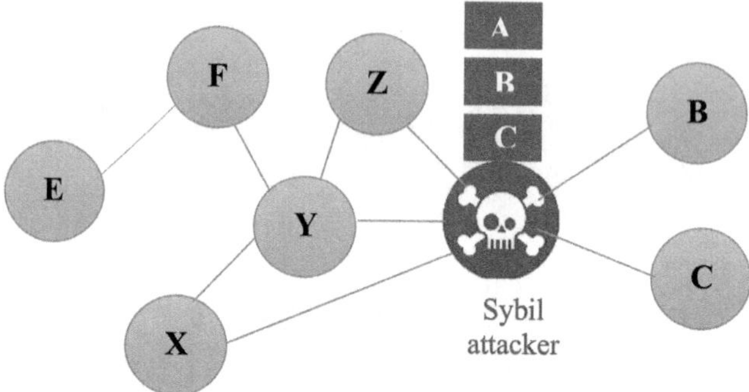

Figure 3.3 Sybil attack.

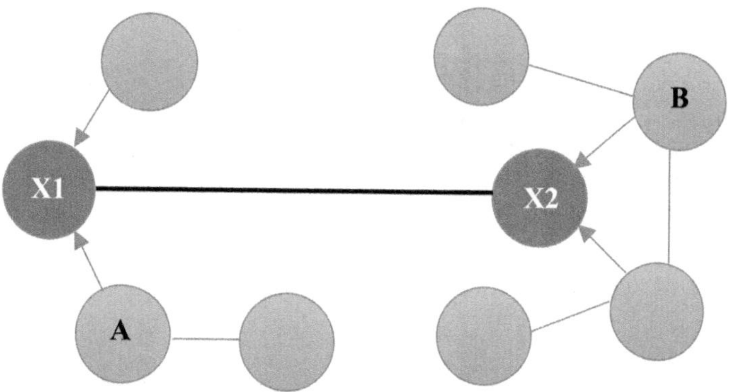

Figure 3.4 Wormhole attack.

3.4.2.1.6 Hello Flood

The attacker in a hello flood attack tricks the network's sensors into thinking it's all okay by sending them a barrage of hello packets. An adversary transfers power from one node to another using a routing protocol hello packet. An attacker with extensive processing capabilities and a wide transmission range sends hello packets to several sensor nodes across the network. As a result, the sensors start to believe the enemy is a nearby neighbor. Consequently, the victim nodes attempt to communicate with the BS by navigating around the attacker, who they see as a neighbor, as shown in Figure 3.5.

3.4.2.1.7 Acknowledgement Spoofing

A further attack in WSNs occurs when a malicious actor copies the contents of an acknowledgement message that a node has transmitted and then sends it back to its original sender. An attacker may employ this method to trick the sender into thinking their message reached the destination node when it did not.

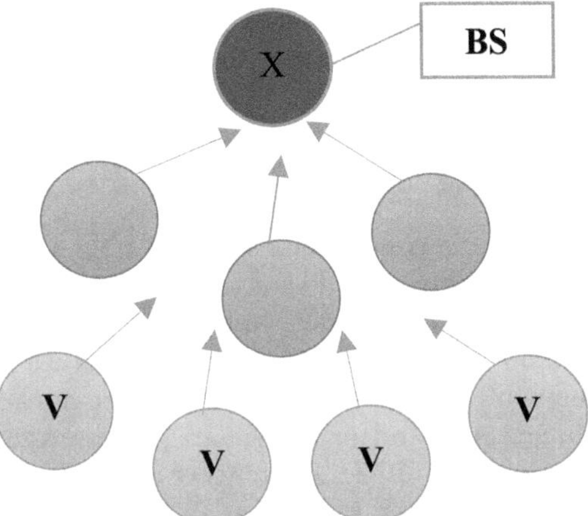

Figure 3.5 Hello flood attack.

3.4.2.1.8 Node Malfunction

Problems with individual nodes seriously threaten the availability and reliability of WSNs. Problems with one node might have a domino effect on the rest of the network, causing data loss or broken connections. In addition, it can potentially create congestion in the network, which can raise latency and lower throughput. The failure of a node can occur for several causes. Possible causes include malfunctioning software or hardware, power outages, or node damage. If the node fails due to these problems, important data can be lost, and the network could crash. In addition, attackers might use vulnerabilities introduced into the network by a faulty node to conduct subsequent assaults.

3.4.2.1.9 Collecting Passive Information

A passive eavesdropping attack is when an outsider gains access to a WSN's data transmission without participating in it themselves. Without interfering with the communication transmission or the sensor nodes' positioning, they may examine the recorded data to learn more about the contents of messages, such as physiological data, location, and other personally identifiable information.

3.4.2.1.10 Artificial Node

In WSNs, an attack known as an artificial node (or fake node) occurs when an adversarial node pretends to be a legitimate node in the network to carry out destructive activities. This node could act like it has sensor readings, sends out false signals, or even tampers with real ones. Such nodes pose a threat to network operations because they can mislead other nodes and cause them to make poor judgments, which in turn can cause the intended job to fail. Authentication and secure communication protocols are two of the many proposed defenses to artificial nodes, a major danger to WSNs.

3.4.3 Passive Attacks

An attacker conducting a passive attack just keeps tabs on network traffic to gather sensitive information; they do not change or manipulate the data in any way. Passwords, credit card details, and other sensitive information might be among the data an attacker tries to capture. Several techniques, including packet sniffing, network scanning, and traffic analysis, can be used to execute passive attacks. Intercepting and analyzing data packets as they go over a network are known as packet sniffing. An attacker can find possible vulnerabilities in a network by scanning it for devices and services and creating a map of them. To deduce information on communication patterns and transmitted content, traffic analysis examines data flow patterns. Passive attacks are hard to spot since they don't change the data, but they may be stopped by securing the data during transmission with authentication and encryption.

3.4.3.1 Congestion

When an attacker deliberately makes the radio frequency (RF) spectrum utilized by the network congested, it can lead to poor network performance or even network failure; this sort of assault is known as a congestion attack on the physical layer. An attacker might launch a congestion attack to disrupt the WBAN nodes' ability to communicate with one another. This interference can be caused by sending out very strong signals on the same channel as the WBAN or by flooding the channel with noise or other signals that lower the Signal-to-Noise Ratio (SNR) and limit the wireless communication's effective range. The assault can cause the sensor nodes to have slower processing speeds, more lost packets, or even a total loss of connectivity, which can affect the WBAN's reliability and performance. As sensor nodes try to retransmit damaged or missing packets, congestion attacks can increase power consumption and shorten battery life.

3.4.3.2 Frequency Transmission

To counteract unforeseen congestion or interferences in WSNs, this approach is employed. The process entails altering the broadcast frequency through a sequence, which the receiver must rebuild to recover the initial message. This method may protect the sensor network from harm even in very loud settings. On the other hand, sensor nodes may find the usage of broad-spectrum systems for frequency transmission to be complicated and costly. Despite these obstacles, frequency transmission is a great way to keep WSNs communicating reliably.

3.4.3.3 Frequency Jump

This technique entails quickly adjusting the broadcast frequency to avoid discovery or interfere with communication. This kind of assault usually comes with a hefty price tag and demands a lot of strength. Because of its potential effectiveness in single-frequency networks, it finds widespread application in WBANs. Since many sensor networks can't rapidly adjust to frequency changes, preventing frequency jump attacks isn't always easy. According to Wood, Stankovic, and Son, jammed-area mapping is one way to lessen the impact of frequency jump assaults. Reducing the effects of congestion or interference is the goal of this method, which entails first pin-pointing and then mapping those regions. To do this, we may use more sophisticated encryption methods, expand the spectrum of frequencies we use, or employ some other strategy to fortify the network.

3.4.3.4 Tapping

The physical layer of WBANs is vulnerable to tapping, a security hazard. Several problems might arise as a result of this assault, which includes illegal access to devices on the network. Due to the vast number of nodes in the network, it might be tough to recognize attackers who may abduct or trap them. The nodes are easy prey for hackers because of their portability and diminutive size. The physical temperature of the devices might be regulated as a possible solution to this problem. If someone tries to tap you, this can assist you to erase sensitive cryptographic data.

Nevertheless, not all WBANs will benefit from this method, which might be expensive. An alternative approach that has shown promise is using algorithms that mitigate the effect of a single critical component on the network. If all the nodes in a network share a secret key with their agents and neighbors, then compromising only one node will have a localized effect.

3.5 KEY MANAGEMENT FOR SMART HEALTHCARE SENSOR NETWORKS

Due to the significant attack vector potential of SHSNs, it is critical to implement security measures to prevent any assaults. Before, during, and after an assault, the system must be defended. Communication between nodes requires exchanging cryptographic keys for authentication and encryption to provide security services (availability, confidentiality, integrity, and secrecy). On the other hand, everyone knows that encryption systems are the first defense against any assault. It is also important that cryptographic methods identify the most harmful assaults in progress.

Furthermore, these methods need to be compact to make do with the restricted resources of the WSN. To address the issue of resource restriction in sensor devices, classic WSN deployments have suggested many important installation and administration techniques. Because of their minimal resource usage, symmetric cryptography primitives are relied upon by the majority of the suggested methods. As far as sensor nodes are concerned, these systems are the most efficient.

3.5.1 Methods and Protocols Classification

Through a pre-distribution phase, most techniques based on symmetric, asymmetric, or hybrid systems address the key setup problem. The practice of storing encryption keys in memory nodes before deployment is known as pre-distribution in a WSN. Various cryptographic key management techniques have been categorized in the literature.

Key sharing between two or more nodes is the foundation of certain classification algorithms, whereas others depend on using probabilities, combinatorial analysis, etc. We categorize everything into two big families: one for distribution models and the other for key management models. The symmetrical designs are in the second family, whereas the asymmetrical schemes are in the first. Figure 3.4 illustrates the process of classifying these objects. Here we will go over the most common models mentioned in published papers. Secure communication is essential for IoT nodes, just as for traditional ones. Authentication, secrecy, integrity, and non-repudiation are the main security criteria. Cryptographic primitives, such as signature and verification techniques and encryption and decryption algorithms, form the basis of these security services.

Therefore, a crucial management mechanism is required for these primitives to accommodate IoT devices' limited capabilities and budgetary restrictions, which do not permit the implementation of intricate security systems. In order to function on the constrained resources of nodes, the existing Internet key formation methods either are overly complex or fail to deliver an adequate degree of security. Protocols for establishing keys allow two or more nodes to share a secret, which may then be used as symmetric keys for different types of cryptography. Several security procedures, including those for protecting the authenticity of the source, ensuring data integrity, and maintaining user privacy, rely on symmetric cyphers and message authentication codes (MACs) to achieve these ends. Schemes that depend on an asymmetric key mechanism and other methods that pre-distribute symmetric keys are the primary types of extant smart sensor security mechanisms and schemes. The categorization utilized in this publication is illustrated in Figure 3.6.

3.5.2 Symmetric Key Pre-distribution Schemes

The symmetric or secret key approach entails encrypting and decrypting messages using the identical secret key. Key loading into the nodes before deployment is the essence of this approach. There are two main types of

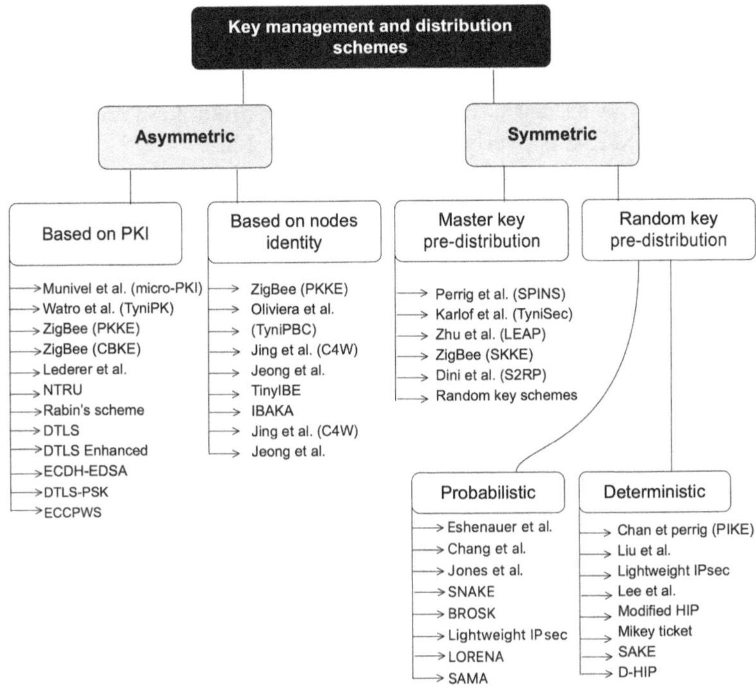

Figure 3.6 Key management models for SHSNs.

solutions for key pre-distribution methods in the IoT: deterministic and probabilistic. The primary pre-distribution processes could vary according to what's laid forth here.

3.5.2.1 SPINS

Security Protocols for Sensor Networks (SPINS) is a suite of security building blocks proposed by Perig and several other authors (Perrig et al. 2002). A security mechanism that was first suggested for the CWHN. Two protocols, namely µTESLA and the Sensor Network Encryption Protocol (SNEP), form its basis. While only adding 8 bytes to each transmission, SNEP guarantees low-cost data secrecy and authentication between two nodes. The enhanced version of TESLA, known as µTESLA, guarantees the broadcast's authenticity. SNEP uses Counter Mode CTR (CounTeR) to implement the RC5 encryption technique. At the outset of the deployment, the network structure only permits communication between the BSs and the sensor nodes. With SPINS, a new way is introduced for nodes to extend trust between themselves and the BS to direct connections between nodes. SPINS implements a secure two-party key agreement and an authenticated routing application independently using SNEP and µTESLA, all while consuming little storage, computation, and communication. But there are still some fundamental issues with SPINS, and they are as follows:

- Due to the security routing protocol's paired key pre-distribution strategy, SPINS is overly dependent on the BS.
- SPINS disregards updating communication keys and fails to account for the potential of a DoS attack.
- To achieve forward security, a practical key updating method is required.
- SPINS cannot address the issue of compromised nodes and concealed channel leaks.

3.5.2.2 LEAP

LEAP is a key management system for sensor networks, which stands for "Localized Encryption and Authentication Protocol." Its primary purpose is to facilitate in-network processing while limiting a compromised node's security effect to its local network neighborhood. An intriguing finding that various kinds of signals sent between sensor nodes have varying security needs inspired the concept of LEAP. Based on these findings, it is clear that a single keying system cannot satisfy these many security needs (Zhu, Setia, and Jajodia 2003). For each node LEAP supports the establishment of four types of keys:

- Individual key: Shared with the BS
- Pairwise key: Shared with another sensor node
- Cluster key: Shared with multiple neighboring nodes
- Global key: Shared by all nodes in the network

The packets that each node exchanged in a sensor network can be classified into several categories, which is based on different criteria, for example:

- Control packets versus data packets
- Broadcast packets versus unicast packets
- Queries or commands versus sensor readings

Depending on its classification, the security requirements for each packet are unique. While secrecy only applies to certain packet types, authentication is required for nearly all types. As stated next, some of the secure communication requirements of sensor networks cannot be met by a single keying technique.

3.5.2.3 LEAP Enhanced

According to LEAP+ (Zhu, Setia, and Jajodia 2006), one of the most important assumptions is that a node cannot be compromised within Tmin. This

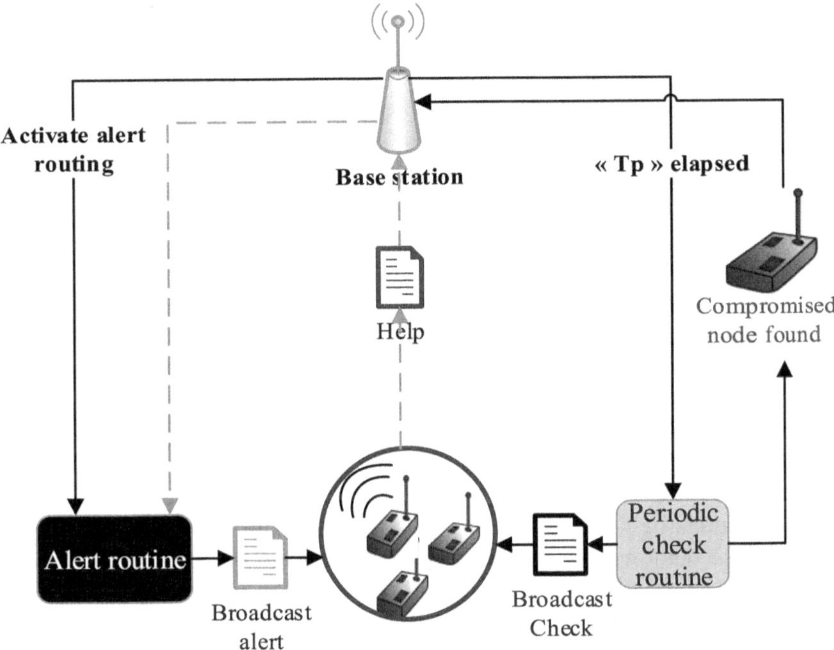

Figure 3.7 LEAP enhanced.

theory sounds reasonable; however, it's only feasible under perfect circumstances that Tmin is larger than the one assumed. Using a periodic verification called "Periodic Check" to identify the compromised node is the first of two strategies suggested by (Yassine and Ezzati 2016) to overcome this problem, as shown in Figure 3.7. The second model decides whether to remove the shared key after executing a sequence number in each node and comparing them with the information contained in the BS. This comparison is done after the pairwise key setup stage.

3.5.2.4 *TinySec*

TinySec was the first comprehensive secure design implemented at the data link layer for WSN, the TinySec protocol was proposed by Karlof et al. (Karlof, Sastry, and Wagner 2004). Two security options are available in this implementation: TinySec-Auth for authentication of messages without data encryption and TinySec-EA for message authentication with data encryption. TinySec employs conventional cryptographic methods, much like SPINS, to provide privacy and message integrity check. While SPINS uses the RC5 method, TinySec's authors believe that the Skipjack algorithm (Brickell and Davenport 1991) is better suited to WSN. A pre-key computation using 104 bytes of RAM is required by RC5, according to TinySec assessments. Instead of SPINS's CTR encryption mode, TinySec employs CBC or Cypher Block

Chaining. Using the same random values, the CTR will encrypt more packets. Due to their primary purpose in generating encryption key sequences, these numbers' recurrence can compromise the solution's security and make message content discoverable by attackers. Rather than proposing a key distribution technique, TinySec is an implementation tailored to the larger network. For symmetric key sharing across nodes, two keys are required. The first is for message encryption and the second for MAC calculation.

Xiong et al. (Li et al. 2017) proposed a lightweight anonymous mutual authentication and key agreement scheme tailored for centralized two-hop WBANs. The scheme ensures confidentiality, mutual authentication, and anonymity in data transmission, crucial for safeguarding patient information.

Xu et al. (2019) presented a lightweight and anonymous mutual authentication and key agreement scheme tailored for WBANs, prioritizing forward secrecy and computational efficiency. Our scheme, leveraging hash function and XOR operations, ensures forward secrecy without resorting to asymmetric encryption. Security verification through the ProVerif tool, along with informal analysis, validates the robustness of our approach. Comparative analysis demonstrates that our scheme offers superior security and computational efficiency compared to existing solutions. The paper discusses related work, outlines network and threat models, presents the proposed scheme, analyses security and performance, and concludes with future directions in WBAN security enhancement.

Chunka et al. (Chunka and Banerjee 2021) focused on analyzing the security vulnerabilities of a previous scheme by Li et al. (2017), proposing a more efficient authentication and key agreement scheme using cryptographic hash functions and XOR operations. The proposed scheme undergoes rigorous informal and formal security analyses, including Burrows-Abadi-Needham (BAN) logic and ProVerif simulation, to ensure its secrecy and authenticity. Additionally, the paper compares the proposed scheme with existing ones regarding computational cost, memory overhead, communication message exchange, and security functionalities. The subsequent sections delve into related work, a review of Li et al.'s scheme, the proposed authentication and key agreement scheme, security analysis, comparison with existing schemes, and finally, the conclusion and future research directions.

3.5.2.5 Probabilistic Key Distribution

In 2002, L. Eschenauer (Eschenauer and Gligor 2002) presented a system for randomly pre-distributing keys. There are usually three steps to a Routing Key Pre-distribution (RKP): distributing pre-keys, discovering shared keys, and establishing path keys. The schema generates a crucial key pool. After that, the sensor nodes receive their keys, chosen from a pool of keys. With some luck, a common commune can share two nodes. When two nodes are not in communication with each other, the third phase has begun. At this point, you can use the secure channel to transition to the key. When key K reaches the opposite node, the procedure terminates. From then on, K and the other node are considered the key pair. This plan proposes several solutions (Chan, Perrig, and Song 2003; Du et al. 2004; Ito, Ohta, Matsuda, and Yoneda 2005). These suggestions focus on enhancing the pre-distribution phase to decrease essential storage space requirements and increase node connection. A pre-distribution system is created by Du et al. (2004) that uses deployment information to prevent key assignments that aren't essential.

A plan based on Du et al. (2004) applied to two-dimensional locations is developed by Ito, Ohta, Matsuda, and Yoneda (2005). They provide an improved key connectivity price-density function. The study by Chan, Perrig, and Song (2003) is also translated into French for the convenience of French speakers. Node A discovers every potential link to node B. This is the fundamental concept. These arbitrary numbers serve to secure the shared keys for A and B. If you don't want to be able to spy on every path between them, the generous key will be shared by both nodes. Establishing the session key between all nodes is not guaranteed by the probabilistic key distribution, even with the path key's setup phase. There is a possibility that no common key exists between any two languages.

3.5.2.6 Deterministic Key Distribution

The key schemes discussed in this section use a predetermined procedure to establish the key pool and disperse the whole network. Including an unbiased third party during key boot is a defining feature of deterministic solutions' key schemas.

The ease of the offline key distribution method makes it a popular choice in WSN. Every node could share a pair of keys, depending on the protocol. The session is subsequently created after the third party has arrived. Since it does not need costly cryptographic computations like asymmetric methods, offline key distribution uses less power. The sensitive information kept in a sensor node can be compromised in the event of a physical assault on the node. That means the criminal can potentially compromise the whole network or even several nodes that share the same secret key as the one they're investigating. The model for secure key exchanges between sensor nodes has been developed in several previous publications using mathematical principles. Even in the IoT setting, these plans have their uses. Bivariate polynomials provide the basis for the most well-known schemes (Fanian, Berenjkoub, Saidi, and Gulliver 2010; Liu, Ning, and Li 2005). Bivariate n-polynomial degree f (x, y) is assigned to a common node A in these systems. The value of f(IdA, IdB), where IdA and IdB are the identities of A and B, respectively, may be derived. Since f (IdA, IdB) is equivalent to f (IdB, IdA), B may obtain the same key pair.

One such approach, the Bloom scheme (Bloom 1984), uses the secret key that nodes A and B share to create a secret symmetric matrix D. It provides a public matrix IA for A and an IB for B, respectively. For A, the private key is privA = DxIA; for B, it is privB = DxIB. The last step is determining the key pair by solving either (privA x IB) or (privB x IA). Both of these cases involve the dilemma of the unchanging. Two key settlement methods that include key management are SNAKE (Seys and Preneel 2002) and BROSK (Lai, Kim, and Verbauwhede 2002). All nodes on the same network are assumed to share a primary secret key by both protocols. Each communicating node in SNAKE uses the pre-shared key to produce two random nonces, forming the session together. The nuncio, an important message in negotiations, is aired by BROSK. After a node has received messages from its neighbors, it may construct the session key by determining the MAC of two nuncios.

According to Raza et al. (2011), an IP-based WSN may be secured using the industry-standard IPsec protocol by using 6LoWPAN. Their proposed methods manage packet sizes while integrating IPsec with the 6LoWPAN layer and compressing the AH and ESP headers. Despite their usefulness for origin authentication, message integrity, and IP packet privacy, the AH and ESP techniques aren't equipped to deal with key exchange. The use of a pre-shared key facilitates the manual establishment of security relationships.

3.5.2.7 LORENA

Coelho et al. (2022) addressed the security challenges in Internet of Health Things (IoHT), particularly in wearable medical devices and remote health monitoring systems. With the increasing proliferation of IoT devices in healthcare, ensuring secure transmission of sensitive patient data becomes paramount. The paper proposes a novel protocol called LORENA (Low memORy symmEtric-key geNerAtion method based on groups) to generate symmetric keys with low resource consumption using physiological signals, particularly electrocardiogram (ECG) data. LORENA establishes secure communication channels and facilitates key device agreement, ensuring data confidentiality and integrity. LORENA achieves efficient key generation and transmission by leveraging the human body as a communication medium and employing approximate computing techniques while minimizing resource usage. The paper's contributions include defining communication protocols, evaluating key generation efficiency, and providing a scalable solution suitable for real-world deployment with low-cost microcontrollers.

3.5.3 Asymmetric Key Schemes

By using a "public" key for encryption and a "private" key for decryption and signing, the asymmetric or public key approach ensures that messages remain secure. According to Nguyen, Laurent, and Oualha (2015), there are primarily two types of asymmetric schemes: public key encryption for key transmission and classic asymmetric approaches for key management. The following sections will concisely analyze several asymmetric key schemes that can be used in the IoT.

3.5.3.1 *Key Transport Based on Public Key Encryption*

This subcategory examines the key establishment schemes in which the public key is used to carry secret data or to negotiate a session key. Several methods are used to generate the public and private key pair. This subcategory classifies these mechanisms according to public/private key generation methods. Figure 3.7 gives an example of a communication scenario between two entities A and B. In this scenario, A and B can use the public keys to create an encrypted channel. The Certificate Authority (CA) can participate to verify the identity of the message sender when certificates are supported. This method can be expensive for resource-constrained sensor nodes, especially when using a traditional algorithm such as Rivest-Shamir-Adleman (RSA). Without a verifiable relationship between the public key and identity (i.e., cryptography based on identity, cryptographic identification, or CA mediation), this approach becomes vulnerable to man in the middle attack. Indeed, A and B cannot authenticate the identity of the other. When communicating with B, an attacker can generate any public/private key and pretend to be A.

3.5.3.2 *Micro-PKI*

A more condensed form of traditional PKI, micro-PKI (Public Key Infrastructure Micro) is the approach that Munivel et al. (Munivel and Ajit 2010) suggest for WSN. A public key and a private key are stored in the BS. Nodes in the network authenticate the BS using the public key, while the BS uses the private key to decode data received by the nodes. Before deployment, every node stores the BS's public key. Two different forms of authentication (handshake) are incorporated into the authors' approach. Nodes in a network initially authenticate with one another and the BS. The node creates a symmetric session key using the BS's public key for encryption. The authors' suggestion includes a MAC that uses the same encryption key as the message to guarantee the authenticity of messages sent and received. To facilitate the addition of new nodes to the network, the public key of the BS is saved in these nodes before deployment.

3.5.3.3 *TinyPK*

Using public keys and the Diffie–Hellman (DH) principle, Watro et al. (2004) provided TinyPK, a technique for establishing a secret key between two WSN nodes. Nodes' public keys are signed by a trustworthy authority in TinyPK. Each node receives the CA key before deployment so that they may verify each other's key neighbors. Nodes use many resources due to the RSA algorithm's selection for encryption. So, even the most fundamental tasks might take a few seconds, which affects responsiveness and shortens the network's lifespan.

3.5.3.4 *PKKE and CBKE*

Key establishment in Zigbee's PKKE and CBKE protocols rely on node identities. Using these IDs, we can generate a unique key that can be used to unlock any two nodes in a network. Still, the two nodes need to communicate to generate the shared key. So, to generate a key, procedures necessitate the exchange of several messages in both directions. Several solutions have been suggested to eliminate these interactions, which would benefit the intermediate and power nodes that wish to keep a secret. The acronym for "Identity-Based Non-Interactive Key Distribution Scheme" is "ID-NIKDS" in the cryptography community (Steinwandt and Suárez 2011).

3.5.3.5 *C4W*

A novel approach, C4W, was put out by Jing, Hu, and Chen (2006), and it relies on the nodes' identities to determine public keys. By using their own identities, nodes may deduce the public keys of other nodes. In what ways may a certificate be superseded? Keys (private/public key ECC) and public information about the network nodes are placed into the BS and the nodes before deployment. Without the need for certificates, using the DH key exchange principle, the C4W technique generates a single shared key between any two nodes.

3.5.3.6 *pDCS (Privacy-Enhanced Data-Centric Sensor Network)*

A privacy-enhanced data-centric sensor networks (pDCS) architecture, "data-centric sensor networks, enhanced privacy,"(Shao et al. 2009), uses rectangular cells divided by Steiner's Euclidean trees to organize the network. Within each cell, there are sensors and cell keys. Mobile data "sinks" collect and transmit this information, but the encryption prevents an unauthorized party from accessing the original sensor that detected an event. Once again, a Bloom filter reduces the volume of control data generated by pDCS. ERP-DCS, "an efficient protocol for key regeneration for DCS networks" (Ming Huang Shun, Chan, and Dai 2013), has been developed to enhance the key management mechanism when an agent is compromised and recognized. An exclusion system known as Exclusion Basis System (EBS) has been employed.

3.5.3.7 *ZigBee*

While Zigbee's (2006) focus is more general, it uses the IEEE 802.15.4 stack, which is utilized in sensor networks on occasion. As things stand, he has the potential to become the de facto norm for all "Internet of Things" linked devices. When coupled with sensors, it safeguards data by encrypting it, authenticating its user, and preventing replay attacks. With the introduction of the concept of a "trust centre" by ZigBee, key management is centralized. Although alternative designs offer additional security, this one comes at the expense of headers and computations.

Using out-of-band communications or pre-distribution of public keys are two examples of how such processes work. These methods allow for a limited amount of message exchanges, but they can't handle large networks since every device has to know everyone else's public key. Some "raw public key encryption" methods have been suggested for WSN networks, including NtruEncrypt (Gaubatz, Kaps, and Ozturk 2005) and Rabin (Rabin 1978). RSA, an algorithm in many cryptosystems, is likewise based on the difficulty of the factorization issue; Rabin's schema is quite close to it. Interestingly, the system's power consumption for decryption processes is same as RSAs, while maintaining the same level of security. Since only one equation is required to encrypt a message, it offers a considerably quicker technique for encryption processes. One of the alternative cryptographic systems is NtruEncrypt, which uses a trellis with RSA and elliptic curve cryptography (ECC) primitives. Smart cards and RFID tags, which have limited resources, are ideal for this technique because of its efficiency. The Rabin method, NtruEncrypt, and ECC are the three suggested PKC techniques for limited devices that are compared in (Gaubatz, Kaps, and Ozturk 2005). According to the findings, NtruEncrypt is the most energy-efficient operation on average.

Nevertheless, this encryption scheme may cause packet fragmentation at lower levels and several retransmissions when communication faults occur, frequently requiring huge messages. If the transmitting power is the most significant and limiting component, protocols based on "raw public key encryption" have a modest message exchange need, which is highly favorable. An authentication approach for the IoT based on Two-level Session Keys (TSKs) was suggested by Mahmood, Ning, and Ghafoor in 2017. Additionally, a technique for associating nodes is presented. End-to-end users may communicate securely and with minimal overhead using TSK.

Many security service standards established by the Internet Engineering Task Force (IETF) include Transport Layer Security (TLS) as their preferred protocol (Turner 2011). Nevertheless, TLS is not recommended for optimal security in the IoT, as stated in (Kothmayr et al. 2012; Raza et al. 2013). TLS is typically used with dependable transport protocols like Transmission Control Protocol (TCP), which aren't ideal for devices with limited resources because of their congestion management method. Datagram Transport Layer Security (DTLS) is a newer proposal to replace TLS in very limited settings. It offers the same robust security as TLS but operates on the unstable User Datagram Protocol (UDP) transport technology. Using a certificate is, at its core, costly. The researchers examined the following software and hardware enhancements to lower energy consumption: implementation of hardware accelerators for cryptography. The computations involved in cryptography are handled by hardware accelerators. A technique for DTLS implementation utilizing sensor node hardware was proposed by (Kothmayr et al. 2012). This method is based on the premise that all sensors have a Trusted Platform Module (TPM) installed. Hardware support for the RSA algorithm and tamper-proof key generation and storage are provided by an integrated device known as a TPM. Before deployment, a publisher with a trusted CA certificate and a trusted publisher certificate integrated with a trusted hardware module (TPM) must be stored on the publisher. We offer authentication using the DTLS pre-shared key encryption key for publishers without TPM chips. This key requires minimal randomly generated bytes to be placed onto publishers before deployment. For the AC server to provide the device keys to those with the proper authority, this secret must also be accessible to them. In addition to a high degree of security in trust building with the aid of an authorized third party, this solution offers inexpensive energy, end-to-end latency, and overhead memory, as well as message integrity, secrecy, and authenticity.

Recent research by Maleh, Ezzati, and Belaissaoui (2016a) aims to mitigate DoS attacks by lowering the communication cost of the DTLS protocol and strengthening the vulnerability of cookie exchange during connection establishment. To lessen the burden on the network and save space, the Constrained Application Protocol (CoAP) incorporates the upgraded DTLS protocol.

Shamir (1984) created the initial version of identity-based cryptography. An individual's or group's public key is defined by this cryptographic method as a known string (identity). A third party, known as a public key generator (PKG), uses each entity's public key to create its private key, as seen in Figure 3.8. This technique is especially beneficial for WSNs since it eliminates certificate requirements. To set up secure communication utilizing their identities, any sensor node may easily produce the public key of any other node. The verification of the legitimate sensor identification also helps the revocation procedure. Since PKG has access to the private keys of every node in the network, ID-based schemas are susceptible to key deposit attacks. According to Yang, Ding, and Wu (2013) and Granjal, Monteiro, and Sa Silva (2013b), the ECC primitive is the most common way to use the IBE paradigm in a limited setting. Other primitives have their implementations; for instance, ElGamal-type RSA or IBE. But, because there are a lot of exponentiation operations, and each one has a big exponent, they are costly for the limited nodes. Using the design from Boneh and Franklin (2003) as inspiration, IBAKA is an IBE system proposed by Yang, Ding, and Wu (2013). To create a session key, though, they modify the IBE technique so it can work with an ECDH key exchange. Every time a secret key is started, their proposal calls for two bilinear pairings and three multiplications of scalar points.

3.5.3.8 Asymmetrical Schemes for Key Agreement

Protocols for key agreement based on asymmetric primitives in the IoT fall under this class. According to many studies, a key agreement protocol is a

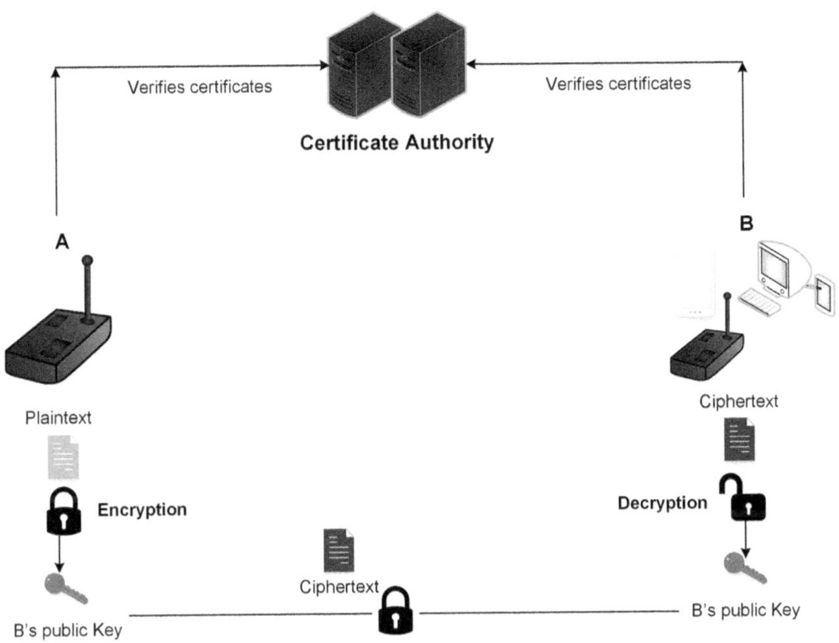

Figure 3.8 Public key transport mechanism.

way for two or more parties to develop a shared secret without anybody else being able to guess how much that secret is worth (Nguyen, Laurent, and Oualha 2015). An example of an asymmetric key agreement is shown in Figure 3.9. A notable example of a symmetric key chord is the DH protocol and its variations (Rescorla. E 1999). Nevertheless, based on how nodes are classified in LWIG terminology according to their resource capacity, DH protocols are deemed inappropriate and costly for limited nodes, namely those in classes 0 and 1 (Bormann and Ersue 2013). Several variants of the DH protocol are contemplated in limited settings, employing ECC (ECDH). Compared to RSA, the key size of the ECDH cryptographic primitive is much less. The US National Institute for Standards and Technology (NIST) has demonstrated that a 256-bit key, generated via an elliptic curve, is preferable to the 3072 bits used by RSA and the DH protocol in order to attain the 128-bit AES key's security level. For example, a framework that enables end-to-end adaptive security in the context of WSNs bound for the Internet and end-to-end address TLS with delegated ECC public key authentication is provided (Granjal, Monteiro, and Silva 2013a). For sensor networks, IBAKA provides a hybrid of ECDH and BIE (Yang, Ding, and Wu 2013). Using the Boneh pattern, which is based on identification, the system ensures that message exchanges remain secret, building on the foundation of the ECDH protocol (Boneh and Franklin 2003).

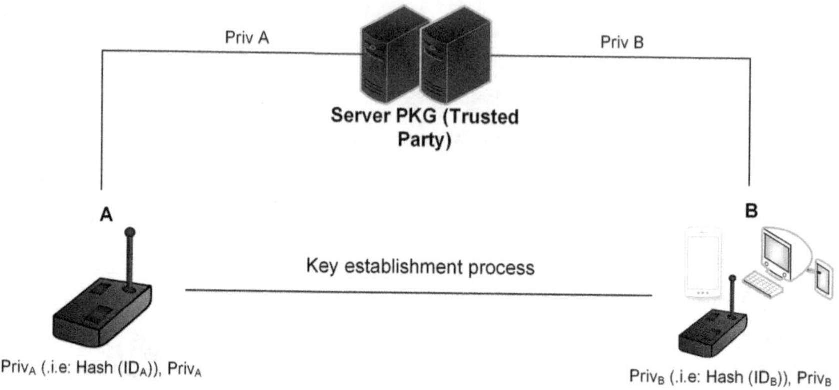

Figure 3.9 Identity-based cryptography scheme.

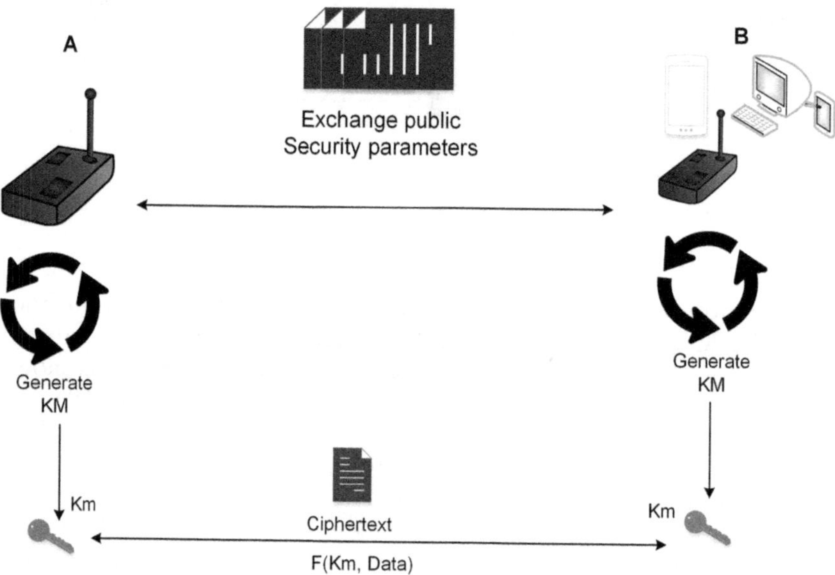

Figure 3.10 Key agreement based on asymmetric mechanisms.

Using public key methods and the Rabin scheme, Hayajneh et al. (2014) presented a lightweight authentication protocol for WBAN, which is well-suited for small devices with limited resources (Figure 3.10). In a medical setting, the technology is intended to be implanted in the bodies of individuals suffering from various ailments. Actuators, a physician, sensors, and a coordinator of nodes are the four components of the system. In the system, these nodes securely communicate with one another.

Building on the work of Lu, Li, Peng, and Yang (2015), the study of Chaudhry, Mahmood, Naqvi, and Khurram Khan (2015) introduces an improved protocol used for authentication in Telecare Medic Information Systems (TMISs). Patients' privacy, their identification, and the TMIS server were all determined to be at risk under the initial protocol, according to the authors. To fix these flaws, they came up with a new protocol that is more secure but also more computationally expensive. against guarantee the protocol's resilience against assaults, the ProVerif tool was used for testing.

In the study by Abdmeziem and Tandjaoui (2015), the authors present a secure key management strategy that e-health apps may use to keep patient data private, intact, and readily available. Key distribution and administration are made easier by the protocol's hybrid method, which mixes symmetric and asymmetric encryption. Key management and setup between the sensors and the server is handled by a trusted third-party authority (TPA) in the protocol. The authors also suggested a safe approach for establishing session keys that employ a one-time password for both the server and sensor to authenticate each other. Results from a simulation test of the proposed protocol demonstrate its efficacy, security, and ability to manage the essential process for e-health applications.

Telecare Medic Information Systems utilized a newly introduced protocol (Chaudhry, Mahmood, Naqvi, and Khurram Khan 2015). The paper suggests a method for authenticating a healthcare server in a telecare Health Information System (HIS) while protecting the patient's privacy. The protocol has four parts: the patient, the trusted authority, the medical server, and the medical sensor node. To ensure the transmitted messages' security, authenticity, and privacy, the protocol employs symmetric key cryptography, MACs, and hash functions. By using a pseudonym rather than the patient's real name, the technique guarantees the patient's privacy.

Feng et al. (2020) proposed a collaborative authentication protocol for Smart Electronic Health Record (SEHR) systems, addressing the challenge of ensuring security and privacy in healthcare data management. The paper highlights the need for robust authentication mechanisms in SEHR systems due to the sensitive nature of patient data and the potential risks associated with unauthorized access. By introducing a collaborative authentication protocol based on two-party computation, the paper aims to enhance efficiency and security while ensuring fairness between patients and doctors. Additionally, the paper thoroughly analyses the proposed protocol's provable security and performance, demonstrating its effectiveness for practical implementation in SEHR systems.

A novel privacy-preserving mutual authentication system for WBANs was proposed by Jegadeesan et al. (2020), who also introduced a privacy-preserving protocol. The protocol aims to provide private and efficient data transfer between a user's wearable sensors and an off-site server. The three main components of the suggested protocol are the user, the proxy node, and the distant server. The protocol protects the user's anonymity, which permits the user to remain anonymous to both the proxy node and the distant server. Its unique encryption and decryption technique, which is based on ECC and hash functions, achieves secure communication between entities. The four primary components of the suggested protocol are signing up, verifying identity, creating a session key, and exchanging messages. The user's authentication and session key generation occur during the registration step. During the authentication phase, the session key is used for mutual authentication between the user and the proxy node.

Additionally, the proxy node verifies the distant server. The user and the remote server establish the session key during the session key establishment phase. The user and the remote server have created a session key and are ready to exchange encrypted communications. WBANs can benefit from the suggested Efficient Privacy-preserving Authentication for WBANs (EPAW) protocol's privacy-preserving mutual authentication approach, which is both efficient and safe. Connecting the user's wearable sensors to a distant server safely, the protocol also protects the user's anonymity. Despite being able to operate in WBANs with limited resources, the simulation-based trials demonstrate that the suggested protocol has little computing costs and overhead.

It was suggested in 2020 that WSNs use a new authentication and key agreement system (Rehman, Altaf, and Iqbal 2020). User nodes (UNs), gateway nodes (GNs), and remote healthcare servers (RHSs) are the three components of the suggested design. The scheme's use of hash functions and symmetric key encryption ensures secure communication between entities. First, the UN and GN create a session key; second, the GN and RHS use the key established during the first session to share the key. This is the first of two steps in the key agreement procedure. To ensure that communications sent between entities are legitimate, the authentication procedure uses MACs. The suggested approach safeguards data from attacks like replay, impersonation, and man-in-the-middle while simultaneously facilitating mutual authentication between entities. To ensure the scheme is secure and works as intended, we ran it using the Automated Validation of Internet Security Protocols and Applications (AVISPA) tool. The security study shows that the suggested scheme is safe and efficient, and hence it may be used in WBANs. Currently, existing techniques use more memory, take more calculation time, and have more communication overhead than the suggested approach.

Olufemi and Adedamola (2020) proposed a Secure Addressing and Mutual Authentication (SAMA) protocol. With the rapid integration of healthcare and IoT technologies, ensuring the secure communication between patients and doctors remotely has become increasingly vital. The paper emphasizes the need for a robust protocol to uniquely identify smart medical devices (SMDs) and establish mutual trust between these devices and the medical authentication server (HS). The SAMA scheme aims to achieve this by utilizing a modified standard IPv6 address format for secure addressing;

incorporating password authentication, unique identity verification of doctors, and SMDs; and establishing secure communication channels with session keys. By encapsulating each packet without increasing packet size, the proposed protocol aims to mitigate various security threats and ensure patient data's integrity and confidentiality.

Pirmoradian, Safkhani, and Dakhilalian (2023) evaluated the security of a recent authentication scheme proposed by Sowjanya, Dasgupta, and Ray (2020) for WHMS, based on ECC. Our analysis reveals vulnerabilities to passive insider secret disclosure and replay attacks in their scheme. To address these weaknesses, we propose a novel ECC-based authentication scheme, ECCPWS, designed to mitigate these vulnerabilities effectively. We provide informal and formal security proofs for ECCPWS, including analysis using the Real-or-Random (ROR) model, Burrows-Abadi-Needham (BAN) logic, and verification using Scyther and AVISPA tools. Our findings demonstrate that ECCPWS offers comprehensive security against various security threats, ensuring the integrity and privacy of patient data in WBANs and WHMS.

3.6 ANALYSES AND COMPARISON

3.6.1 Analyses Method

To compare the various key management approaches, a number of characteristics are considered. Figure 3.11 displays the primary criteria. We start by limiting the resources that nodes have. Now that the nodes have been installed to gather the data, the suggested key management mechanism must

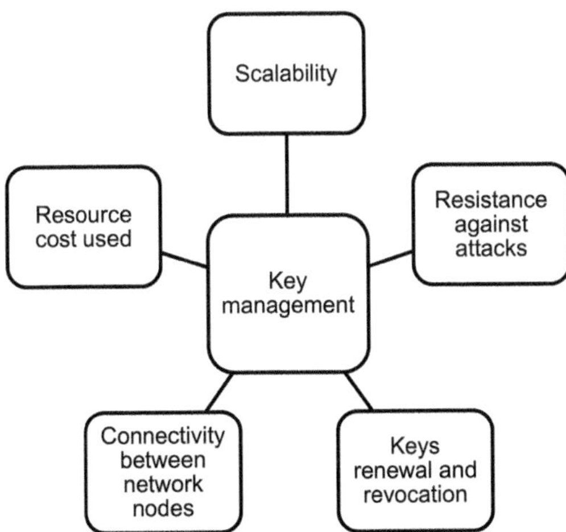

Figure 3.11 The criteria for comparison of methods of key management.

consider that. They rely on their embedded energy and memory space for data storage and application role assurance.

Additionally, the solution needs to be scalable, dynamic, and flexible. Resistance to assaults is another need that must be met. If an adversary manages to capture a node and stores information about it, they can use that data to launch more attacks or otherwise control the network. Before dispersing keys, the key management system should be able to identify compromised nodes and verify their authenticity. Key renewal and revocation is the last requirement. It can be considered just as crucial as key distribution. Keys that have expired or detected by an adversary must be revoked. It is also necessary to refresh the keys for the secure links regularly. A network's connection ensures nodes have more secure pathways to transmit data. Key distribution methods should be able to guarantee reliable network connectivity. If a node leaves or is captured, it might affect the ability of other nodes to connect to the network. This aspect has to be considered by the distribution technique when suggesting new safe pathways.

3.6.2 Comparison and Discussion

We have analyzed various key management schemes for SHSNs and categorized their diagrams in Figure 3.6. Table 3.3 shows the results of comparing these diagrams using the same criteria as shown in Figure 3.11. Be aware that the table's evaluation of memory storage just considers the number of keys stored in the nodes, ignoring the size of code algorithms and cryptographic primitives.

3.7 CONCLUSION

This chapter thoroughly analyses security protocols for safeguarding the integrity, confidentiality, and availability of sensitive patient data within e-Health applications. Employing an SLR methodology, this chapter meticulously examines the intricacies of securing communications within smart sensor networks, emphasizing the critical role of cryptographic methodologies and intrusion detection systems in bolstering the resilience of communication channels. Through a comprehensive exploration of security requirements, threats, and key management strategies specific to healthcare sensor networks, this chapter offers invaluable insights into the evolving landscape of healthcare cybersecurity. This chapter lays a solid foundation for future research endeavors to advance secure and trustworthy e-Health applications by elucidating fundamental questions concerning security paradigms in healthcare environments. Moreover, its synthesis of existing literature and recommendations for enhancing security practices contribute significantly to the ongoing discourse surrounding secure healthcare infrastructure development.

Table 3.3 Key Management Techniques for WSN as Suggested and Compared. Memory, Connectivity, Resilience, Computational Complexity, Communication Complexity, and Renewal and Revocation Are the Five Evaluation Metrics. These Metrics Have Two Possible Values, Representing the Degree to Which a Particular Protocol Supports a Property: + (Good or Medium Performance–Level) and − (Poor Performance Level)

Schemes			*Criteria of Comparison*								
					Resistance against attacks				*Resource cost used*		
Type	*Authors*	*Based on*	*Scalability*	*Connectivity*	*Information collection*	*Communication perturbation*	*Data aggregation and resource exhausted*	*Capture of physical nodes*	*Memory (key store)*	*Calculation and energy consumption*	*Renewal and revocation*
Symmetric key schemes	SNAKE (Seys and Preneel 2002)	Deter.	−	+		−		−	+	−	−
	BROSK (Lai, Kim, and Verbauwhede 2002)	Deter.	−	+		−		−	−	−	−
	(Chan, Perrig, and Song 2003)	Proba.	−	+		−		+	−	+	−
	(Chan and Perrig 2005)	Deter.	−	+		−		+	+	−	−
	(Perrig et al. 2002)	MK + BS	−	+		−		−	+	+	+
	(Zhu, Setia, and Jajodia 2003)	MK	+	+		−		−	+	−	+
	lightweight IPsec (Raza et al. (Raza et al. 2011)	Deter.	+	+		−		−	+	+	−
	DTLS-PSK (Granjal, Monteiro, and Sa Silva 2013b)	PKI	+	+		−		−	+	−	+
	(Yassine and Ezzati 2016)	MK + BS	+	+		−		+	+	−	−
	LORENA (Coelho et al. 2022)	Proba.	+	+		−		+	+	−	+

(*Continued*)

Table 3.3 (*Continued*) Key Management Techniques for WSN as Suggested and Compared. Memory, Connectivity, Resilience, Computational Complexity, Communication Complexity, and Renewal and Revocation Are the Five Evaluation Metrics. These Metrics Have Two Possible Values, Representing the Degree to Which a Particular Protocol Supports a Property: + (Good or Medium Performance–Level) and − (Poor Performance Level)

Schemes			*Criteria of Comparison*								
					Resistance against attacks				*Resource cost used*		
Type	*Authors*	*Based on*	*Scalability*	*Connectivity*	*Information collection*	*Communication perturbation*	*Data aggregation and resource exhausted*	*Capture of physical nodes*	*Memory (key store)*	*Calculation and energy consumption*	*Renewal and revocation*
Public key schemes	(Zigbee 2006)	ID	+	−		+		+	−	−	+
	(Munivel and Ajit 2010)	PKI	−	−		+		−	+	+	−
	(Watro et al. 2004)	PKI	−	−		−		+	−	−	+
	DTLS modified (Raza et al. 2013)		+	+		−		+	+	−	−
	IBAKA (Yang, Ding, and Wu 2013)	Node identity	+	−		−		+	−	−	+
	DTLS Enhanced (Yassine, Ezzati, and Belaissaoui 2016b)	PKI	+	+		+		+	−	+	−
	Feng et al. 2019	PKI	+	+		−		+		−	+
	EPAW (Jegadeesan et al. 2020)	PKI	+	+		+		−	+	+	−
	SAMA (Olufemi and Adedamola 2020)	Proab.	+	+		+		+	−	+	+
	ECCPWS (Pirmoradian, Safkhani, and Dakhilalian 2023)	PKI	+	+		+		−		−	+

REFERENCES

Abdmeziem, Mohammed Riyadh, and Djamel Tandjaoui. 2015. "An End-to-End Secure Key Management Protocol for e-Health Applications." *Computers & Electrical Engineering* 44: 184–97.

Abouzakhar, Nasser S., Andrew Jones, and Olga Angelopoulou. 2017. "Internet of Things Security: A Review of Risks and Threats to Healthcare Sector." In *2017 IEEE International Conference on Internet of Things (IThings) and IEEE Green Computing and Communications (GreenCom) and IEEE Cyber, Physical and Social Computing (CPSCom) and IEEE Smart Data (SmartData)*, IEEE, 373–78.

Bloom, B. S. (1984). The 2 sigma problem: The search for methods of group instruction as effective as one-to-one tutoring. Educational researcher, 13(6), 4-16.

Boneh, Dan, and Matt Franklin. 2003. "Identity-Based Encryption from the Weil Pairing." *SIAM Journal on Computing* 32(3): 586–615.

Bormann, Caster, M. Ersue, and A. Keranen. 2013. "Terminology for Constrained Node Networks." *Draft-Internet.*

Brickell, E. F., & Davenport, D. M. (1991). On the classification of ideal secret sharing schemes. Journal of Cryptology, 4(2), 123-134.

Butt, Shariq Aziz, Jorge Luis Diaz-Martinez, Tauseef Jamal, Arshad Ali, Emiro De-La-Hoz-Franco, and Muhammad Shoaib. 2019. "IoT Smart Health Security Threats." In *2019 19th International Conference on Computational Science and Its Applications (ICCSA)*, IEEE, 26–31.

Chan, Haowen, and Adrian Perrig. 2005. "PIKE: Peer Intermediaries for Key Establishment in Sensor Networks." *IEEE Infocom* 1(Cc): 524–35. doi:10.1109/INFCOM.2005.1497920.

Chan, Haowen, Adrian Perrig, and Dawn Song. 2003. "Random Key Predistribution Schemes for Sensor Networks." *Proceedings—IEEE Symposium on Security and Privacy* 2003-January: 197–213. doi:10.1109/SECPRI.2003.1199337.

Chaudhry, Shehzad Ashraf, Khalid Mahmood, Husnain Naqvi, and Muhammad Khurram Khan. 2015. "An Improved and Secure Biometric Authentication Scheme for Telecare Medicine Information Systems Based on Elliptic Curve Cryptography." *Journal of Medical Systems* 39: 1–12.

Chunka, Chukhu, and Subhasish Banerjee. 2021. "An Efficient Mutual Authentication and Symmetric Key Agreement Scheme for Wireless Body Area Network." *Arabian Journal for Science and Engineering* 46(9): 8457–73. doi:10.1007/s13369-021-05532-8.

Coelho, Kristtopher Kayo, Michele nogueira, Mateus Coutinho Marim, Edelberto Franco Silva, Alex Borges Vieira, and José Augusto M. Nacif. 2022. "LORENA: Low MemORy SymmEtric-Key GeNerAtion Method for Based on Group Cryptography Protocol Applied to the Internet of Healthcare Things." *IEEE Access* 10: 12564–79. doi:10.1109/ACCESS.2022.3143210.

Du, Wenliang, Shigang Chen, Wenliang Du, Jing Deng, Yunghsiang S Han, Shigang Chen, and Pramod K Varshney. 2004. "A Key Management Scheme for Wireless Sensor Networks Using Deployment Knowledge." *Electrical Engineering and Computer Science. In IEEE INFOCOM 2004 (Vol. 1). IEEE.*

Eschenauer, L., and V. D. Gligor. 2002. "A Key-Management Scheme for Distributed Sensor Networks." *In Proceedings of the 9th ACM Conference on Computer and Communications Security (pp. 41-47).*

Fanian, A., M. Berenjkoub, H. Saidi, and T. A. Gulliver. 2010. "A Scalable and Efficient Key Establishment Protocol for Wireless Sensor Networks." *2010 IEEE Globecom Workshops, GC'10*: 1533–38. doi:10.1109/GLOCOMW.2010.5700195.

Feng, Q., D. He, H. Wang, L. Zhou, and K.-K. R. Choo. 2020. "Lightweight Collaborative Authentication With Key Protection for Smart Electronic Health Record System." *IEEE Sensors Journal* 20(4): 2181–96. doi:10.1109/JSEN.2019.2949717.

Gaubatz, Gunnar, J. P. Kaps, and E. Ozturk. 2005. "State of the Art in Ultra-Low Power Public Key Cryptography for Wireless Sensor Networks." In *Proceedings of the Third IEEE International Conference on Pervasive Computing and Communications*, IeEE, 146–50. doi:10.1109/PERCOMW.2005.76.

Granjal, J., E. Monteiro, and J. S[a] Silva. 2013a. "A Framework towards Adaptable and Delegated End-to-End Transport-Layer Security for Internet-Integrated Wireless Sensor Networks." In *2nd joint ERCIM EMobility and MobiSense Workshop*, 34. *University of Bern, Bern, Switzerland.*

Granjal, J., E. Monteiro, and J. S. Silva. 2013b. "End-to-End Transport-Layer Security for Internet-Integrated Sensing Applications with Mutual and Delegated ECC Public-Key Authentication." *IFIP Networking Conference* 2013: 1–9.

Hayajneh, Thaier, Athanasios V .Vasilakos, Ghada Almashaqbeh, Bassam J. Mohd, Muhammad A Imran, Muhammad Z. Shakir, and Khalid A. Qaraqe. 2014. "Public-Key Authentication for Cloud-Based WBANs." *ACM*, In *Proceedings of the 9th International Conference on Body Area Networks*, 286–92.

Ito, Takashi, Hidenori Ohta, Nori Matsuda, and Takeshi Yoneda. 2005. "A Key Pre-Distribution Scheme for Secure Sensor Networks Using Probability Density Function of Node Deployment." *Proceedings of the 3rd ACM Workshop on Security of Ad Hoc and Sensor Networks—SaSN '05*: 69. doi:10.1145/1102219.1102233.

Jegadeesan, S., M. Azees, N. Ramesh Babu, U. Subramaniam, and J. D. Almakhles. 2020. "EPAW: Efficient Privacy Preserving Anonymous Mutual Authentication Scheme for Wireless Body Area Networks (WBANs)." *IEEE Access* 8: 48576–86. doi:10.1109/ACCESS.2020.2977968.

Jing, Qi, Jianbin Hu, and Zhong Chen. 2006. "C4W: An Energy Efficient Public Key Cryptosystem for Large-Scale Wireless Sensor Networks." *2006 IEEE International Conference on Mobile Ad Hoc and Sensor Systems*: 827–32. doi:10.1109/MOBHOC.2006.278660.

Karlof, Chris, Naveen Sastry, and David Wagner. 2004. "TinySec: A Link Layer Security Architecture for Wireless Sensor Networks." *Proceedings of the 2nd ACM International Conference on Embedded Networked Sensor Systems (SenSys)*: 162–75. doi:http://0-doi.acm.org.library.unl.edu:80/10.1145/1031495.1031515.

Kothmayr, Thomas, Corinna Schmitt, Wen Hu, and Michael Brünig, and G. Carle. 2012. "A DTLS Based End-T o-End Security Architecture for the Internet of Things with Two-Way Authentication." In *Local Computer Networks Workshops (LCN Workshops), 2012 IEEE 37th Conference On*, 956–63. http://www.cse.unsw.edu.au/~wenh/kothmayr_senseapp12.pdf.

Lai, Bocheng, Sungha Kim, and Ingrid Verbauwhede. 2002. "Scalable Session Key Construction Protocol for Wireless Sensor Networks." *IEEE Workshop on Large Scale RealTime and Embedded Systems (LARTES)*. http://citeseerx.ist.psu.edu/viewdoc/download?doi=10.1.1.1.8316&rep=rep1&type=pdf.

Li, Xiong, Maged Hamada Ibrahim, Saru Kumari, Arun Kumar Sangaiah, Vidushi Gupta, and Kim-Kwang Raymond Choo. 2017. "Anonymous Mutual Authentication and Key Agreement Scheme for Wearable Sensors in Wireless

Body Area Networks." *Computer Networks* 129: 429–43. doi:10.1016/j.comnet.2017.03.013.

Liu, Donggang, Peng Ning, and Rongfang Li. 2005. "Establishing Pairwise Keys in Distributed Sensor Networks." *ACM Transactions on Information and System Security* 8(1): 41–77. doi:10.1145/1053283.1053287.

Lu, Yanrong, Lixiang Li, Haipeng Peng, and Yixian Yang. 2015. "An Enhanced Biometric-Based Authentication Scheme for Telecare Medicine Information Systems Using Elliptic Curve Cryptosystem." *Journal of Medical Systems* 39: 1–8.

Maleh, Yassine, Abdellah Ezzati, and Mustapha Belaissaoui. 2016a. "An Enhanced DTLS Protocol for Internet of Things Applications." In *Proceedings—2016 International Conference on Wireless Networks and Mobile Communications, WINCOM 2016: Green Communications and Networking. IEEE.* doi:10.1109/WINCOM.2016.7777209.

Maleh, Yassine, Abdellah Ezzati, and Mustapha Belaissaoui. 2016b. "DoS Attacks Analysis and Improvement in DTLS Protocol for Internet of Things." *Proceedings of the International Conference on Big Data and Advanced Wireless Technologies* 54(1–54): 7. doi:10.1145/3010089.3010139.

Maleh, Yassine, Abdellah Ezzati, and Mustapha Belaissaoui. 2018. *Security and Privacy in Smart Sensor Networks.* IGI Global. doi:10.4018/978-1-5225-5736-4.

Maleh, Yassine, Youssef Qasmaoui, Khalid El Gholami, Yassine Sadqi, and Soufyane Mounir. 2022. "A Comprehensive Survey on SDN Security: Threats, Mitigations, and Future Directions." *Journal of Reliable Intelligent Environments. 9(2), 201-239.* doi:10.1007/s40860-022-00171-8.

Maleh, Yassine, Abdelkebir Sahid, Abdellah Ezzati, and Mustapha Belaissaoui. 2018. "Key Management Protocols for Smart Sensor Networks." In *Security and Privacy in Smart Sensor Networks.* IGI Global: 1–23.

Ming Huang Shun, J., B. Chan, and L. Dai. 2013. "An Efficient Key Management Scheme for Data-Centric Storage Wireless Sensor Networks." *IERI Procedia* 4: 25–31. doi:10.1016/J.IERI.2013.11.005.

Mucchi, Lorenzo, Sara Jayousi, Alessio Martinelli, Stefano Caputo, and Patrizio Marcocci. 2019. "An Overview of Security Threats, Solutions and Challenges in Wbans for Healthcare" In *2019 13th International Symposium on Medical Information and Communication Technology (ISMICT)*, IEEE, 1–6.

Munivel, E., and G. M. Ajit. 2010. "Efficient Public Key Infrastructure Implementation in Wireless Sensor Networks." *2010 International Conference on Wireless Communication and Sensor Computing (IcWCSC)*: 1–6. doi:10.1109/ICWCSC.2010.5415904.

Nguyen, Kim Thuat, Maryline Laurent, and Nouha Oualha. 2015. "Survey on Secure Communication Protocols for the Internet of Things." *Ad Hoc Networks* 32(February): 17–31. doi:10.1016/j.adhoc.2015.01.006.

Olufemi, Olakanmi Oladayo, and Dada Adedamola. 2020. "SAMA: A Secure and Anonymous Mutual Authentication with Conditional Identity-Tracking Scheme for a Unified Car Sharing System." *International Journal of Autonomous and Adaptive Communications Systems* 13(1): 84–101.

Perrig, Adrian, Robert Szewczyk, J. D. Tygar, Victor Wen, and David E. Culler. 2002. "SPINS: Security Protocols for Sensor Networks." *Wireless Networks* 8(5): 521–34. doi:10.1023/A:1016598314198.

Pirmoradian, Fatemeh, Masoumeh Safkhani, and Seyed Mohammad Dakhilalian. 2023. "ECCPWS: An ECC-Based Protocol for WBAN Systems." *Computer Networks* 224: 109598. doi:10.1016/j.comnet.2023.109598.

Rabin, Michael O. 1978. "Digitalized Signatures and Public-Key Functions as Intractable as Factorization." *Foundations of Secure Computations*: 155–68. doi:10.1080/09720529.2013.858478.

Raza, S., S. Duquennoy, T. Chung, D. Yazar, T. Voigt, and U. Roedig, U. 2011. "Securing Communication in 6LoWPAN with Compressed IPsec. In Distributed Computing in Sensor Systems And." In *IEEE Workshops (DCOSS)*, 1–8. *IEEE.*

Raza, Shahid, Hossein Shafagh, Kasun Hewage, Hummen Rene, and Thiemo Voigt. 2013. "Lithe: Lightweight Secure CoAP for the Internet of Things." *IEEE Sensors Journal* 13(10): 3711–20. doi:10.1109/JSEN.2013.2277656.

Rehman, Z. U., S. Altaf, and S. Iqbal. 2020. "An Efficient Lightweight Key Agreement and Authentication Scheme for WBAN." *IEEE Access* 8: 175385–97. doi:10.1109/ACCESS.2020.3026630.

Rescorla, E. (1999). RFC2631: Diffie-Hellman key agreement method. RFC Editor.

Seys, S., and B. Preneel. 2002. "Key Establishment and Authentication Suite to Counter DoS Attacks in Distributed Sensor Networks." *Unpublished manuscript, COSIC.*

Shamir, A. 1984. "ID-BasedCryptoSystem.Pdf." In *Crypto'84*, 47–54.

Shao, Min, Sencun Zhu, Wensheng Zhang, Guohong Cao, and Yi Yang. 2009. "PDCS: Security and Privacy Support for Data-Centric Sensor Networks." *IEEE Transactions on Mobile Computing* 8(8): 1023–38. doi:10.1109/TMC.2008.168.

Sikder, Amit Kumar, Giuseppe Petracca, Hidayet Aksu, Trent Jaeger, and A. Selcuk Uluagac. 2021. "A Survey on Sensor-Based Threats and Attacks to Smart Devices and Applications." *IEEE Communications Surveys & Tutorials* 23(2): 1125–59.

Sowjanya, K., Mou Dasgupta, and Sangram Ray. 2020. "An Elliptic Curve Cryptography Based Enhanced Anonymous Authentication Protocol for Wearable Health Monitoring Systems." *International Journal of Information Security* 19(1): 129–46. doi:10.1007/s10207-019-00464-9.

Steinwandt, Rainer, and Adriana Suárez. 2011. "Identity-Based Non-Interactive Key Distribution with Forward Security." *Test*: 195–96. doi:10.1007/s10623-011-9486-0.

Watro, Ronald, Derrick Kong, Sue-Fen Cuti, Charles Gardiner, Charles Lynn, and Peter Kruus. 2004. "TinyPK: Securing Sensor Networks with Public Key Technology." *2nd Workshop on Security of Ad Hoc and Sensor Networks SASN'04* (October): 59–64. doi:10.1145/1029102.1029113.

Xu, Guangxia, Qun Wu, M. Daneshmand, Yan-bing Liu, and Manman Wang. 2015. "A Data Privacy Protective Mechanism for WBAN." *Wireless Communications and Mobile Computing* (February 2015): 421–30. doi:10.1002/wcm.

Xu, Z., C. Xu, W. Liang, J. Xu, and H. Chen. 2019. "A Lightweight Mutual Authentication and Key Agreement Scheme for Medical Internet of Things." *IEEE Access* 7: 53922–31. doi:10.1109/ACCESS.2019.2912870.

Yang, Lijun, Chao Ding, and Meng Wu. 2013. "Establishing Authenticated Pairwise Key Using Pairing-Based Cryptography for Sensor Networks." *2013 8th International ICST Conference on Communications and Networking in China, CHINACOM 2013—Proceedings*: 517–22. doi:10.1109/ChinaCom.2013.6694650.

Yassine, Maleh, and Abdellah Ezzati. 2015. "Performance Analysis of Routing Protocols for Wireless Sensor Networks." In *Colloquium in Information Science and Technology, CIST. IEEE.* doi:10.1109/CIST.2014.7016657.

Yassine, Maleh, and Abdellah Ezzati. 2016. "LEAP Enhanced: A Lightweight Symmetric Cryptography Scheme for Identifying Compromised Node in WSN." *International Journal of Mobile Computing and Multimedia Communications (IJMCMC)* 7(3): 42–66. doi:10.4018/IJMCMC.2016070104.

Zhu, Sencun, Sanjeev Setia, and Sushil Jajodia. 2003. "LEAP: Efficient Security Mechanisms for Large-Scale Distributed Sensor Networks." *CCS '03: Proceedings of the 10th ACM Conference on Computer and Communications Security*: 62–72. doi:10.1145/948109.948120.

Zhu, Sencun, Sanjeev Setia, and Sushil Jajodia. 2006. "Leap+." *ACM Transactions on Sensor Networks* 2(4): 500–28. doi:10.1145/1218556.1218559.

Zigbee, A. 2006. "Zigbee Specification." *ZigBee document 053474r13*.

Chapter 4

Securing Digital Health

A Comprehensive Ethical Hacking Framework and Comparative Analysis Using a Novel Hybrid Quality Evaluation Model

Gauhar Ali, Mohammed El-Affendi, and Ahmed A. Abd El-Latif

4.1 INTRODUCTION

The healthcare industry has seen a dramatic change in recent years toward digitalization, utilizing technology to improve patient care, expedite processes, and spur innovation in medical research [1]. However, this shift to digital has also presented several complex difficulties in protecting private patient information and strengthening healthcare systems against ever-changing cyber threats [2]. Healthcare security practices have been greatly influenced by the ethical hacking frameworks that are currently in place, including MITRE Adversarial Tactics, Techniques, and Common Knowledge (MITRE ATT&CK) [3], National Institute of Standards and Technology (NIST) Cybersecurity Framework [4], The Open Web Application Security Project (OWASP) [5], and Health Insurance Portability and Accountability Act (HIPAA) [6]. However, a more thorough examination of these frameworks reveals important flaws and restrictions. These drawbacks make it harder for them to effectively address the quickly changing field of healthcare cybersecurity.

One of the mainstays of healthcare security laws, HIPAA, is not as technological or flexible as it should be to keep up with new and developing threats [7]. Furthermore, although beneficial, frameworks such as MITRE ATT&CK and OWASP have limitations when providing detailed instructions for securing huge amounts of medical devices [8, 9] and dealing with new attack vectors at the necessary level of detail. Furthermore, despite its comprehensiveness, the NIST Cybersecurity Framework cannot keep up with the quick advancement of healthcare technology, leaving large gaps in its ability to mitigate new risks and solve interoperability issues [9].

This study presents a novel, complete ethical hacking methodology specifically designed to meet the complexities of healthcare cybersecurity to address these serious shortcomings. This innovative framework seeks to address the shortcomings of previous frameworks while combining their

DOI: 10.1201/9781003470038-4

best features. Strengthening technological specificity, improving threat coverage granularity, and guaranteeing adaptability to the ever-changing healthcare technology ecosystem are its main goals. Most importantly, it emphasizes critical elements such as medical device security, risks related to people, and the necessity of smooth interoperability between various healthcare systems.

Furthermore, this research aims to provide a thorough assessment system by comparing existing frameworks using a score system. By highlighting their advantages and disadvantages, this in-depth review hopes to provide a thorough grasp of their suitability and drawbacks. Moreover, it aims to create thorough standards for evaluating the caliber of any healthcare security system, offering priceless information to interested parties looking to strengthen their cybersecurity defenses. This study intends to lay the foundation for a more robust healthcare cybersecurity infrastructure by addressing current weaknesses and suggesting improvements. It hopes to enable healthcare organizations to protect patient information, proactively reduce risks, and move more confidently and effectively through the constantly changing threat landscape.

4.1.1 Our Contributions

- We propose a novel and comprehensive ethical hacking framework to improve threat coverage, technical specificity, medical device security, and human-centric risks.
- We propose a novel hybrid quality scoring system by integrating and enhancing the strengths of the state-of-the-art quality evaluation model and overcoming their limitations.
- Despite no pre-industry peer review score, the proposed framework scores higher than all the existing frameworks except the NIST framework using a hybrid quality evaluation model. The score will improve after industry peer review.

4.2 LITERATURE REVIEW

This section is divided into three sections. First, we discuss the existing well-known quality evaluation models. Second, we provide an overview of well-known ethical hacking frameworks. At last, we discuss the weakness of the existing ethical hacking frameworks.

4.2.1 Existing Quality Evaluation Models

The following are the well-known existing quality evaluation models.

4.2.1.1 ISO/IEC 25010

A standard called ISO/IEC 25010 [10] guides metrics and features related to software quality. It offers a framework for analyzing and rating software product quality based on a range of characteristics and standards. The standard highlights eight primary attributes of quality. The standard highlights six primary attributes of quality, that is, efficiency, functionality, maintainability, portability, reliability, security, compatibility, and usability. This standard provides an organized approach to analyzing software quality by defining these attributes and offering metrics and guidelines for evaluating and enhancing software quality throughout the development lifecycle.

4.2.1.2 FURPS Model

A framework for software development called the FURPS model [11, 12] aids in the definition and assessment of software quality attributes. It stands for Functionality, Usability, Reliability, Performance, and Supportability. Throughout the software development lifecycle, developers, designers, and stakeholders should take into account the important characteristics of software quality that are represented by each piece. It aids in directing the development process by concentrating on important facets of software quality, guaranteeing that the finished result satisfies user expectations and intended standards.

4.2.1.3 Generic, Multilayered, and Customizable Quality Model (GEQUAMO)

GEQUAMO [13] is developed by E. Georgiadou. This model gradually broke down features and characteristics into sublayers to encapsulate the varied user requirements flexibly and dynamically. The end user, developer, and management can construct their model in this fashion, indicating the weight assigned to each characteristic and/or requirement.

4.2.2 Existing Ethical Hacking Frameworks

In this section, we discuss the state-of-the-art ethical hacking frameworks.

4.2.2.1 Ethical Hacker

A person who tries to lawfully breach a network or computer system to identify its weak points. Penetration tester is another name for an ethical hacker [14].

4.2.2.2 Ethical Hacking Framework

It is an organizational security control testing technique. The US military and other organizations started employing "red teams" or "penetration testers" in the 1960s to try computer security breaches and thereby aid in identifying and mitigating vulnerabilities; ethical hacking has been a professional endeavor [15].

4.2.2.3 HIPAA Security Rule

A collection of guidelines created under the HIPAA in the United States is known as the HIPAA Security Rule [16]. It describes particular specifications and security measures for protected health information (PHI) [17] that covered entities and their business partners hold or transfer electronically. HIPAA security rules consist of the following essential components.

- **Administrative safeguards**: These are guidelines and protocols created to oversee the choice, creation, application, and upkeep of security measures to safeguard electronic protected health information (ePHI) [18].
- **Physical safeguards**: These deal with the physical entry to buildings, workstations, and other equipment that contain or are used to access ePHI.
- **Technical safeguards**: These include the systems and tools used to secure and manage ePHI access.
- **Organizational requirements**: Contracts or agreements between covered entities and their business associates must ensure that the latter abide by HIPAA regulations about the protection of ePHI.

4.2.2.4 OWASP Framework

OWASP is a nonprofit organization established in 2001 by Mark Curphey that raises public awareness of security issues. Prominent entities such as the US Federal Trade Commission (FTC) [19] and the Payment Card Industry Data Security Standard (PCI DSS) [20] have all cited it. This framework provides a web application penetration testing methodology that can identify vulnerabilities often seen in web and mobile applications, as well as sophisticated logic problems stemming from risky development practices. With a total of over 66 controls to assess and thorough instructions for every penetration testing method, the new manual helps testers identify vulnerabilities in a broad variety of functionalities found in modern apps. The following are a few OWASP projects and resources that are related to protecting systems and applications in industries like healthcare, e-commerce, etc.

- **OWASP Top 10**: This is a well-known ranking of the biggest security threats that online applications must contend with. The vulnerabilities listed in the OWASP Top 10 are pertinent to healthcare applications and must be mitigated to safeguard patient data and system integrity, even though they are not specifically related to healthcare [21, 22]. The OWASP Top 10 list was initially released in 2003. In 2004, 2007,

2010, 2013, and 2017 there were updates. In 2021, the most recent upgrade was released. It focuses on web apps especially and makes tool recommendations at every testing phase. It also offers executive and technical staff reporting guidelines.

- **OWASP Application Security Verification Standard** (ASVS): This standard [23] offers a structure for formulating security criteria for applications. Healthcare applications may make sure they adhere to security guidelines and address common vulnerabilities by utilizing ASVS.
- **OWASP Mobile Security Project**: Mobile applications are frequently used in healthcare for remote monitoring, data collection, and patient care [24]. This project [25] provides recommendations on mobile app security, which is important for the healthcare industry.

4.2.2.5 NIST Cybersecurity Framework

The US National Institute of Standards and Technology released this framework in 2014. Compared to other information security publications, NIST offers penetration testers more comprehensive guidance. One excellent resource for improving an organization's overall cybersecurity is the guidebook provided by the NIST. The most recent version 1.1, gives Critical Infrastructure Cybersecurity more focus. Regulations mandate that many American service providers and business partners follow the NIST framework. It helps businesses to manage and safely own their essential infrastructure. It is a framework that the populace developed in collaboration with business, academia, and governmental institutions. The NIST framework is categorized into three sections, that is, core, profile, and tiers [26]. A variety of activities, findings, and references about cybersecurity-related subjects and techniques are included in the "core" of the framework. An organization will choose a set of outcomes from the categories and subcategories to construct a "framework profile" based on its needs and risk assessments. Similarly, cybersecurity risk and the degree of sophistication of its management strategy are categorized into "tiers" section. The NIST framework is composed of five essential elements, that is, identify, protect, detect, respond, and recover [27].

4.2.2.6 MITRE ATT&CK Framework

The MITRE ATT&CK (Adversarial methods, Techniques, and Common Knowledge) framework lists and arranges the many strategies, methods, and practices that cyber attackers employ during different phases of a cyberattack [28]. It offers a thorough and organized perspective of the strategies attackers employ to enter, reroute, and retrieve data from systems they have targeted. The framework is designed in the form of a matrix that describes techniques and tactics for the various stages of an attack.

- **Tactics:** The high-level goals that opponents want to accomplish during an attack are represented by tactics [29]. Initial access, execution, persistence, defense evasion, privilege escalation, credential access, discovery, lateral movement, collection, exfiltration, and impact are a few examples of techniques.
- **Techniques:** Within each technique, some particular procedures or approaches are employed. Techniques describe how enemies achieve their goals. For example, "Command-Line Interface" or "Scripting" are two prominent techniques used by attackers to run malicious code on a victim's system and fall under the "Execution" approach.

MITRE ATT&CK focuses on the wider variety of strategies and tactics that adversaries use throughout an attack, rather than just concentrating on particular vulnerabilities or threats. By using this strategy, businesses can strengthen defenses, enhance threat detection and response capabilities, and comprehend possible assault routes.

The MITRE ATT&CK architecture can be used by healthcare security teams to better align their protection tactics with observed attack behaviors [30, 31]. To prevent, detect, and react to assaults more skillfully, they might proactively deploy procedures to discover potential vulnerabilities or weaknesses in their security posture.

4.2.3 Weaknesses in the Existing Frameworks

This study assessed existing frameworks and discovered the following four common main issues.

(1) Lack of human factor emphasis
(2) Insufficient/complex documentation
(3) Insufficient tools recommendation
(4) Insufficient domain coverage

4.3 THE PROPOSED FRAMEWORK

The proposed framework is not just a simple compilation of methods and approaches. It also provides a step-by-step methodology to identify vulnerabilities in the system. The proposed framework for ethical hacking consists of the following components as shown in Figure 4.1.

4.3.1 System Decomposition

Divide the system into smaller components to better understand the fundamental controls and system flow.

Figure 4.1 High-level proposed framework.

4.3.2 Identification of Potential Threats

After the system has been broken down into parts, every major point of entry and any potential danger that could lead to data loss, illegal access, system failure, or denial-of-service attack must be located.

4.3.3 Identification of Vulnerabilities

An ethical hacker can run manual tests or use tools that are recommended to find vulnerabilities in the system.

4.3.4 Identification of Appropriate Controls

Make sure that the appropriate controls are chosen for the target system after a thorough analysis of the system and consideration of all possible threats and vulnerabilities.

4.3.4.1 Control and Subcontrols

The controls and subcontrols of the suggested framework are described in this part along with how they relate to test performance and impact value. Every organization has varied risks, threats, vulnerabilities, and risk appetites. The suggested framework enables tailored security procedures according to the organizational context, particularly addressing domains that are neglected or underappreciated in the current frameworks. These include physical system security, human resource security, risk and incident management, and changeability. This framework proposes 13 controls and 41 subcontrols to maintain availability, confidentiality, and integrity.

(1) **Physical system hardening:** Lowering the attack surface accessible to malevolent parties. There are four subcontrols in this category.
   i. **Authorized physical access:** For a restricted period of time, servers, routers, and switches may only be physically accessible to authorized individuals. Time and activity logs need to be appropriately documented.
   ii. **Audit:** Thorough examination of the current infrastructure.
   iii. Maintenance.

iv. **System change procedure**: Keep an eye on modifications and their causes to make sure their systems aren't being undermined by shoddy or malevolent development.

(2) **Operating system security**: This category contains eight subcontrols that must be met for the application to operate in a stable and secure environment.
   i. **User accounts**: Assign local users to limited user accounts. Administrator rights are only to be granted to reliable users.
   ii. **Account policies**: Establish guidelines for password length, time-outs for sessions, and changing passwords after a predetermined amount of time.
   iii. **File system**: Access to authorized users with the necessary rights for a predetermined amount of time, with activity duly documented in logs.
   iv. **System minimization**: Eliminate unnecessary programs and components.
   v. **Logging**: Every action needs to be noted and stored for a predetermined amount of time.
   vi. **Restore points**: Maintain backup copies of the operating system in case of unauthorized access or emergency.
   vii. **Updates**: Apply all of the most recent security patches and updates.
   viii. **Virtualization**: To improve security coverage, hardware and software must be kept apart.

(3) There are five subcontrols under database security.
   i. **Segregation**: The web servers must be separated from database servers.
   ii. **Encryption**: Data must be encrypted before storing in the database and sending.
   iii. **Physical security**: Secure the database server physically.
   iv. **Strong authentication**: Authentication is required for any users or services connecting to the database.
   v. **Firewall**: The firewall must be configured to protect the database from external attacks.

(4) **Information disclosure**: Giving unauthorized actors access to private personal information. There are two subcontrols in this category.
   i. Sensitive information should not be stored in clear text.
   ii. Strong encryption for sensitive data.

(5) **Data integrity**: Only authorized users can alter data and system resources, protecting them from manipulation and spoofing.

(6) **Application security**: This section includes nine relevant subcontrols for desktop, online, and mobile apps.
   i. Buffer overflows
   ii. Race conditions
   iii. Tainted input
   iv. Format string issues

  v. Third-party dependency check
  vi. Input validation
  vii. Temporary files
  viii. Strong encryption
  ix. Logging and auditing

(7) **Network security**: There are nine subcontrols under network security.
  i. **Prevent data loss**: Lower the possibility of data loss by keeping an eye on the locations of sensitive data transfers.
  ii. Restricted online entry.
  iii. **Virtual private network**: After users establish a connection to a virtual private network, they can access applications and services.
  iv. **Physical security of network devices**: Only those with permission can access switches, routers, and other network devices.
  v. **Firmware**: To protect against programs and tools, network devices need to be patched and have their firmware updated.
  vi. **Traffic filtering**: An intrusion detection system must be installed to reject traffic that contains malware, spam, or phishing.
  vii. **Examining vulnerability**: Identification and affirmation of vulnerability in the network connecting devices.
  viii. **Backup and restore**: Data and power backup and restore mechanisms must be implemented.

(8) **Transmission security**: There are two subcontrols under transmission security.
  i. Routing protocols
  ii. Security of protocols

(9) **Service security**: Services such as File Transfer Protocol (FTP), Domain Name Services (DNS), and telnet are computer programs that execute to offer standard features to users, applications, and other services. There are two subcontrols in this category.
  i. Specialized access to additional system resources
  ii. Inaccuracies in configurations

(10) **Information Security policy**: Describe the methods and acceptable uses that will keep the required level of security in place. It includes policies, procedures, and standards for both new and seasoned workers.

(11) **Risk management**: Tolerance, identification, and assessment

(12) **Denial of service**: Defense against intrusions that could cause a service to go down.

(13) **Human resource security**: To maintain the appropriate level of security, employment contracts must include recommendations. Before recruiting, background checks must be implemented.

4.3.5 Documentation

Every security issue discovered needs to be recorded using the provided report template, which has sections for technical and executive (non-technical) staff. The seriousness of the problem and potential solutions are also included in this report to assist allay worries. A single language for comprehending, controlling, and communicating cybersecurity threats both within and internationally is provided by the report.

4.3.6 Reporting

Every issue that is found needs to be communicated in a way that makes replication simple for other similar issues. This could be in the form of easily understood textual instructions or even videos or pictures showing the procedure.

4.3.7 Use Case: Implementation of the Proposed Framework

In this section, we discuss the proposed framework's application on hospital organizations to test its applicability, as well as present artifacts that will help in the evaluation of the framework.

4.3.7.1 System Decomposition

After performing documentation examination, log evaluation, scope provided by the XYZ Hospital, and inventory list, XYZ Hospital was found to have the following resources.

- Hardware, that is, servers, workstations, and medical equipment
- Software, that is, Hospital Information Management System (HMIS), operating system, and utility software
- Information, that is, patient health record (PHR) and employee data

4.3.7.2 Identification of Threat, Vulnerability, and Selection of Appropriate Security Control

The proposed framework uses a multi-level technique to investigate application/network vulnerabilities. The assessment process begins with scanning the network devices on the private network, identifying potential exploits on all open ports, and scanning web services for vulnerabilities. Information collection is done actively, which involves direct involvement with the target, such as running an Nmap scan on the target IP addresses. Alternatively, it can be accomplished passively by exploring open-source platforms for information about the subject, which may include search engines, that is, Google, or social networking platforms, that is, Twitter. Network mapping and scanning allow for the identification of the operating system as well as other relevant information like the number of nodes and open ports. Following the collection of preliminary data, vulnerability scanning can begin, using either automated technologies or human approaches. If initial access is secured, the next step is to try privilege escalation, which gives the attacker more rights and raises the possibility of infecting additional parts of the network. Backdoors are installed to maintain long-term access to the target, which may include actions such as setting up new user or administrative accounts on the machine or network, changing scripts, and installing new scripts or programs. Finally, a thorough analysis is performed to identify flaws and offer the most effective remedial techniques based on the severity of the threat. The proposed framework divides evaluation results into segments to identify their impact on the aim as shown in Table 4.1.

Several vulnerabilities have been identified while assessing the security of XYZ Hospital. However, Tables 4.2–4.5 depict only a few selected critical-, high-, medium-, and low-risk threats/vulnerabilities along with their corresponding mitigation strategies.

Table 4.1 Threat/Vulnerability Severity Levels

Risk	*Description*
Critical	Immediate action is necessary to perform the mitigation measures.
High	Take immediate action and try to fix it as swiftly as possible.
Medium	Define priorities and resolve the issue within 14 days.
Low	Resolve the issue in 30 days.
Info	It provides information.

Table 4.2 Critical Risk: Threat/Vulnerability and the Mitigation Strategy

Risk: Critical
Threat: Hacker **Vulnerability:** A blind SQL injection vulnerability has been found, presenting the risk of remote code injection or potential database dumping. **Control/subcontrol:** Application security and tainted input **Mitigation:** Make sure the use of parameterized queries.

Table 4.3 High Risk: Threat/Vulnerability and the Mitigation Strategy

Risk: High
Threat: Malicious insider **Vulnerability:** Hospital employees have access to critical physical resources, that is, database server and web server. **Control/subcontrol:** Physical system hardening and authorized physical access **Mitigation:** Physical resources need to be placed in a secured room, accessible only to authorized persons, and all activity should be logged.

Table 4.4 Medium Risk: Threat/Vulnerability and the Mitigation Strategy

Risk: Medium
Threat: Hacker **Vulnerability:** When there is no index page, web servers can be set to display directory contents automatically. This functionality allows for easy discovery of resources along a specified path, aiding study and potential exploitation by attackers. Notably, it improves access to sensitive information in the directory, such as temporary files and crash dumps that are not intended for user access. **Control/subcontrol:** Information disclosure **Mitigation:** The web server must be configured to stop directory listings for all paths under the root.

Table 4.5 Low Risk: Threat/Vulnerability and the Mitigation Strategy

Risk: Low
Threat: Malicious insider **Vulnerability:** No internal or external audit has been performed. **Control/subcontrol:** Physical system hardening and audit **Mitigation:** Audit must be performed for all hospital resources yearly or quarterly.

4.3.7.3 Documentation and Reporting

The final deliverable, presented in report format, described the detected vulnerabilities and offered remediation as a mitigation strategy. A sample of the report is depicted in Table 4.6.

4.4 PROPOSED HYBRID QUALITY EVALUATION MODEL (HQEM)

The quality models given in the literature review are used to develop an innovative hybrid evaluation model, which is employed to determine the quality of ethical hacking frameworks.

During the literature review, three assessment models were examined; however, none of them matched all of the requirements, that is, covering all domains, being quantifiable, flexible, and score-based. Thus, an HQEM is proposed using the best factors of the models discussed in the literature review. While compiling a list of factors from current quality models, it was discovered that some terms are duplicated or have significant overlap. Therefore, those terms are selected to maintain only the most critical factors in the proposed hybrid model. Moreover, because the quality model's primary objective is to evaluate an ethical hacking framework, erroneous

Table 4.6. Final Report

Target Organization: XYZ Hospital *Purpose: Security assessment of the hospital's IT assets* *Date: xx-xx-xxxx*					
ID	*Status*	*Risk*	*Risk Level*	*Suggested Control/ Subcontrol*	*Suggested Mitigation Strategy*
1	New	A blind SQL injection vulnerability has been found, presenting the risk of remote code injection or potential database dumping.	Critical	Control: Physical system Hardening Subcontrol: Authorized physical access	Make sure to use parameterized queries.
2	New	Hospital employees have access to critical physical resources, that is, database servers and web servers.	High	Control: Application security Subcontrol: Tainted input	Physical resources need to be placed in a secured room, accessible only to authorized persons, and all activity should be logged.
3	New	When there is no index page, web servers can be set to display directory contents automatically. This functionality allows for easy discovery of resources along a specified path, aiding study and potential exploitation by attackers. Notably, it improves access to sensitive information in the directory, such as temporary files and crash dumps that are not intended for user access.	Medium	Control: Information disclosure	The web server must be configured to stop directory listings for all paths under the root.
4	New	No internal or external audit has been performed.	Low	Control: Physical system hardening Subcontrol: Audit	The audit must be performed for all hospital resources yearly or quarterly.

cybersecurity terms are removed because this hybrid model aims to evaluate ethical hacking frameworks. The proposed HQEM consists the following:

- **Open source:** This factor refers to the license type making it available for utilization and distribution with its original privileges. This factor is scored either 1 or 0 based on whether the quality evaluated system is open source or not.
- **Peer reviewed:** This quality factor provides insight into the acceptably reviewed framework by industry experts or reputable organizations. This factor shows the percentage of positive reviews of a framework by survey.
  - 0: Has not been acceptably surveyed.
  - 1: Positive reviews are less than 50%.
  - 2: Positive reviews are more than 50%.
- **Operating system security:** This factor is scored based on whether the hacking framework supports operating system security or not. This factor can be scored as either 1 or 0.
- **Web application security:** This factor is scored based on whether the hacking framework covers web application security. This factor can be scored as either 1 or 0.
- **Desktop application security:** It shows how the hacking framework covers desktop security. It can be scored as either 1 or 0, based on whether the target framework covers desktop application security.
- **Human resource security:** It involves performing a background check of employees' rights security. It can be scored as either 1 or 0.
- **Tools recommendation:** This factor is scored based on whether the framework suggests a suitable tool to use for a specific control or not. This factor can be scored as either 1 or 0.
- **Domain coverage:** This factor shows whether the target framework supports all types of systems, that is, Internet of Things, computer/mobile operating systems, networks, and web/desktop applications. The scoring criteria for this factor are given as follows.
  - 0: Has single-domain support.
  - 1: Has two domains support.
  - 2: Has more than two domains support.
- **Maintainability:** It represents the success and efficiency with which the target framework may be rectified, enhanced, or adjusted to accommodate changing requirements and environmental conditions. It can be scored as either 1 or 0, based on whether the target framework accepts rectification for improvements.
- **Operability:** This factor shows whether a system or product is simple to operate. It can be scored as either 1 or 0, based on whether the evaluated framework contains this feature.
- **Changeability:** It represents the target framework's capacity for the acceptance of specific changes. This factor can be scored as either 1 or 0.

- **Installability:** It represents the degree of success and efficiency needed to implement and remove a system or product. Installability can be scored as either 1 or 0, depending on the availability of this feature in the target framework.
- **Fault tolerance:** It tells how well a system or component executes as intended despite having problems. Similarly, this factor can be scored as either 1 or 0, based on the system fault tolerance feature.
- **Documentation:** Effective documentation is required to convey a clear message, provide evidence about planning, or facilitate knowledge transfer. It reflects the comprehensiveness of the user guidelines offered by the framework. It can be scored as follows:

  - 0: no documentation available
  - 1: brief and complex documentation
  - 2: comprehensive and easy documentation

4.4.1 Evaluation and Comparison among Proposed and Existing Quality Evaluation Models

The proposed framework has been evaluated and compared with the state-of-the-art frameworks using the hybrid quality model. The evaluation result and comparison are given in Table 4.7.

The proposed framework achieved a score of 15 on the HQEM, with the potential for improvement after peer review by industry experts, potentially

Table 4.7 Evaluation and Comparisons among Proposed and Existing Quality Evaluation Models

Quality Factor	*OWASP*	*HIPAA*	*MITRE ATT&CK*	*NIST*	*Proposed Framework*
Open source	1	0	1	1	1
Peer reviewed	2	2	2	2	0
Operating system security	1	0	1	0	1
Desktop application security	0	1	1	1	1
Web application security	1	0	0	1	1
Human resource security	0	1	1	1	1
Tools recommendation	1	1	1	1	1
Documentation	1	2	2	2	2
Domain coverage	1	1	2	2	2
Maintainability	1	1	1	1	1
Operability	1	1	1	1	1
Changeability	1	1	1	1	1
Installability	1	1	0	1	1
Fault tolerance	1	0	0	1	1
Total score	**12**	**12**	**14**	**16**	**15**

allowing it to get the highest score on the HQEM. Currently, it scores just below the NIST framework.

4.5 CONCLUSION

The study explored many existing ethical hacking frameworks, such as MITRE ATT&CK, OWASP Healthcare Project, HIPAA, and NIST Cybersecurity Framework, and found substantial inadequacies in their capacity to meet the intricacies of modern healthcare technology. HIPAA lacks technical depth and flexibility, whereas OWASP and MITRE ATT&CK for healthcare provide insufficient guidance on medical device security and fail to address emerging attack routes adequately. The NIST Cybersecurity Framework, while comprehensive, struggles to keep up with the fast-changing healthcare IT world.

To overcome these deficiencies, this chapter presents a new, complete ethical hacking framework that builds on the benefits of previous frameworks while resolving their weaknesses. The new framework intends to improve technical specificity, granularity in threat coverage, and flexibility to changing healthcare technologies. Improving medical device security, addressing human-centric vulnerabilities, and guaranteeing interoperability across varied health systems are all key areas of study.

In addition, this chapter proposed a novel HQEM to evaluate the quality of existing frameworks. The proposed framework gets a score of 15 that is just below the leading NIST framework. However, the score may improve after peer review by experts from the industry.

Acknowledgment: The authors would like to acknowledge Prince Sultan University and EIAS Lab for their valuable support.

REFERENCES

[1] Gjellebæk, C., Svensson, A., Bjørkquist, C., Fladeby, N., & Grundén, K. (2020). Management challenges for future digitalization of healthcare services. *Futures*, 124, 102636.

[2] Kaplan, B. (2020). Revisiting health information technology ethical, legal, and social issues and evaluation: Telehealth/telemedicine and COVID-19. *International Journal of Medical Informatics*, 143, 104239.

[3] Strom, B. E., Applebaum, A., Miller, D. P., Nickels, K. C., Pennington, A. G., & Thomas, C. B. (2018). Mitre attack: Design and philosophy. In *Technical report*. The MITRE Corporation.

[4] NIST Cybersecurity Framework. (n.d.). https://www.nist.gov. Retrieved February 15, 2024, from https://www.nist.gov/itl/smallbusinesscyber/nist-cyber security-framework-0

[5] OWASP Cybersecurity Framework. (n.d.). https://owasp.org/. Retrieved February 15, 2024, from https://owasp.org/www-project-top-ten/

[6] Health Information Privacy. (n.d.). https://www.hhs.gov/. Retrieved February 15, 2024, from https://www.hhs.gov/hipaa/for-professionals/security/laws-regulations/index.html.

[7] Chen, J. Q., & Benusa, A. (2017). HIPAA security compliance challenges: The case for small healthcare providers. *International Journal of Healthcare Management*, 10(2), 135–146.

[8] Williams, P. A., & Woodward, A. J. (2015). Cybersecurity vulnerabilities in medical devices: A complex environment and multifaceted problem. *Medical Devices: Evidence and Research*, 305–316.

[9] Kioskli, K., Fotis, T., & Mouratidis, H. (2021, August). The landscape of cybersecurity vulnerabilities and challenges in healthcare: Security standards and paradigm shift recommendations. In *Proceedings of the 16th International Conference on Availability, Reliability and Security* ACM, (pp. 1–9).

[10] ISOIEC. (n.d.). ISO/IEC 25010:2011. https://www.iso.org/. Retrieved February 16, 2024, from https://www.iso.org/standard/35733.html.

[11] Grady, R. B., & Caswell, D. L. (1987). *Software metrics: establishing a company-wide program*. Prentice-Hall, Inc.

[12] Grady, R. B. (1992). *Practical software metrics for project management and process improvement*. Prentice-Hall, Inc.

[13] Georgiadou, E. (2003). GEQUAMO—a generic, multilayered, customisable, software quality model. *Software Quality Journal*, 11, 313–323.

[14] Hawamleh, A. M. A., Alorfi, A. S. M., Al-Gasawneh, J. A., & Al-Rawashdeh, G. (2020). Cyber security and ethical hacking: The importance of protecting user data. *Solid State Technology*, 63(5), 7894–7899.

[15] Solomon, M. G., & Oriyano, S. P. (2022). *Ethical hacking: Techniques, tools, and countermeasures*. Jones & Bartlett Learning.

[16] Evans, B. J. (2023). *The HIPAA privacy rule at age 25: Privacy for equitable AI*. Florida State University Law Review, Forthcoming.

[17] Cohen, I. G., & Mello, M. M. (2018). HIPAA and protecting health information in the 21st century. *JAMA*, 320(3), 231–232.

[18] Saha, B. (2023). *Analysis of the adherence of mHealth applications to HIPAA technical safeguards*, Kennesaw State University

[19] Ward, P. C. (2023). *Federal trade commission: Law, practice, and procedure*. Law Journal Press.

[20] Williams, B., & Adamson, J. (2022). *PCI compliance: Understand and implement effective PCI data security standard compliance*. CRC Press.

[21] Priambodo, D. F., Ajie, G. S., Rahman, H. A., Nugraha, A. C. F., Rachmawati, A., & Avianti, M. R. (2022, November). Mobile health application security assessment based on OWASP top 10 mobile vulnerabilities. In *2022 international conference on information technology systems and innovation (ICITSI)* (pp. 25–29). IEEE.

[22] Gómez, J., Olivero, M. Á., García-García, J. A., & Escalona, M. J. (2022). A practical experience applying security audit techniques in an industrial healthcare system. In *Illumination of artificial intelligence in cybersecurity and forensics* (pp. 1–20). Springer International Publishing.

[23] OWASP-Application Security Verification Standard. (n.d.). www.owasp.org. Retrieved February 18, 2024, from https://owasp.org/www-project-application-security-verification- standard/

[24] Schmeelk, S., & Tao, L. (2022). A case study of mobile health applications: The OWASP risk of insufficient cryptography. *Journal of Computer Science Research*, 4(1), 22–31.

[25] OWASP- Mobile Application Security. (n.d.). www.owasp.org. Retrieved February 18, 2024, from https://owasp.org/www-project-mobile-app-security/

[26] Gordon, L. A., Loeb, M. P., & Zhou, L. (2020). Integrating cost–benefit analysis into the NIST Cybersecurity Framework via the Gordon–Loeb Model. *Journal of Cybersecurity*, 6(1), tyaa005.

[27] Staves, A., Anderson, T., Balderstone, H., Green, B., Gouglidis, A., & Hutchison, D. (2022). A cyber incident response and recovery framework to support operators of industrial control systems. *International Journal of Critical Infrastructure Protection*, 37, 100505.

[28] Mitre att&ck. (n.d.). Corporation the MITRE. https://attack.mitre.org/. Retrieved February 18, 2024, from https://attack.mitre.org/versions/v9.

[29] Al-Sada, B., Sadighian, A., & Oligeri, G. (2023). Analysis and characterization of cyber threats leveraging the MITRE ATT&CK database. *IEEE Access*, 12, 1217-1234

[30] Abeysinghe, A. M. S. B., De Zoysa, M. T. R., Samuditha, K. M. Y., DJDHT, D., Yapa, K., & Dharmkeerthi, U. (2023). Security operation center for healthcare sector. *International Research Journal of Innovations in Engineering and Technology*, 7(11), 299.

[31] Lopez Martinez, A., Gil Pérez, M., & Ruiz-Martínez, A. (2023). A comprehensive review of the state-of-the-art on security and privacy issues in healthcare. *ACM Computing Surveys*, 55(12), 1–38.

Chapter 5

Biometric Security and Access Management in E-health Services

Mohamed Hammad

5.1 INTRODUCTION

In modern healthcare, the digitalization of medical records and the widespread use of e-health services have transformed how patient information is obtained, kept, and shared [1]. Although these advancements have greatly improved the efficiency and accessibility of healthcare services, they have also introduced new challenges in maintaining the security and privacy of confidential medical information [1]. Due to the rise in cyber threats and the increased complexity of criminal actors, traditional authentication methods, such as passwords and PINs, are now insufficient to protect against unauthorized access and data breaches [2]. These traditional procedures, previously deemed effective, are now inadequate in safeguarding against the advanced tactics employed by cybercriminals to breach healthcare networks and obtain unauthorized entry to confidential information. Data breaches in healthcare can have serious effects, such as compromising patient confidentiality and manipulating medical information, underscoring the need to enhance security measures [3]. To address these difficulties, there is an increasing interest in utilizing biometric security technology to strengthen access control in e-health services [4]. Biometric identification utilizes distinct biological traits like fingerprints [5–10], iris patterns [11–15], facial features [16–20], voiceprints [21–25], and electrocardiogram (ECG) signals [26–30] to verify identity. Biometric identifiers are more secure and dependable than traditional authentication methods since they are linked to an individual's physiological or behavioral characteristics, unlike knowledge-based elements that can be compromised or forgotten [31–33].

The healthcare industry has increasingly become a prime target for cyberattacks due to its vast data holdings, leading to a significant rise in data breaches with millions of compromised patient records annually [34]. These breaches not only endanger patient privacy but also result in financial losses, reputational harm, and regulatory fines for healthcare organizations. The digitalization of medical data and the widespread use of electronic health records (EHRs) have made healthcare systems more vulnerable to cyber threats, exacerbated by the growing interconnection of networks and the

DOI: 10.1201/9781003470038-5

use of mobile devices and cloud platforms [35, 36]. Ransomware attacks, phishing scams, malware infections, and insider threats are prevalent in the healthcare sector, with ransomware posing a significant threat by encrypting healthcare data and demanding ransom payments [37]. Compliance with stringent data protection regulations such as the Health Insurance Portability and Accountability Act (HIPAA) is crucial, as non-compliance can lead to severe penalties [38, 39]. Healthcare organizations have been investing in cybersecurity measures, including network segmentation, encryption, and security awareness training, to mitigate cyber risks. Authentication methods in healthcare have evolved from manual and paper-based procedures to more secure options like multi-factor authentication (MFA) and biometric authentication [40]. Biometric authentication, which utilizes unique biological traits, offers enhanced security and user convenience but presents challenges such as privacy concerns, compatibility issues, and regulatory compliance requirements [41]. Despite these challenges, incorporating biometric authentication into healthcare systems can improve access control integrity and reduce the risks of unauthorized access and data breaches.

Biometric security adoption in the healthcare industry is driven by several compelling factors that underscore its significance in addressing the evolving challenges of cybersecurity and access management [42]. Following are elaborations on the key reasons behind the increasing interest in biometric authentication:

- **Enhanced security**: Biometric authentication offers a higher level of security compared to traditional methods like passwords or PINs. Unlike static credentials, such as passwords, biometric identifiers are unique to each individual and are inherently difficult to forge or replicate. This uniqueness makes biometric authentication highly resistant to unauthorized access and identity theft, significantly reducing the risk of data breaches and fraud within healthcare systems [43].
- **Improved accuracy and reliability**: Biometric authentication systems rely on physiological or behavioral characteristics, such as fingerprints, iris patterns, or ECG signals, to verify the identity of users. These biometric traits are highly distinctive and difficult to spoof, ensuring greater accuracy and reliability in identity verification processes. As a result, healthcare organizations can have greater confidence in the integrity of access control mechanisms and the protection of sensitive patient information [44].
- **User convenience**: Biometric authentication offers a seamless and user-friendly experience for both patients and healthcare personnel. Unlike passwords or PINs, which can be forgotten, lost, or shared, biometric identifiers are inherently tied to an individual's biological characteristics. This eliminates the need for users to remember complex passwords or carry physical tokens, streamlining the authentication process and enhancing user satisfaction [45].

- **Compliance with regulatory standards**: Healthcare organizations are subject to stringent regulatory requirements, such as HIPAA, which mandates the protection of patient confidentiality and the secure handling of medical information. Biometric authentication provides a robust mechanism for ensuring compliance with these regulations by offering a secure method for verifying the identity of users and controlling access to sensitive data. By implementing biometric security solutions, healthcare organizations can demonstrate their commitment to safeguarding patient privacy and upholding regulatory standards [46, 47].
- **Mitigation of insider threats**: Insider threats, including unauthorized access by employees or healthcare staff, pose a significant risk to the security of healthcare systems. Biometric authentication helps mitigate these risks by ensuring that only authorized individuals can access sensitive patient information. By binding user identities to unique biometric traits, healthcare organizations can prevent unauthorized access and detect suspicious behavior more effectively, thereby reducing the likelihood of insider-related security incidents [48].
- **Future-proofing security infrastructure**: With the continuous evolution of cyber threats and technological advancements, healthcare organizations must adopt security solutions that can adapt and scale to meet emerging challenges. Biometric authentication provides a future-proof solution for enhancing access control and cybersecurity in healthcare settings. By investing in biometric security technologies, healthcare organizations can build a resilient security infrastructure capable of mitigating evolving threats and ensuring the long-term integrity of patient data [49]. Figure 5.1 shows a schematic illustrating the architecture of a biometric security system in an e-health setting.

This chapter analyses the use of biometric security in e-health services, investigating authentication technologies such as fingerprint and facial recognition, as well as ECG. It emphasizes the role of biometric authentication in mitigating risks associated with unauthorized access, identity theft, and data breaches in healthcare applications. Advantages include enhanced precision, ease of use, and adherence to rules such as HIPAA. This chapter

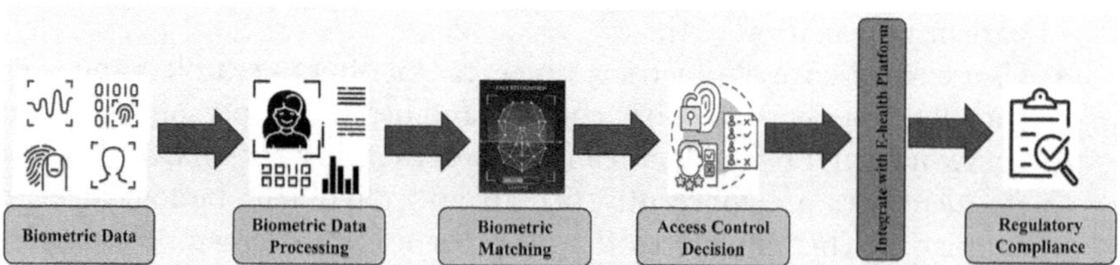

Figure 5.1 Architecture of a biometric security system in an e-health setting.

examines the merits, limitations, and future implications of biometric security, including innovations such as multimodal biometrics and behavioral biometrics. It also covers legal constraints, ethical considerations, and upcoming technology including wearable sensors and biometric encryption. It finally provides guidance for healthcare organizations to improve security and integrity in digital healthcare ecosystems.

5.2 UNDERSTANDING BIOMETRIC SECURITY

In a time characterized by digital transformation and growing dependence on technology, the importance of strong security measures is more crucial than ever. The healthcare industry has notable difficulties in protecting confidential patient data due to the swift integration of EHRs and the digitalization of healthcare procedures [50]. Conventional authentication techniques such as passwords and PINs have shown significant weaknesses, making healthcare organizations susceptible to cyber threats and data breaches. Biometric security has developed as an attractive approach to strengthen access control and protect patient data in response to these problems. Biometric authentication uses distinct biological characteristics or behavioral patterns to confirm people's identities, providing a higher level of security compared to conventional approaches. Biometric systems authenticate individuals by capturing and analyzing unique characteristics including fingerprints, iris patterns, face features, ECG, and voiceprints, ensuring great accuracy and reliability. Authentication methods in healthcare have evolved from manual, paper-based operations to modern digital alternatives [51]. In the past, healthcare organizations used manual verification methods such as physical signatures and identity badges to confirm the identities of patients and healthcare workers [52]. The emergence of EHRs and computerized systems highlighted the necessity for more secure and efficient authentication techniques. During the initial stages of digitization, basic authentication methods such as username–password combinations were implemented to provide entry to electronic systems. Although these approaches provided some protection, they were vulnerable to different weaknesses such as password theft and phishing assaults. Healthcare organizations acknowledged the constraints of conventional authentication systems as cyber threats advanced and grew more complex, prompting them to investigate alternatives.

Biometric security's rise signifies a major change in healthcare authentication methods. Biometric authentication provides superior security, ease, and precision compared to traditional techniques. Biometric systems use distinct biological characteristics or behavioral qualities to accurately confirm the identification of users, hence decreasing the likelihood of unauthorized access and data breaches. Healthcare organizations have been using biometric solutions more frequently to deal with changing security risks and regulatory demands [53]. Biometric methods, including fingerprint recognition, facial recognition,

ECG, and voice recognition, are increasingly being used in healthcare settings because of their efficiency and dependability. Technological progress has made it easier to incorporate biometric authentication into current healthcare systems, allowing for smooth and safe access control procedures.

5.2.1 Fundamental Concepts of Biometric Security

Biometric security is based on various biological characteristics or behavioral qualities that are unique to individuals and serve as indicators of their identity. These characteristics are seen as inherent, unchangeable, and unique, distinguishing them from conventional authentication methods like passwords or PINs, which are prone to being forgotten, stolen, or shared. To comprehend the basic principles of biometric security, one must explore the foundational notions that support its effectiveness and dependability in verifying persons.

5.2.1.1 Biometric Data

Biometric data serves as the cornerstone of biometric security systems, encapsulating the unique biological or behavioral attributes that distinguish individuals from one another. Biometric data can be broadly categorized into two main types: physiological and behavioral.

- *Physiological biometrics* are physical features that are inherent to an individual's biology. This includes characteristics such as fingerprints, iris patterns, facial geometry, hand geometry, vein patterns, and DNA. These characteristics are usually unchanging and remain generally stable over the course of an individual's life, which makes them well-suited for verifying one's identification [54].
- *Behavioral biometrics* center on the behavioral patterns displayed by people. These attributes can encompass characteristics such as typing rhythm, mouse behavior, signature style, voiceprints, gait analysis, and patterns of engagement with electronic gadgets. Behavioral biometrics are dynamic and can change over time, yet they provide vital insights into an individual's behavior patterns, adding an extra layer of verification [55]. Figure 5.2 shows a block diagram for the categorization of biometric data.

5.2.1.1.1 Characteristics of Biometric Data

Biometric data possesses several unique characteristics that distinguish it from traditional forms of authentication:

(1) **Uniqueness:** Biometric data is characterized by its inherent distinctiveness. Physiological characteristics like fingerprints or iris patterns are unique to each person, guaranteeing that no two sets of biometric data

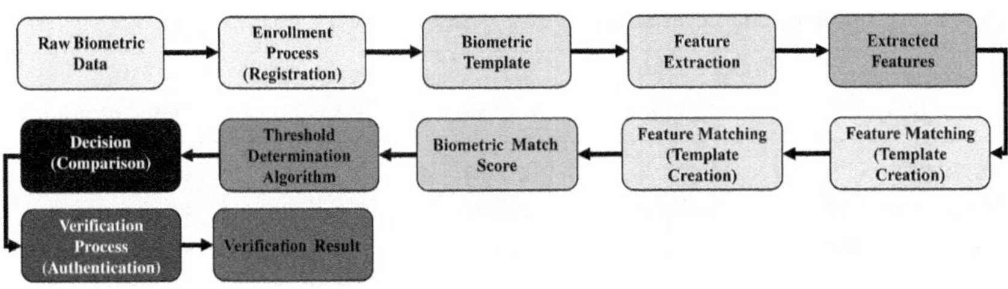

Figure 5.2 Types of biometric data.

are identical. This distinctiveness serves as the foundation for dependable identity authentication.

(2) **Permanence**: Physiological biometric features are typically seen as enduring and consistent over time. Although age or injury may lead to modest alterations, the fundamental attributes of biometric data generally remain stable during an individual's lifetime. The durability of biometric authentication systems is improved by this permanence, increasing their reliability and lifespan.

(3) **Universality**: Biometric traits are present in individuals throughout all human populations, irrespective of their ethnicity, nationality, or demographic factors. This universality guarantees that biometric authentication technologies can be widely used among various demographics.

(4) **Non-repudiation:** It is enhanced by biometric data due to its ability to provide strong evidence of an individual's identification, surpassing previous authentication methods. Biometric data, once acquired and matched to an individual, provides undeniable evidence of their identification, reducing the possibility of rejection or denial. Table 5.1 shows comparison of biometric characteristics between some common biometrics [56–60].

5.2.1.1.2 Significance in Security

Biometric data is essential for improving security in different areas:

(1) **Improved precision**: Biometric authentication solutions provide superior levels of precision and dependability in comparison to conventional techniques such as passwords or PINs. Biometric systems can accurately confirm an individual's identity using unique physiological or behavioral characteristics, leaving little room for error.

(2) **Enhanced convenience**: Biometric authentication removes the necessity for users to recall intricate passwords or carry physical tokens, improving user convenience and simplifying the authentication process. This convenience is especially important in situations where quick and smooth authentication is crucial, like in access control or online transactions.

Table 5.1 Biometric Characteristics

Biometric Characteristic	*Uniqueness*	*Permanence*	*Universality*	*Non-repudiation*
Fingerprint	High	Medium	High	High
Iris pattern	High	Medium	Medium	High
Facial geometry	Medium	Medium	Medium	Medium
Hand geometry	Medium	High	Medium	Medium
Vein pattern	High	High	Low	High
DNA	High	High	High	High
Typing rhythm	Medium	Low	High	Low
Mouse dynamics	Medium	Low	High	Low
Signature dynamics	Medium	Medium	Medium	Medium
Voiceprint	High	Medium	High	High
Gait analysis	Medium	Low	Medium	Low
ECG	High	High	High	High

(3) Biometric data is very secure and difficult to fake, copy, or steal, making it very effective for improving security. Biometric features are unique to each individual and cannot be easily copied, providing strong protection against unauthorized access or identity theft, unlike passwords or PINs that can be forgotten, shared, or stolen.

Biometric data provides substantial advantages in security and convenience, but its gathering, retention, and application present crucial privacy and ethical concerns. These concerns involve issues related to consent, openness, data privacy, and the possibility of biometric information being misused or abused. Organizations implementing biometric authentication systems must create strong privacy policies, obtain informed consent from users, and enforce strict security measures to safeguard biometric data from unauthorized access or exploitation.

5.2.1.2 Biometric Recognition Systems

Biometric recognition systems, often called biometric authentication or identification systems, are technical solutions that identify and confirm individuals by their distinct physiological or behavioral traits. These systems are essential for improving security and access control in many sectors such as healthcare, banking, government, and law enforcement. Biometric recognition systems typically consist of several key components:

- **Sensor**: The sensor acquires biometric data from the individual, including fingerprint impressions, iris patterns, facial features, voice samples, and behavioral traits like typing rhythm or walking patterns. Sensors can differ according to the modality employed and may consist of fingerprint scanners, iris scanners, cameras, microphones, or other specialized devices.

- **Feature extraction:** After capturing biometric data, algorithms are used to process the raw data and extract specific features or templates that represent the individual's unique qualities. These qualities are used for comparison and matching in the authentication process.
- **Database:** Biometric traits are kept in a database along with user IDs or biometric templates. The database functions as a storage place for reference templates used to compare incoming biometric samples for identification or verification.
- **Matching algorithm:** It evaluates the biometric characteristics obtained from the input sample against the reference templates saved in the database. The algorithm computes a similarity score or distance metric to assess the level of similarity between the input sample and the stored templates.
- **Decision module:** It uses the similarity score or distance metric from the matching algorithm to make a binary decision on the individual's identity. The decision module in verification situations assesses if the input sample corresponds to the enrolled template of a claimed identity. During identification scenarios, the decision module scans the entire database to locate the most similar match or highest-ranked candidates for the input sample. Figure 5.3 shows the components of biometric recognition.

Biometric recognition systems find applications in a wide range of sectors, including:

- **Access control:** Biometric systems are utilized for access control to secure locations, sensitive information, or digital gadgets. Fingerprint

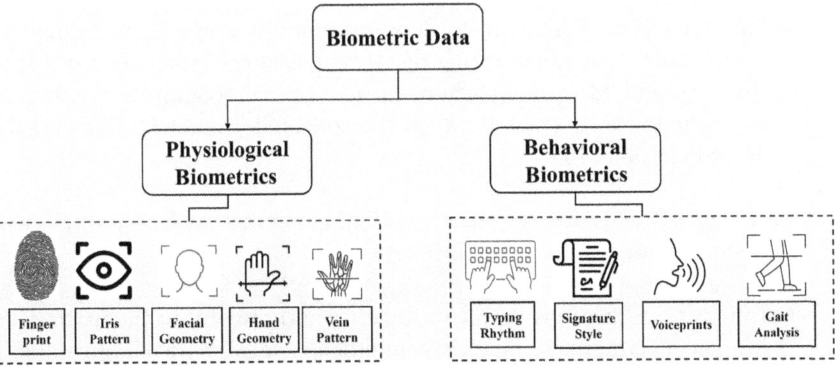

Figure 5.3 Block diagram outlining the key components of a biometric recognition system.

scanners can be used to control access to high-security facilities, and facial recognition technologies can be incorporated into smartphones for user verification [61, 62].

- **Identity verification**: Biometric systems are used to confirm the identity of persons in different activities or interactions, such as banking, border crossings, or online account access [63, 64]. Biometric authentication offers a more dependable and safe option compared to conventional approaches such as passwords or PINs.
- **Surveillance and security**: Biometric systems are used in surveillance and security to identify and monitor specific individuals in public areas, airports, stadiums, and other busy places [65]. Facial recognition technology has become prominent in security and law enforcement applications.
- **Forensic analysis**: It utilizes biometric techniques to identify persons through physical or behavioral evidence found at crime scenes. Forensic investigations typically utilize fingerprint analysis, DNA profiling, and voice recognition to connect suspects with criminal activity [66].

5.2.1.3 Biometric Matching Algorithms

Biometric matching algorithms are essential in biometric recognition systems. The algorithms compare biometric data obtained during authentication or verification with stored template data to identify a match [67]. Biometric matching algorithms can be categorized into two main types based on their approach to comparison:

(1) Feature-based matching algorithms: Feature-based matching algorithms extract distinct features from the biometric data and compare them with features in the template. Feature-based matching involves comparing specific points such as minutiae in fingerprint recognition or landmarks in facial recognition [68].
(2) Template-based matching algorithms: Template-based matching algorithms compare complete biometric templates instead of individual characteristics. These algorithms commonly employ mathematical approaches like correlation, distance measures (such as Euclidean distance and Hamming distance), or pattern recognition techniques to evaluate the likeness between the collected biometric data and the stored template [69].

Despite their effectiveness, biometric matching algorithms face several challenges and considerations as the following:

- Matching algorithms need to be precise and resilient to fluctuations in biometric data due to factors including ageing, climatic circumstances, and sensor quality.
- Real-time applications necessitate rapid and efficient matching algorithms to deliver prompt results during authentication.

- Matching algorithms need to prioritize security and privacy by using encryption methods and secure storage systems to safeguard biometric data.
- Template management involves effectively handling biometric templates, including storage, retrieval, and update methods, to guarantee scalability and performance in extensive biometric systems.

5.2.1.4 Security and Privacy Considerations

Security and privacy are crucial factors in the development, execution, and maintenance of biometric systems. These factors are crucial for preserving sensitive biometric data, upholding individual privacy rights, and maintaining the integrity and reliability of the biometric system.

(1) **Data security** [70, 71]:
   a. **Encryption**: Biometric data must be encrypted when sent and stored to avoid unauthorized access or interception by hostile individuals. Utilize robust encryption algorithms and protocols to safeguard the confidentiality and integrity of biometric data.
   b. **Access control**: Access to biometric databases and systems must be limited to authorized persons. Implement role-based access control systems and strong authentication methods to deter unauthorized access to sensitive biometric data.
   c. **Data integrity**: Ensure the integrity of biometric data at all stages of its existence. Hashing methods and digital signatures can authenticate and ensure the integrity of biometric templates and authentication transactions.

(2) **Privacy protection**:
   a. **Anonymization** of biometric data should be prioritized to disconnect it from individual identities. This helps reduce privacy risks related to the improper use or unauthorized release of biometric data.
   b. **Purpose limitation**: Biometric data must only be collected, processed, and retained for clearly defined and lawful purposes. Organizations must precisely outline the reasons for collecting biometric data and secure explicit agreement from individuals.
   c. **Data minimization**: Organizations should only gather and store the essential quantity of biometric data required to fulfill the intended objectives. To reduce privacy risks, it is important to avoid collecting an excessive amount of biometric data.
   d. **Transparency**: Individuals should get straightforward and succinct details on the collection, processing, and utilization of their biometric data. Clear privacy rules and consent methods should be established to enhance user awareness and comprehension.
   e. **User control**: Individuals should have autonomy over their biometric data and be able to assert their rights concerning its

utilization and disclosure. This may involve choices for data access, correction, deletion, and opting out of specific biometric applications.

(3) **Biometric template protection** [72–74]:
   a. **Secure storage**: Biometric templates must be securely maintained using cryptographic methods to avoid unwanted access or manipulation. Template databases should have limited access and strong authentication methods to safeguard template repositories.
   b. **Template revocation**: Procedures must be established to revoke and reissue biometric templates in case of a security breach or compromise to avoid unauthorized use. This may require developing rules for updating biometric templates and keeping records of template access and changes.

(4) **Compliance with regulations**:
   a. **Legal compliance**: Biometric systems must adhere to applicable laws, regulations, and industry standards for the acquisition, handling, and safeguarding of biometric data. This involves adhering to data privacy laws such as the General Data Privacy Regulation (GDPR), HIPAA, and restrictions related to biometrics.
   b. **Ethical considerations**: The design and operation of biometric systems should be guided by ethical concepts such justice, openness, accountability, and respect for individual autonomy. Utilizing ethical review boards and privacy impact assessments can guarantee that biometric technologies comply with ethical standards and concepts.

5.2.2 Types of Biometric Modalities

Types of biometric modalities refer to the various physiological or behavioral characteristics used for biometric identification or verification. These modalities capture unique traits inherent to individuals, allowing for reliable and secure authentication. Table 5.2 shows an overview of biometric modalities and their applications in healthcare.

5.2.3 Advantages of Biometric Security

The advantages of biometric security are the following:

- Biometric security provides a superior level of security in comparison to conventional authentication techniques such as passwords or PINs. Biometric identifiers, like fingerprints or iris patterns, are distinct to each person and challenging to copy or imitate. Biometric authentication solutions are very resistant to illegal access and identity theft, considerably lowering the risk of data breaches and fraud due to their uniqueness.

Table 5.2 Overview of Biometric Modalities and Their Applications

Type	*Biometric Modality*	*Description*	*Healthcare Applications*
Physiological biometrics	Fingerprint recognition	Analyzes unique patterns of ridges and valleys on fingertip	Patient identification; access to electronic health records
	Iris recognition	Captures unique patterns of the iris	Patient identification; access control in hospitals
	Facial recognition	Analyzes unique facial characteristics	Patient identification; tracking patient movements in hospitals
	Hand geometry	Measures physical characteristics of the hand	Physical access control in healthcare facilities
	Retina recognition	Scans unique patterns of blood vessels at the back of the eye	Patient identification; access to sensitive medical information
Behavioral biometrics	Voice recognition	Analyzes unique characteristics of an individual's voice	Voice-based patient authentication; remote patient monitoring
	Signature recognition	Assesses dynamic features of an individual's signature	Electronic signature for medical documents
	Keystroke dynamics	Captures typing rhythm and timing patterns when typing on a keyboard	Keyboard-based patient authentication
	Gait recognition	Analyzes unique walking patterns of individuals	Gait analysis for diagnosing neurological disorders
Electrophysiological biometrics	ECG recognition	Measures electrical activity of the heart to generate a unique biometric signature	Patient identification; continuous health monitoring

- Biometric authentication systems utilize distinct physiological or behavioral traits specific to each person. Biometric features such as fingerprints or speech patterns are unique and tend to remain consistent over time. Biometric authentication provides more accuracy and dependability than traditional systems, which are vulnerable to human error, theft, or loss.
- Biometric authentication offers a smooth and user-friendly experience for individuals accessing secure systems or facilities, enhancing convenience and user experience. Biometric identifiers are linked to an individual's biological traits, unlike passwords or PINs, which can be forgotten, lost, or traded. This removes the necessity for users to recall intricate passwords or carry physical tokens, simplifying the authentication process and improving user satisfaction.
- Biometric authentication systems can decrease administrative costs related to monitoring and changing passwords, issuing physical access cards, or dealing with stolen credentials. Upon registration, users can conveniently verify their identity using their biometric characteristics without requiring extra credentials or administrative involvement.
- Biometric authentication aids in mitigating internal threats, such as unlawful access by workers or individuals with privileged access. Linking user identities to distinct biometric characteristics enables enterprises to thwart unwanted entry and identify questionable actions more efficiently, thus decreasing the chances of security breaches caused by insiders.
- Biometric authentication aids firms in meeting strict regulatory standards concerning data protection and privacy, including the HIPAA in healthcare. Organizations can show their dedication to protecting sensitive data and complying with regulations by using biometric security solutions.
- Biometric authentication offers a long-lasting solution for improving access control and cybersecurity across many sectors. Organizations can establish a strong security framework and safeguard sensitive data by investing in biometric security solutions to counter emerging threats effectively.

5.2.4 Challenges and Considerations

The challenges and considerations associated with biometric security are as follows:

- Privacy is a major issue when it comes to biometric security. Biometric data, such as fingerprints or iris patterns, is extremely sensitive and distinctive to each person. Hence, there is a potential for privacy violation if this data is accessed or misused. Organizations need to establish strong privacy policies and security protocols to safeguard biometric data from unwanted access or disclosure.

- Biometric data, like other personal information, is vulnerable to cyber dangers such as hacking, theft, or illegal access. Organizations need to establish robust encryption and authentication measures to protect biometric data during transmission and storage. Regular security audits and vulnerability assessments can assist in identifying and addressing potential security problems.
- Biometric authentication typically provides excellent accuracy and reliability, although its performance might be influenced by specific conditions. Environmental factors, including inadequate lighting or background noise, might affect the precision of biometric devices. Changes in an individual's physiological or behavioral features over time, such as age or injury, might impact the reliability of biometric authentication. Organizations need to consider these concerns and take steps to improve the precision and dependability of biometric systems.
- Interoperability issues may arise when biometric technologies need to integrate with current infrastructure or third-party systems. Various biometric methods may utilize exclusive algorithms or formats, which can hinder smooth integration. Organizations should prioritize interoperability when choosing biometric solutions to prevent implementation challenges and operational interruptions by ensuring compatibility with current systems.
- User acceptability and adoption play a vital role in the success of biometric security projects. Some people could be reluctant to sign up for biometric systems because of privacy worries or the perception of intrusiveness. Organizations need to be clear and open with users regarding the purpose and handling of biometric data, and they should resolve any worries or misunderstandings to encourage acceptance and implementation.
- Biometric security systems must adhere to regulatory regulations for data protection, privacy, and security. Healthcare firms must comply with standards such as HIPAA to guarantee the secure management of patient information. Noncompliance with regulations can lead to legal consequences, financial penalties, or harm to reputation.
- Ethical considerations, such as consent and autonomy, are important factors in the implementation of biometric security systems. Organizations are required to get informed consent from individuals prior to gathering or utilizing their biometric data and guarantee transparency in the utilization of this data. Organizations must also deal with ethical issues about potential biases or prejudice in biometric systems, especially in fields like law enforcement or job screening.

5.3 BIOMETRIC MODALITIES IN E-HEALTH

In the realm of E-healthcare, the utilization of biometric modalities offers a promising avenue for enhancing security, efficiency, and patient care.

Biometric technologies, which encompass various physiological and behavioral characteristics unique to individuals, are increasingly being integrated into healthcare systems to provide robust identification and authentication mechanisms. This section delves into the diverse array of biometric modalities employed within E-healthcare settings, exploring their applications, advantages, and considerations in ensuring secure and seamless patient management and access control.

5.3.1 Fingerprint Recognition in Healthcare

Fingerprint recognition, a commonly used biometric method, shows great potential for transforming healthcare systems by providing strong identity verification solutions. Fingerprint recognition is widely used in healthcare for tasks such as patient identification, safe access control, and medication monitoring.

Fingerprint recognition is mostly used in healthcare for patient identification. Healthcare facilities can verify the identity of patients seeking medical care correctly and effectively by assigning each patient a unique fingerprint template. This guarantees that patients are provided with tailored care and avoids mistakes linked to misidentification, such giving medication to the wrong person or accessing inaccurate medical files. Fingerprint identification is essential for improving security in healthcare facilities. Healthcare firms can implement strong access control measures by incorporating fingerprint scanners at access points, including entrances to restricted areas or drug storage units. Access is restricted to authorized people with registered fingerprints to reduce the chance of unlawful entrance into sensitive locations and protect precious medical resources.

Fingerprint recognition in medication management ensures medication adherence and prevents medication errors. Healthcare professionals can accurately dispense prescriptions and manage administration data by associating patients' fingerprints with their medication profiles. Patients can verify their identity using their fingerprints before obtaining prescription medications, which decreases the chances of medication errors and improves medication safety. Fingerprint recognition technology enables rapid and safe access to EHR. Healthcare personnel can utilize their registered fingerprints to efficiently and securely access EHR systems, ensuring prompt retrieval of patient information during consultations, operations, or emergencies. This improved access to medical records optimizes clinical processes, boosts patient care coordination, and guarantees data protection and confidentiality.

Although fingerprint identification in healthcare offers many advantages, it also poses certain obstacles. Environmental elements including dirt, dampness, or even injuries to the fingertips might impact the accuracy of fingerprint scans, which may result in authentication errors. Furthermore, hygiene difficulties may occur in environments where numerous users must use fingerprint scanners one after the other. Healthcare institutions need to maintain fingerprint scanning devices properly and follow hygiene guidelines to ensure reliable and hygienic fingerprint authentication operations.

5.3.2 Iris Recognition in Healthcare

Iris recognition is an advanced biometric technique that provides a precise and secure way to verify identify in healthcare environments. Iris recognition has great potential to improve patient safety, data security, and operational efficiency in healthcare institutions because to its unique benefits.

Healthcare utilizes iris recognition mostly for patient identification and access control. Healthcare companies can generate unique biometric templates for individuals by capturing and analyzing the detailed patterns in the iris. Iris recognition systems can properly match patients with their medical records during registration or admission, ensuring exact identification and lowering the risk of errors related to misidentification. This feature is especially beneficial in situations where accurate patient identification is essential for providing prompt and suitable medical treatment, such as emergency rooms or intensive care units.

Iris recognition technology is crucial for implementing access control measures in healthcare institutions. Healthcare businesses can control access to sensitive areas and resources by incorporating iris scanners at entrances to restricted areas, pharmaceutical storage units, or secure laboratories. Access is restricted to authorized individuals with registered iris patterns to prevent unlawful entrance and safeguard precious medical assets, sensitive information, and regulated drugs. Iris recognition is also used in healthcare for secure authentication when accessing EHRs. Healthcare practitioners can use iris recognition technologies to securely access EHR platforms, allowing fast and convenient retrieval of patient information during clinical interactions. Improving access to medical records boosts healthcare efficiency, aids in making well-informed decisions, and promotes continuity of care between various healthcare environments.

Additionally, iris recognition technology has advantages in maintaining patient confidentiality and enhancing data protection. Iris patterns are distinct to each person and cannot be easily copied or imitated, unlike conventional means of identification like ID cards or passwords. The inherent uniqueness of iris recognition systems provides great resistance against identity theft, fraud, and illegal access, ensuring the protection of sensitive patient information and confidentiality in healthcare operations.

Although iris recognition offers many benefits, its integration into healthcare also presents specific obstacles. Deploying iris recognition systems in healthcare companies may face financial challenges due to the high initial setup expenses, which include hardware acquisition, installation, and connection with existing infrastructure. Furthermore, it is essential to address concerns regarding user acceptance, privacy consequences, and regulatory compliance to enable the ethical and responsible implementation of iris recognition technology in healthcare environments.

5.3.3 Facial Recognition in Healthcare

Facial recognition technology, an advanced biometric method, offers a flexible and promising approach for verifying identity and controlling access in healthcare environments. By utilizing distinct face characteristics, facial recognition systems provide a non-invasive, touchless way to precisely identify individuals, improving patient safety, operational effectiveness, and data protection in healthcare settings. Facial recognition technology is used in healthcare for patient identification, access control, and patient monitoring. Facial recognition technology is mostly used for patient identification processes. Healthcare organizations can develop individualized biometric templates by recording and analyzing facial features including eye, nose, and mouth size and shape. Facial recognition systems used during patient registration or admission can effectively match patients with their medical information, assuring correct identification and minimizing the chances of errors related to misidentification. This capacity is especially important in instances where quick and precise identification is necessary to provide prompt and suitable medical treatment, like in emergencies or intensive care units.

Facial recognition technology is important for controlling access in healthcare institutions. Healthcare businesses can control access to sensitive areas and resources by implementing facial recognition systems at entrances to restricted areas, pharmaceutical storage units, or secure laboratories. Access is restricted to authorized individuals with registered face biometrics to reduce the chances of unlawful entrance and safeguard precious medical resources, personal data, and regulated substances. Facial recognition in healthcare is also crucial for patient monitoring and surveillance. Highly sophisticated facial recognition systems with real-time monitoring can help healthcare providers monitor patient movements in healthcare facilities, ensure adherence to treatment programs, and improve patient safety. Facial recognition technology can be combined with video surveillance systems to recognize patients who are at risk of straying or leaving without permission, allowing healthcare professionals to intervene quickly and avoid negative incidents.

Facial recognition technology provides advantages by increasing the effectiveness of administrative duties and promoting patient satisfaction. Facial recognition technologies automate identification verification operations including patient check-ins and appointment confirmations, improving administrative efficiency, decreasing wait times, and enhancing the patient experience. Facial recognition technology can help healthcare providers obtain patient-specific information and preferences rapidly, allowing for personalized interactions with patients and a more customized approach to care delivery. Although facial recognition technology in healthcare offers advantages, its extensive use also brings forth specific obstacles and factors to consider. Privacy, data security, algorithm bias, and regulatory compliance issues must be meticulously handled to guarantee the ethical and responsible implementation of facial recognition technologies in healthcare environments. Healthcare institutions need to invest in strong cybersecurity measures to protect facial biometric data from illegal access, abuse, or breaches.

5.3.4 Voice Recognition in Healthcare

Voice recognition technology, an advanced biometric approach, provides a unique and convenient way for verifying identity and controlling access in healthcare environments. Voice recognition systems use unique speech patterns and traits to identify individuals, improving patient safety, operational efficiency, and data security in healthcare settings. Voice recognition technology is utilized in healthcare for tasks such as patient identification, authentication, dictation, and transcription. Voice recognition technology is mostly used in patient identification processes. Healthcare companies can develop distinctive biometric voiceprints for each person by recording and examining vocal characteristics like pitch, tone, rhythm, and pronunciation. Voice recognition systems may reliably match people with their medical records during patient encounters or phone-based inquiries, facilitating seamless identification and minimizing errors linked to manual identification procedures.

Voice recognition technology is important for authentication and access control in healthcare institutions. Healthcare organizations can limit access to restricted locations, medical devices, and EHR systems by combining voice recognition technologies with access control techniques. Authorized personnel can utilize their voice for secure authentication, guaranteeing that only authenticated individuals can access important information and resources. This feature improves data security and reduces the chance of unwanted access, safeguarding patient confidentiality and organizational integrity. Furthermore, speech recognition technology provides advantages in clinical documentation and workflow improvement. Healthcare practitioners can utilize speech recognition technology to dictate clinical notes, capture patient encounters, and create medical transcripts instantly. This efficient documentation method minimizes manual data entry, decreases administrative tasks, and enables doctors to concentrate on patient care. Voice recognition technology facilitates remote dictation and transcription, allowing healthcare personnel to access and update patient information and medical records from any place, improving care coordination and continuity.

Voice recognition technology also enhances patient experiences and involvement in healthcare delivery. Patients can utilize voice-activated devices or apps to book appointments, renew prescriptions, and retrieve customized health data through natural language instructions. This user-friendly interface encourages patient empowerment, autonomy, and adherence to treatment programs, resulting in improved health outcomes and patient satisfaction. Although speech recognition technology in healthcare offers many benefits, it also presents specific challenges and factors to consider. Environmental noise, speech variability, language obstacles, and voice-based security risks need to be resolved to guarantee the precision, dependability, and security of voice recognition systems in healthcare environments. Healthcare institutions must adhere to regulatory regulations such as the HIPAA to safeguard patient privacy and confidentiality while gathering and handling voice biometric data.

5.3.5 ECG Authentication in Healthcare

ECG authentication is a new biometric method that uses the distinct electrical signals of a person's heart to verify their identification and control access in healthcare environments. This advanced technology uses a non-invasive method based on physiology to authenticate individuals by analyzing the unique patterns of the heart's electrical signals. ECG authentication shows potential for improving patient safety, data security, and operational efficiency in healthcare settings. ECG authentication can be used in healthcare for patient identity, access control, and medical device authentication. The method entails capturing the electrical signals produced by the heart using specialized sensors or electrodes positioned on the patient's body. ECG waveforms are distinct patterns that possess individual-specific traits, akin to biometric modalities like fingerprints or iris patterns.

ECG authentication is mostly used in healthcare for patient identification. Healthcare companies can generate biometric templates based on the distinctive ECG patterns of patients, which act as digital representations of each person's cardiac activity. ECG authentication systems can compare acquired ECG signals with stored templates during patient contacts or admission processes to correctly validate patient identity, ensuring proper matching with medical records and lowering the possibility of misidentification. Furthermore, ECG authentication technology can improve access control systems in healthcare facilities. Healthcare organizations can control access to sensitive information and resources by combining ECG authentication systems with secure entry points, EHR systems, or medical devices, using the unique cardiac signatures of authorized individuals. Access to restricted locations, medical records, or diagnostic equipment is limited to those with registered ECG biometrics to enhance data security and reduce the chance of unwanted entry.

Moreover, ECG authentication shows potential for improving the security of medical devices and guaranteeing patient safety. Healthcare professionals can use ECG authentication in wearable health monitoring devices, implanted medical devices, or infusion pumps to confirm patients' identities before providing treatments or enabling device interactions. This additional authentication layer aids in preventing illegal entry to medical devices, reducing the chances of device misuse or tampering, therefore improving patient safety and treatment effectiveness. Moreover, ECG authentication method has advantages in remote patient monitoring and telemedicine applications. Patients can utilize ECG-enabled wearable devices or smartphone apps to record and send their ECG signals to healthcare providers for remote verification and monitoring. This remote authentication feature allows secure and convenient access to healthcare services, especially for persons in remote or underdeveloped areas, elderly patients, or those with chronic diseases that need constant monitoring.

Although ECG authentication in healthcare has intriguing uses, its implementation also brings along certain obstacles and factors to consider. Signal variability, motion artifacts, integration with existing systems, and regulatory compliance are crucial factors that need to be resolved to guarantee the precision, dependability, and safety of ECG authentication systems in healthcare environments. Healthcare businesses need to establish strong cybersecurity protocols to safeguard ECG biometric data against unauthorized access, abuse, or breaches, in accordance with regulations such as HIPAA. Table 5.3 summarizes the modalities in E-health.

Table 5.3 Overview of Biometric Modalities in E-healthcare

Biometric Modality	*Description*	*Characteristics*	*Applications*
Fingerprint recognition	Utilizes distinctive patterns present on the fingertip for identification	— High accuracy—cost-effective—user-friendly—widely deployable	— Patient identification—access control—medication dispensing
Iris recognition	Analyzes unique patterns within the iris of the eye for identification	— Exceptionally high accuracy—variable cost—non-invasive—stable and unique characteristics	— Patient identification—access control—patient tracking
Facial recognition	Identifies individuals based on facial features and characteristics	— Moderate to high accuracy—variable cost—non-intrusive—broad acceptance	— Patient identification—access control—patient monitoring
Voice recognition	Analyzes distinctive vocal patterns for identification	— Moderate accuracy—cost-effective—non-contact—convenient	— Patient identification—access control—clinical documentation
ECG authentication	Utilizes unique electrical signals of the heart for identification	— high accuracy—cost-effective—physiological-based—non-intrusive	— Patient identification—Access control—medical device authentication

5.4 BENEFITS OF BIOMETRIC SECURITY IN E-HEALTH

Biometric security solutions offer numerous advantages in e-healthcare settings, addressing critical challenges while enhancing security, efficiency, and patient care. Below are some key benefits of implementing biometric security in e-health:

- **Enhanced security**: Biometric authentication offers an exceptionally secure approach to authenticating the identities of authorized personnel, healthcare professionals, and patients. Biometric systems considerably reduce the likelihood of unauthorized access and identity theft by utilizing distinctive biological characteristics such as fingerprints, iris patterns, or voiceprints.
- **Accuracy and reliability**: Biometric modalities provide exceptional accuracy and dependability when it comes to the identification of individuals, thereby reducing the likelihood of erroneous positive or negative results. By restricting access to sensitive medical records to authorized personnel, the likelihood of data breaches and unauthorized disclosures is significantly mitigated.
- **Convenience and user experience**: User experience and convenience are key attributes of biometric authentication systems, which benefit healthcare providers and patients alike. In contrast to conventional authentication techniques like PINs and passwords, which are susceptible to loss or theft, biometric identifiers are intrinsic to the subject, thereby obviating the necessity for physical tokens or memorization.
- **Enhanced workflow optimization**: Biometric security solutions optimize workflow and alleviate administrative duties for healthcare personnel through the automation of the authentication process. This facilitates expedited and streamlined retrieval of patient records, thereby empowering medical practitioners to allocate greater attention toward providing high-quality care.
- **Regulatory compliance**: Biometric security systems assist healthcare organizations in adhering to rigorous regulatory requirements, including but not limited to the HIPAA. Healthcare providers exhibit their dedication to protecting patient confidentiality and adhering to regulatory standards through the implementation of secure protocols, which may include biometric authentication.
- **Fraud prevention**: In healthcare contexts, biometric authentication aids in the prevention of identity theft and fraud by limiting access to sensitive data and medical resources to authorized personnel only. This mitigates the potential for fraudulent activities, including but not limited to prescription drug abuse, insurance fraud, and unauthorized medical procedures.
- **Patient trust and confidentiality**: Healthcare organizations foster patient confidence and trust in the security and confidentiality of their medical information through the implementation of advanced

security measures, including biometric authentication. This promotes improved patient satisfaction and the development of more robust provider–patient relationships.

5.5 CHALLENGES AND CONSIDERATIONS

While biometric security offers numerous benefits in E-healthcare, its implementation also presents various challenges and considerations that healthcare organizations must address:

- **Privacy concerns**: These arise due to the inherently intimate and unique nature of biometric data, which is collected from individuals. To safeguard patient privacy and adhere to regulatory requirements like HIPAA, healthcare organizations must guarantee the appropriate collection, storage, and handling of biometric data.
- **Ethical considerations**: The implementation of biometric technology within the healthcare sector gives rise to concerns of an ethical nature concerning potential misuse of biometric data, transparency, and consent. In addition to establishing transparent policies and procedures for obtaining patients' informed consent, healthcare providers must be transparent concerning the storage and utilization of biometric data.
- **Data security risks**: Although biometric authentication bolsters security measures, it concurrently presents novel vulnerabilities pertaining to intrusions and data breaches. Healthcare organizations are required to establish and enforce strong cybersecurity protocols in order to safeguard biometric databases against illicit access, hacking, or tampering.
- **Difficulties in interoperability**: The integration of biometric systems with pre-existing healthcare IT infrastructure may present obstacles in terms of interoperability. In order to facilitate the smooth exchange of data and integration of biometric solutions with EHR systems, medical devices, and other healthcare technologies, it is imperative for healthcare organizations to ensure such compatibility.
- **Accuracy and reliability**: Notwithstanding the progress made in biometric technology, specific modalities might demonstrate constraints in terms of precision and dependability. The performance of biometric systems may be impacted by environmental conditions, variations in biometric characteristics, or technical defects, which may result in false positives or negatives.
- **Financial and resource limitations**: Due to financial and resource limitations, the implementation of biometric security solutions in electronic healthcare necessitates substantial hardware, software, and infrastructure investments. Healthcare organizations are required to evaluate the cost-effectiveness of biometric solutions, taking into account factors such as resource availability, budgetary limitations, and long-term viability.

- **User acceptance and training**: Patients, healthcare professionals, or personnel who are not well-versed in the technology may exhibit opposition toward the implementation of biometric authentication. Healthcare organizations are obligated to furnish sufficient training and support in order to resolve concerns pertaining to privacy, usability, reliability, and user acceptance.
- **Healthcare organizations**: Healthcare organizations are confronted with the intricate task of adhering to the legal and regulatory framework that regulates the implementation of biometric technology within the healthcare sector. Ensuring adherence to state-specific privacy laws, HIPAA and the GDPR are critical in order to prevent legal liabilities and penalties.
- **Precautionary measures**: As a precautionary measure against biometric authentication failures and system outages, healthcare organizations must establish dependable failsafe mechanisms to maintain uninterrupted access to vital healthcare services and patient records. This may encompass backup strategies for manual verification or alternative methods of authentication.
- **Long-term sustainability**: In order to maintain their efficacy in the face of evolving threats and technologies, biometric security solutions necessitate continuous maintenance, updates, and enhancements. In order to ensure the enduring viability of biometric systems, healthcare organizations must devise strategies that address scalability, interoperability, and the ability to adapt to forthcoming developments in biometric technology.

5.6 CONCLUSION

The incorporation of biometric security technology into electronic health (E-health) services offers a substantial prospect for augmenting security, operational effectiveness, and patient welfare within healthcare environments. We have examined the various facets of biometric security, including its applications, benefits, challenges, and considerations, throughout this chapter. E-healthcare benefits from the unique advantages provided by biometric modalities such as retinal recognition, facial recognition, voice recognition, and ECG authentication, which include increased security, precision, convenience, and regulatory compliance. These technologies facilitate the fortification of access control protocols, the optimization of operational processes, and the protection of patient privacy in a progressively digitalized setting for healthcare organizations. However, there are obstacles to the implementation of biometric security in e-health services. Thorough consideration must be given to technological limitations, privacy concerns, interoperability challenges, and regulatory compliance in order to guarantee a successful implementation. Furthermore, in order to safeguard against unauthorized access and data breaches, healthcare organizations must consistently update their security measures and maintain a state of constant vigilance regarding emergent cyber threats. Notwithstanding these obstacles, the prospective advantages of biometric security in electronic healthcare are considerable. Healthcare providers can enhance operational efficiency, develop patient trust, and improve patient outcomes through the implementation of robust biometric authentication systems, which serve as a tangible manifestation of their dedication to safeguarding sensitive medical data.

REFERENCES

[1] Ahmad, G. I., Singla, J., & Giri, K. J. (2021). Security and Privacy of E-health Data. *Multimedia Security: Algorithm Development, Analysis and Applications*, 199–214.

[2] Aslan, Ö., Aktuğ, S. S., Ozkan-Okay, M., Yilmaz, A. A., & Akin, E. (2023). A comprehensive review of cyber security vulnerabilities, threats, attacks, and solutions. *Electronics*, *12*(6), 1333.

[3] Seh, A. H., Zarour, M., Alenezi, M., Sarkar, A. K., Agrawal, A., Kumar, R., & Ahmad Khan, R. (2020, May). Healthcare data breaches: insights and implications. In *Healthcare* (Vol. 8, No. 2, p. 133). MDPI.

[4] Mehmood, Z., Ghani, A., Chen, G., & Alghamdi, A. S. (2019). Authentication and secure key management in E-health services: A robust and efficient protocol using biometrics. *IEEE Access*, *7*, 113385–113397.

[5] Maltoni, D., Maio, D., Jain, A. K., & Prabhakar, S. (2009). *Handbook of fingerprint recognition* (Vol. 2). Springer.

[6] Kaushal, N., & Kaushal, P. (2011). Human identification and fingerprints: A review. *Journal of Biometrics & Biostatistics*, *2*(123), 2.

[7] Allen, R., Sankar, P., & Prabhakar, S. (2005). Fingerprint identification technology. In *Biometric systems: Technology, design and performance evaluation* (pp. 22–61). Springer London.

[8] Ghafoor, M., Tariq, S. A., Zia, T., Taj, I. A., Abbas, A., Hassan, A., & Zomaya, A. Y. (2019). Fingerprint identification with shallow multifeature view classifier. *IEEE Transactions on Cybernetics*, *51*(9), 4515–4527.

[9] Yang, W., Wang, S., Hu, J., Zheng, G., & Valli, C. (2019). Security and accuracy of fingerprint-based biometrics: A review. *Symmetry*, *11*(2), 141.

[10] Singh, G., Bhardwaj, G., Singh, S. V., & Garg, V. (2021). Biometric identification system: Security and privacy concern. *Artificial Intelligence for a Sustainable Industry 4.0*, 245–264.

[11] Ali, E. M., Ahmed, E. S., & Ali, A. F. (2007). Recognition of human iris patterns for biometric identification. *Journal of Engineering and Applied Science-Cairo*, *54*(6), 635.

[12] Ma, L., Tan, T., Wang, Y., & Zhang, D. (2003). Personal identification based on iris texture analysis. *IEEE Transactions on Pattern Analysis and Machine Intelligence*, *25*(12), 1519–1533.

[13] Mabrukar, S. S., Sonawane, N. S., & Bagban, J. A. (2013). Biometric system using Iris pattern recognition. *International Journal of Innovative Technology and Exploring Engineering*, *2*(5), 54–57.

[14] Chirchi, V. R. E., Waghmare, L. M., & Chirchi, E. R. (2011). Iris biometric recognition for person identification in security systems. *International Journal of Computer Applications*, *24*(9), 1–6.
[15] Sarode, N. S., & Patil, A. M. (2014). Review of iris recognition: An evolving biometrics identification technology. *International Journal of Innovative Science and Modern Engineering (IJISME)*, *2*(10), 34–40.
[16] Srivastava, R., Tomar, R., Sharma, A., Dhiman, G., Chilamkurti, N., & Kim, B. G. (2021). Real-time multimodal biometric authentication of human using face feature analysis. *Computers, Materials & Continua*, *69*(1).
[17] Omoyiola, B. O. (2018). Overview of biometric and facial recognition techniques. *IOSR Journal of Computer Engineering (IOSRJCE)*, *20*(4), 1–5.
[18] Umer, S., Dhara, B. C., & Chanda, B. (2015, December). Biometric recognition system for challenging faces. In *2015 fifth national conference on computer vision, pattern recognition, image processing and graphics (NCVPRIPG)* (pp. 1–4). IEEE.
[19] Arigbabu, O. A., Ahmad, S. M. S., Adnan, W. A. W., & Yussof, S. (2015). Recent advances in facial soft biometrics. *The Visual Computer*, *31*, 513–525.
[20] Srivastava, S., Kumar, A., Singh, A., Prakash, S., & Kumar, A. (2022). An improved approach towards biometric face recognition using artificial neural network. *Multimedia Tools and Applications*, *81*(6), 8471–8497.
[21] Markowitz, J. A. (2000). Voice biometrics. *Communications of the ACM*, *43*(9), 66–73.
[22] Babu, A. A., Tumula, S., & Ramadevi, Y. (2019). Voiceprint-based biometric template identifications. *The Biometric Computing: Recognition and Registration*, 53.
[23] Duraibi, S. (2020). Voice biometric identity authentication model for IoT devices. *International Journal of Security, Privacy and Trust Management (IJSPTM)*, *9*.
[24] Saquib, Z., Salam, N., Nair, R., & Pandey, N. (2011). Voiceprint recognition systems for remote authentication-a survey. *International Journal of Hybrid Information Technology*, *4*(2), 79–97.
[25] Ajimah, N., Ezukwoke, N., Dialoke, I., Odaba, A., & Iloanusi, O. (2020). Overview of voice biometric systems: Voice person identification and challenges. *TECHISD Proceedings*, *2020*, 57–62.
[26] Hammad, M., Ibrahim, M., & Hadhoud, M. M. (2016). A novel biometric based on ECG signals and images for human authentication. *The International Arab Journal of Information Technology*, *13*(6A), 959–964.
[27] Prakash, A. J., Patro, K. K., Samantray, S., Pławiak, P., & Hammad, M. (2023). A deep learning technique for biometric authentication using ECG beat template matching. *Information*, *14*(2), 65.
[28] Prakash, A. J., Patro, K. K., Hammad, M., Tadeusiewicz, R., & Pławiak, P. (2022). BAED: A secured biometric authentication system using ECG signal based on deep learning techniques. *Biocybernetics and Biomedical Engineering*, *42*(4), 1081–1093.
[29] Hammad, M., Iliyasu, A. M., Elgendy, I. A., & Abd El-Latif, A. A. (2022). End-to-end data authentication deep learning model for securing IoT configurations. *Human-centric Computing and Information Sciences*, *12*(4).
[30] Hammad, M., Liu, Y., & Wang, K. (2018). Multimodal biometric authentication systems using convolution neural network based on different level fusion of ECG and fingerprint. *IEEE Access*, *7*, 26527–26542.

[31] Hammad, M., Pławiak, P., Wang, K., & Acharya, U. R. (2021). ResNet-Attention model for human authentication using ECG signals. *Expert Systems*, *38*(6), e12547.
[32] Hammad, M., Zhang, S., & Wang, K. (2019). A novel two-dimensional ECG feature extraction and classification algorithm based on convolution neural network for human authentication. *Future Generation Computer Systems*, *101*, 180–196.
[33] Hammad, M., & Wang, K. (2019). Parallel score fusion of ECG and fingerprint for human authentication based on convolution neural network. *Computers & Security*, *81*, 107–122.
[34] Bhosale, K. S., Nenova, M., & Iliev, G. (2021, September). A study of cyber attacks: In the healthcare sector. In *2021 sixth junior conference on lighting (lighting)* (pp. 1–6). IEEE.
[35] Shah, S. M., & Khan, R. A. (2020). Secondary use of electronic health record: Opportunities and challenges. *IEEE Access*, *8*, 136947–136965.
[36] Luna, R., Rhine, E., Myhra, M., Sullivan, R., & Kruse, C. S. (2016). Cyber threats to health information systems: A systematic review. *Technology and Health Care*, *24*(1), 1–9.
[37] Minnaar, A., & Herbig, F. J. (2021). Cyberattacks and the cybercrime threat of ransomware to hospitals and healthcare services during the COVID-19 pandemic. *Acta Criminologica: African Journal of Criminology & Victimology*, *34*(3), 155–185.
[38] Oakley, A. (2023). HIPAA, HIPPA, or HIPPO: What really is the health insurance portability and accountability act? *Biotechnology Law Report*, *42*(6), 306–318.
[39] Silva, I., & Soto, M. (2022). Privacy-preserving data sharing in healthcare: An in-depth analysis of big data solutions and regulatory compliance. *International Journal of Applied Health Care Analytics*, *7*(1), 14–23.
[40] Sciarretta, G., Carbone, R., Ranise, S., & Viganò, L. (2020). Formal analysis of mobile multi-factor authentication with single sign-on login. *ACM Transactions on Privacy and Security (TOPS)*, *23*(3), 1–37.
[41] Jain, A. K., & Kumar, A. (2012). Biometric recognition: An overview. *Second Generation Biometrics: The Ethical, Legal and Social Context*, 49–79.
[42] Laux, D., Luse, A., Mennecke, B., & Townsend, A. M. (2011). Adoption of biometric authentication systems: Implications for research and practice in the deployment of end-user security systems. *Journal of Organizational Computing and Electronic Commerce*, *21*(3), 221–245.
[43] Ogbanufe, O., & Kim, D. J. (2018). Comparing fingerprint-based biometrics authentication versus traditional authentication methods for e-payment. *Decision Support Systems*, *106*, 1–14.
[44] Dargan, S., & Kumar, M. (2020). A comprehensive survey on the biometric recognition systems based on physiological and behavioral modalities. *Expert Systems with Applications*, *143*, 113114.
[45] Abdulkareem, A. M., & Gordon, A. (2023). Evaluating the usability and user acceptance of biometric authentication in different applications. *Quarterly Journal of Emerging Technologies and Innovations*, *8*(2), 1–10.
[46] Gostin, L. O., Levit, L. A., & Nass, S. J. (Eds.). (2009). *Beyond the HIPAA privacy rule: enhancing privacy, improving health through research*. National Academies Press.

[47] Habibu, T., Luhanga, E. T., & Sam, A. E. (2021). A study of users' compliance and satisfied utilization of biometric application system. *Information Security Journal: A Global Perspective*, *30*(3), 125–138.

[48] Hamidi, H. (2019). An approach to develop the smart health using Internet of Things and authentication based on biometric technology. *Future Generation Computer Systems*, *91*, 434–449.

[49] Flores Zuniga, A. E., Win, K. T., & Susilo, W. (2010). Biometrics for electronic health records. *Journal of Medical Systems*, *34*, 975–983.

[50] Argaw, S. T., Troncoso-Pastoriza, J. R., Lacey, D., Florin, M. V., Calcavecchia, F., Anderson, D.,. . .Flahault, A. (2020). Cybersecurity of hospitals: Discussing the challenges and working towards mitigating the risks. *BMC Medical Informatics and Decision Making*, *20*, 1–10.

[51] Rink, S., & Baeumner, A. J. (2023). Progression of paper-based point-of-care testing toward being an indispensable diagnostic tool in future healthcare. *Analytical Chemistry*, *95*(3), 1785–1793.

[52] Anand, D., & Khemchandani, V. (2019). Identity and access management systems. *Security and Privacy of Electronic Healthcare Records: Concepts, Paradigms and Solutions*, *61*.

[53] Sun, Y., Lo, F. P. W., & Lo, B. (2019). Security and privacy for the internet of medical things enabled healthcare systems: A survey. *IEEE Access*, *7*, 183339–183355.

[54] Alsaadi, I. M. (2015). Physiological biometric authentication systems, advantages, disadvantages and future development: A review. *International Journal of Scientific & Technology Research*, *4*(12), 285–289.

[55] Revett, K. (2008). *Behavioral biometrics: A remote access approach*. John Wiley & Sons.

[56] Jain, A., Bolle, R., & Pankanti, S. (1996). *Introduction to biometrics* (pp. 1–41). Springer US.

[57] Wayman, J. L., Jain, A. K., Maltoni, D., & Maio, D. (Eds.). (2005). *Biometric systems: Technology, design and performance evaluation*. Springer Science & Business Media.

[58] Li, S. Z., & Jain, A. (2015). *Encyclopedia of biometrics*. Springer Publishing Company, Incorporated.

[59] Li, L., Correia, P. L., & Hadid, A. (2018). Face recognition under spoofing attacks: Countermeasures and research directions. *Iet Biometrics*, *7*(1), 3–14.

[60] Hammad, M., Luo, G., & Wang, K. (2019). Cancelable biometric authentication system based on ECG. *Multimedia Tools and Applications*, *78*, 1857–1887.

[61] Mittal, Y., Varshney, A., Aggarwal, P., Matani, K., & Mittal, V. K. (2015, December). Fingerprint biometric based access control and classroom attendance management system. In *2015 annual IEEE India conference (INDICON)* (pp. 1–6). IEEE.

[62] Chen, S., Pande, A., & Mohapatra, P. (2014, June). Sensor-assisted facial recognition: An enhanced biometric authentication system for smartphones. *ACM*, In *Proceedings of the 12th annual international conference on Mobile systems, applications, and services* (pp. 109–122).

[63] Blanco-Gonzalo, R., Miguel-Hurtado, O., Lunerti, C., Guest, R. M., Corsetti, B., Ellavarason, E., & Sanchez-Reillo, R. (2019). Biometric systems interaction assessment: The state of the art. *IEEE Transactions on Human-Machine Systems*, *49*(5), 397–410.

[64] Labati, R. D., Genovese, A., Muñoz, E., Piuri, V., Scotti, F., & Sforza, G. (2016). Biometric recognition in automated border control: A survey. *ACM Computing Surveys (CSUR)*, *49*(2), 1–39.

[65] Hutchins, B., & Andrejevcic, M. (2021). Olympian surveillance: Sports stadiums and the normalization of biometric monitoring. *International Journal of Communication*, *15*, 20.

[66] Jobling, M. A., & Gill, P. (2004). Encoded evidence: DNA in forensic analysis. *Nature Reviews Genetics*, *5*(10), 739–751.

[67] Lumini, A., & Nanni, L. (2017). Overview of the combination of biometric matchers. *Information Fusion*, *33*, 71–85.

[68] Babri, U. M., Tanvir, M., & Khurshid, K. (2016). Feature based correspondence: A comparative study on image matching algorithms. *International Journal of Advanced Computer Science and Applications*, *7*(3).

[69] Hashemi, N. S., Aghdam, R. B., Ghiasi, A. S. B., & Fatemi, P. (2016). Template matching advances and applications in image analysis. *arXiv preprint* arXiv:1610.07231.

[70] Jain, A. K., Ross, A., & Pankanti, S. (2006). Biometrics: A tool for information security. *IEEE Transactions on Information Forensics and Security*, *1*(2), 125–143.

[71] Uludag, U., Pankanti, S., Prabhakar, S., & Jain, A. K. (2004). Biometric cryptosystems: Issues and challenges. *Proceedings of the IEEE*, *92*(6), 948–960.

[72] Sakr, A. S., Pławiak, P., Tadeusiewicz, R., & Hammad, M. (2022). Cancelable ECG biometric based on combination of deep transfer learning with DNA and amino acid approaches for human authentication. *Information Sciences*, *585*, 127–143.

[73] Sardar, A., Umer, S., Rout, R. K., & Khan, M. K. (2022). A secure and efficient biometric template protection scheme for palmprint recognition system. *IEEE Transactions on Artificial Intelligence*. 4(5), 1051-1063.

[74] Rajasekar, V., Saračević, M., Karabašević, D., Stanujkić, D., Dobardžić, E., & Krishnamoorthi, S. (2022). Efficient cancelable template generation based on signcryption and bio hash function. *Axioms*, *11*(12), 684.

Chapter 6

Investigating the Effectiveness of Different GNN Models for IoT-Healthcare Systems Botnet Traffic Classification

Phuc Hao Do, Thanh Liem Tran, Van Dai Pham, Abdelhamied A. Ateya, and Tran Duc Le

6.1 INTRODUCTION

The Internet of Things (IoT) has emerged as a transformative force in modern society, with an ever-increasing number of interconnected devices shaping various domains, including smart homes, healthcare, agriculture, and transportation [1]. Deploying IoT for healthcare systems provides an efficient way for all remote medical applications [2]. With the proliferation of IoT devices, ensuring their security has become a paramount priority. The prevalence of IoT malware attacks that exploit vulnerabilities in these devices has been on the rise, as highlighted by recent studies [3]. Developing effective techniques to identify and analyze malicious activities in IoT networks is crucial to safeguard these ecosystems and mitigate the potential consequences of botnet attacks. Such consequences include data breaches, privacy violations, and compromised critical infrastructure.

IoT malware traffic classification is one promising approach to address this challenge [4]. This technique leverages machine learning algorithms [5, 6] or deep learning models [7–9] to detect and analyze patterns indicative of malware attacks. Accurately classifying network traffic enables the identification, prevention, and mitigation of IoT malware attacks, thereby enhancing the security and resilience of these systems. In recent years, graph neural networks (GNNs) have gained significant attention as a powerful class of deep learning models well-suited for IoT malware traffic classification [10]. GNNs are particularly effective in this context because they can model complex relationships between data points, learn from graph-structured data, and adapt to dynamic network changes. There are maybe some advantages that can be leveraged in this context as follows:

- **Representation learning:** GNNs effectively capture complex relationships within network traffic data, enabling the identification of patterns and anomalies associated with IoT malware.

DOI: 10.1201/9781003470038-6

- **Graph-structured data handling:** GNNs natively handle graph-structured data, making them suitable for modeling and analyzing the complex, irregular, and dynamic topologies of IoT networks.
- **Local and global information:** GNNs combine local and global information in graphs, allowing them to identify malware activities with varying locality levels.
- **Scalability:** Some GNN models are designed to be scalable to large graphs, a crucial property for analyzing extensive IoT networks.
- **Robustness to noisy data:** GNNs can be robust to imperfect data, maintaining performance in real-world IoT networks with noisy or incomplete information.
- **Transfer learning:** GNNs can use transfer learning by using pre-trained models or knowledge from related tasks to improve performance. This approach can result in faster training and better generalization across IoT network settings.

Given the nascent state of research in this domain, it is crucial to investigate the effectiveness of different GNN models for IoT malware traffic classification. Conducting a comprehensive comparison of other GNN models, such as graph convolutional networks (GCNs), GraphSAGE, and graph attention networks (GATs), can yield valuable insights into their strengths and weaknesses. This, in turn, can inform future research and the development of more efficient and accurate classification techniques for IoT botnet traffic.

The primary objective of this chapter is to investigate the effectiveness of different GNN models systematically and experimentally in the context of IoT malware, especially IoT botnet traffic classification. We aim to conduct a rigorous evaluation of the performance of these models on benchmark datasets to uncover each model's unique characteristics that make them suitable for specific classification tasks. Additionally, we aim to identify potential avenues for improvement by carefully analyzing the results of our evaluation. This analysis will contribute to developing robust and effective IoT botnet traffic classification methods, ultimately improving security and protection for IoT devices and networks.

The potential impact of this research is two-fold. First, it aims to enhance our understanding of the emerging threats facing IoT ecosystems and the potential of GNNs in addressing these challenges. Second, it seeks to provide a foundation for future research in developing more advanced techniques for classifying IoT malware traffic. Ultimately, the findings of this research can contribute to improving the security and resilience of IoT devices and the broader digital infrastructure.

This chapter is organized as follows: background information and a literature review are provided in Section 6.2. Section 6.3 explains the methodology implemented in the experimental setup. Section 6.4 shows a comprehensive overview of the main outcome of this research, a novel IoT botnet dataset, and its verification. Lastly, Section 6.5 summarizes the study and highlights its significant contributions.

6.2 LITERATURE REVIEW

This section presents recent advancements in GNNs for traffic classification and malware detection. GNNs have gained attention in recent years for their ability to model complex and non-Euclidean data, making them well-suited for traffic classification and malware detection tasks. Ji and Meng (2020) [11] introduced a traffic classification method based on GCNs that achieved a classification accuracy rate of 97.35%, demonstrating the potential of GNNs for traffic classification tasks. However, the study's applicability is mainly limited to small-scale networks, indicating the need for future exploration of other GNN variants in actual computer network data.

In their recent study, Pang et al. (2021) [12] proposed a novel traffic classification method known as Chained Graph Neural Network (CGNN), which utilizes GNNs to capture both structural and semantic relationships in network traffic automatically. The CGNN model improves prediction accuracy for application classification by 23% to 29% and for malicious traffic classification by 2% to 37%, outperforming state-of-the-art neural network-based traffic classifiers. The proposed approach demonstrates robust performance regarding recall and precision metrics, making it an effective solution for traffic classification.

Busch et al. (2021) [13] introduced a graph-based approach for detecting and classifying malware. The proposed method involves extracting flow graphs from network traffic data and organizing them using a novel edge feature-based GNN model. Their approach significantly improves detection performance compared to baseline models across various prediction tasks, including supervised binary, category, family classification, and unsupervised detection. The approach offers an effective solution for malware detection and classification.

Liu, T. et al. (2021) [14] presented a practical and accurate approach for detecting Android malware using a network traffic graph-based model called NT-GNN. In evaluations conducted on the CICAndMal2017 and AAGM datasets, NT-GNN exhibited remarkable results, achieving an accuracy rate of 97%. This outperformed conventional machine learning models such as Decision Tree (DT), Random Forest (RF), and Convolutional Neural Network (CNN) in malware detection. The findings of this research highlight the potential of GNNs in malware detection and classification. By utilizing network traffic characteristics and avoiding the need for handcrafted features, this approach offers promising prospects for the future of malware detection and classification.

Huoh et al. (2022) [15] proposed a GNN model for classifying encrypted network traffic that outperforms Convolutional Neural Networks (CNN) and Recurrent Neural Networks (RNN) in terms of sensitivity, precision, and F1 score. The model maps network traffic flows into graph representations, utilizing data from non-Euclidean domains and preserving data integrity. The authors compared various network input combinations and classification tasks, showing that their GNN model outperforms other GNN variants and reference methods. The study demonstrates the potential of GNNs in classifying encrypted network traffic and opens up new possibilities for future research.

The paper [16] "CFGExplainer: Explaining Graph Neural Network-Based Malware Classification from Control Flow Graphs" proposes CFG-Explainer. This deep learning-based model helps to interpret malware classification results. The proposed model identifies a subgraph of malware control flow graphs (CFGs) that contributes most toward malware classification and provides insight into the importance of the nodes within these subgraphs. CFGExplainer outperforms three state-of-the-art graph explanation solutions, namely GNNExplainer, SubgraphX, and PGExplainer, in identifying top equitized subgraphs with higher classification accuracy. The paper's contributions can be summarized as follows: First, proposing CFG-Explainer is the first work that explains GNN-based malware classification. Second, it analyzes subgraphs containing the top 20% of nodes of malware samples produced by CFGExplainer. Lastly, offering valuable insights into malware patterns would be beneficial for further examination by human experts. The proposed model can be used in tandem with tools such as IDA-Pro and Ghidra to alleviate the complexity of identifying malicious patterns. The methodology proposed in the paper bridges the gap in the existing literature by providing insights into GNN-based malware classification, which was previously considered a black box.

Dvorak et al. (2022) [17] proposed an automatic approach to identify malicious network entities in large-scale network data by leveraging relations between entities and building a heterogeneous graph. The graph is used for classification by applying GNNs to identify malicious domains. The proposed solution simplifies the graph representation and reduces the processed graph size from hundreds of billions of edges to thousands, allowing for GNN application to information retrieval tasks that are computationally infeasible on the original graph. The paper evaluates the proposed method, benchmarking it against reference models, and shows promising results in identifying high-risk malware and legitimate domain classification.

Pujol-Perich et al. (2022) [18] proposed using GNNs to develop accurate and robust Network Intrusion Detection Systems (NIDS) by presenting a graph representation that structures the properties of flows and their relationships in the network and a novel GNN architecture specifically designed to learn and generalize over this graph-structured information. The proposed GNN-based Network Intrusion Detection System (NIDS) achieved comparable accuracy to state-of-the-art machine learning (ML)-based NIDS in the well-known CIC-IDS2017 dataset. Additionally, it exhibited unparalleled robustness against common adversarial attacks aimed at intentionally modifying relevant flow features on attack-related flows.

Overall, the findings presented in the literature review provide valuable insights into the use of GNNs for traffic classification and malware detection, offering promising prospects for the future of these fields.

6.3 METHODOLOGY

Figure 6.1 illustrates the approach adopted in this study to investigate the effectiveness of different GNN models for IoT botnet traffic classification. The approach involves several modules, including dataset, data processing, building graphs, and classifier. The first step consists of collecting the dataset, which includes IoT botnet traffic data, to use as the basis for developing and testing the GNN models. The data-processing module is then used to clean and pre-process the data to ensure it is in the appropriate format for the subsequent stages.

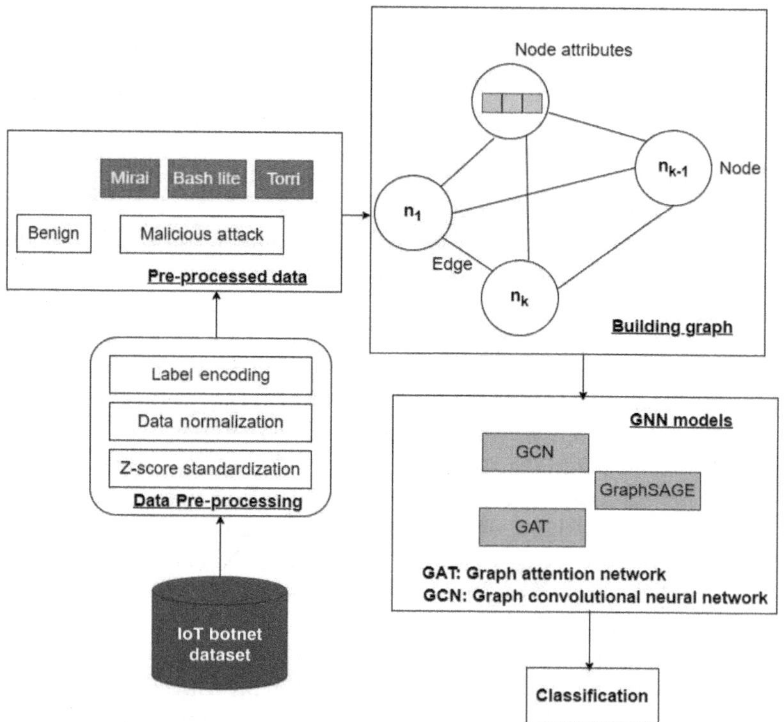

Figure 6.1 The research flow.

6.3.1 Data Collection and Pre-processing

Collecting and pre-processing the appropriate data are essential to evaluate the performance of different GNN models for IoT botnet traffic classification. This section will provide an overview of the data collection process, including the data sources and pre-processing methods to ensure the data is suitable for analysis.

Normalization of data through standardization and minimum-maximum normalization (min-max normalization) is a critical step in data preparation. Standardization is a technique that involves rescaling the data so that it has a mean of 0 and a standard deviation of 1. To enable the comparison of different features that may have varying ranges of values, the min-max normalization technique is employed to scale the values of these features within a fixed range between 0 and 1.

After the pre-processing step, the subsequent step involves constructing a graph using the data, where each data point is depicted as a node in the graph. The edges represent the connections between the nodes, signifying the connections between the data points. The GNN models are then applied to the graph to classify the IoT botnet traffic data.

6.3.1.1 Dataset

In this research, we will conduct experiments using the MedBIoT [19] dataset and implement various GNN models to assess their effectiveness for traffic data. The network packets gathered from the IoT LAN network are redirected to the monitoring network using the port mirroring technique. In this case, we employed Splunk, SIEM (security information and event management) software, to process and label the data. This facilitated the creation of the final dataset in both structured format (features are computed and extracted from the raw data) and non-structured format (raw pcap files). The total number of packets captured during the experimental setup is provided in Table 6.1.

The experimental setup captured a total of 17,845,567 network packets. Of this traffic, roughly 30% was classified and labeled as malicious, while the remaining 70% corresponds to legitimate network traffic. The generated dataset is publicly available at *https://cs.taltech.ee/research/data/medbiot.*

Table 6.1 Dataset Composition

Data Source	*Number of Devices*	*Number of Packets*	*Proportion*
Normal	83	12,540,478	70.27%
BashLite	40	4,143,276	23.22%
Mirai	25	842,674	4.72%
Torii	12	319,139	1.79%

For this study, we will concentrate on binary classification and use a portion of the dataset to experiment. The binary classification will be evaluated as part of our investigation.

6.3.1.2 Pre-processing

This study utilizes label encoding, min-max normalization, and standardization as pre-processing techniques. When the values of the columns in a dataset have different ranges, the performance of regression and classification models is adversely affected. In [20], Mahfouz et al. demonstrated how this issue could cause a decline in model performance when uneven feature scales are present in a dataset. Establishing acceptable ranges for insignificant and dominant values is crucial to addressing this issue. To achieve this, commonly used techniques include min-max normalization and z-score standardization.

The former involves transforming the feature values of a dataset into the [0, 1] range using the following equation:

$$X_{\text{normalized}} = \frac{X - X_{min\_value}}{X_{\max\_value} - X_{min\_malue}} \tag{6.1}$$

Where $X_{\text{normalized}}$ is the normalized value, and X_{min_malue} and $X_{\max\_value}$ are the boundaries of the intended interval. The latter technique, z-score standardization, involves rescaling dataset features to reflect a normal distribution with a mean $\mu = 0$ and standard deviation $\sigma = 1$, as shown below:

$$X_{\text{normalized}} = \frac{X - \mu}{\sigma} \tag{6.2}$$

6.3.1.3 Building the Graph

After processing the data, we transformed it into graph structure data. The graph construction process (refer to Figure 6.2) was carried out as follows:

- For each type of traffic, whether normal or malware, we built a separate graph. Each packet in the traffic was considered a node in the graph.
- The information for each node was a vector containing the packet's data, which was extracted from the original dataset.
- To connect the nodes, we experimented with connecting neighboring packets sequentially.

After representing the data as a graph, we will proceed to experiment with popular GNN models: GCN [21], GAT [22], and GraphSAGE [23]. In addition, we will compare the results and execution time with traditional

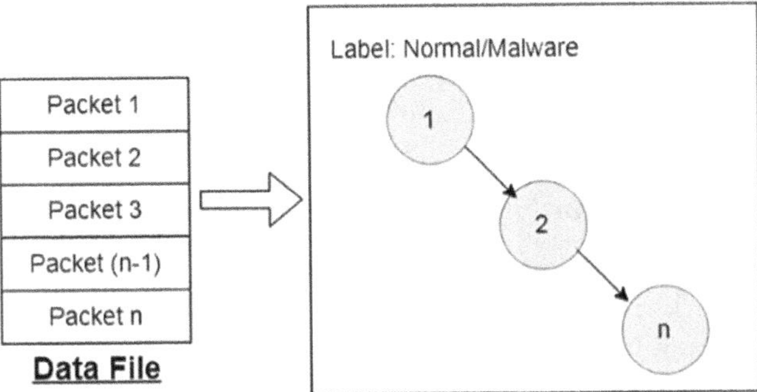

Figure 6.2 Represent data in graph form.

models such as MLP (multilayer perceptron). There are some reasons for this choice:

- **Popularity**: GCN, GAT, and GraphSAGE are some of the most commonly used and well-known GNN models widely used in many research domains. As such, it is essential to investigate how these models perform in the context of traffic classification and malware detection tasks.
- **Different architectures**: GCN, GAT, and GraphSAGE are all based on different GNN architectures, each with strengths and weaknesses. By comparing these models, we can gain insights into which architectures are most effective for traffic classification and malware detection.
- **Performance**: While GCN, GAT, and GraphSAGE are all popular and well-known GNN models, they may perform differently depending on the specific task and dataset used. By comparing the performance of these models on the MedBIoT dataset, we can determine which model is most effective for this particular task.
- **Benchmarking**: Comparing the performance of GCN, GAT, and GraphSAGE can provide a benchmark for future research. Other researchers can use these results as a baseline for comparison when developing new GNN models for traffic classification and malware detection.

Besides, comparing the performance of GNN models with traditional models, such as MLP, can provide insights into the effectiveness and efficiency of GNN models in traffic classification tasks. MLP is a widely used traditional model for classification tasks, and comparing its performance with GNN models can help identify the strengths and weaknesses of each approach. Moreover, such comparisons can guide the selection of models for various scenarios, such as instances with limited computational resources or specific needs for accuracy or execution time.

6.3.2 GNN Models for Traffic Classification

This section will describe the graph convolutional neural network (GCN), graph attention network (GAT), and GraphSAGE models.

6.3.2.1 *Graph Convolutional Neural Network (GCN)*

GCN is a robust neural network architecture that can deeply learn graph data. In network traffic classification, the task is to classify edges. To track traffic in a graph, it is necessary to represent the adjacency of edges, much like the adjacency matrix utilized to represent the adjacency of nodes. Let's call the current adjacency matrix $A \in R^{N \times N}$ The GCN model comprises multilayer graph convolution, where at time t, the l-th layer takes the adjacency matrix At and the embedding node matrix $H_t^{(l)}$ as input and uses the weight matrix $W_t^{(l)}$ to update the embedding node matrix $H_t^{(l=1)}$ as output. This process can be represented as follows:

$$H_t^{(l=1)} = \text{GCONV}\left(A_t, H_t^{(l)}, W_t^{(l)} = \sigma\left(\hat{A}_t, H_t W_t^{(l)}\right)\right) \tag{6.3}$$

Where σ is the activation function (usually ReLU).

The GCONV layer, a crucial component of the GCN, resembles the perceptron, functioning as a fully connected layer. However, the GCONV layer differs from the perceptron in that it obtains its weight matrix by using spectrum filtering of the graph Laplacian matrix. This allows the GCONV layer to learn representations that capture the structure of the graph data and enable practical graph-based classification tasks.

Refer to the parameterized model in [9]:

$$g_\theta * x = U g_\theta U^T x \tag{6.4}$$

Where $\theta \in R^N$. The parameterized model described in [24] involves a matrix U composed of the eigenvectors of the Laplacian matrix of the normalized graph. The Laplacian matrix of a graph is used in this context to represent the graph's structure and is defined as follows:

$$L = I_N - D^{-\frac{1}{2}} - AD^{-\frac{1}{2}} = U \Lambda U \tag{6.5}$$

where D is the degree matrix (a diagonal matrix with the degree of each node on its diagonal), A is the adjacency matrix, and Λ is the corresponding eigenvalue matrix (a diagonal matrix with the eigenvalues on its diagonal). The graph Fourier transform of a signal x can be represented by $U^T x$.

In Equation (6.4), the function g_θ is dependent on the eigenvalues of L. Due to the high complexity of directly computing the L-eigenvalue decomposition, a truncated expansion of the Chebyshev polynomial $T_k(x)$ up to the *k-th* order is used to approximate $g_\theta(\Lambda)$ [24]:

$$g_\theta'(\Lambda) \approx \sum_{k=0}^{k} \theta_k' T_K\left(\tilde{\Lambda}\right) \tag{6.6}$$

Where $\tilde{\Lambda} = \frac{2}{\lambda_{\max}}\Lambda - I_N$ and are the maximum eigenvalues of the L eigenvalues, and $\theta' \in R^k$ is the coefficient vector of Chebyshev. Chebyshev polynomials are defined as follows:

$$T_k(x) = 2xT_{k-1} - T_{k-2}(x) \tag{6.7}$$

Where $T_0(x) = 1, T_1(x) = x$

The GCN model can be constructed by utilizing convolutional layers arranged in a stacked multilayer equation, as shown in Equation (6.8):

$$g_{\theta*} * x \approx \sum_{k=0}^{k} \theta'_k T_K(\tilde{L}) \tag{6.8}$$

Where $\tilde{L} = \frac{2}{\lambda_{\max}} L - I_N$

Now we limit the convolution layer to k = 1, that is:

$$g_\theta * x \approx \theta'_0 T_0(\tilde{L})x + \theta'_1 T_1(\tilde{L})x = \theta'_0 x + \theta'_1 \tilde{L}x \tag{6.9}$$

Taking the approximation $\lambda_{max} = 2$, we can get the following.

$$g_\theta * x \approx \theta'_0 x + \theta'_1 (L - L_N)x = \theta'_0 x - \theta'_0 D^{-\frac{1}{2}} A D^{-\frac{1}{2}} x \tag{6.10}$$

Furthermore, to prevent overfitting, we can limit the number of learnable parameters:

$$g_\theta * x \approx \theta \left(I_N + D^{-\frac{1}{2}} A D^{-\frac{1}{2}} \right) x \tag{6.11}$$

Note that $\theta = \theta'_0 = -\theta'_1$ in Equation (6.6)

The range of feature values of $I_N + D^{-\frac{1}{2}} A D^{-\frac{1}{2}}$ is [0, 2]. However, when this operation is repeatedly applied in a deep neural network model, it can result in unstable values and gradient explosion. To address this issue, an additional normalization method is introduced in [24]:

$$I_N + D^{-\frac{1}{2}} A D^{-\frac{1}{2}} \rightarrow \tilde{D}^{-\frac{1}{2}} \tilde{A} \tilde{D}^{-\frac{1}{2}} \tag{6.12}$$

Where $\tilde{A} = A + I_N, D_{ii} = \sum_j \tilde{A}_{ij}$.

6.3.2.2 *Graph Attention Network (GAT)*

The attention mechanism has shown promising results in many sequence-based tasks. This section will describe the theoretical derivation of the GAT and discuss its application advantages. GAT consists of only one graph attention layer. Any graph attention network can be constructed by stacking multiple layers. The attention coefficient for node pair (i, j) in this layer is calculated using the following formula:

$$\alpha_{i,j} = \frac{e^{\{\text{LeakyReLu}[a^T(Wh_i \| Wh_j)]\}}}{\sum_{K \in N_i} e^{\{\text{LeakyReLu}[a^T(Wh_i \| Wh_j)]\}}} \tag{6.13}$$

GAT utilizes a single graph attention layer; any graph attention network is constructed by stacking this layer. The attention coefficient $\alpha_{i,j}$ for node j with respect to node i, where Ni represents the neighbor node set of nodes i in the graph, is calculated using the concatenated vectors notation $\|$ and the formula given in Equation (6.13). The input set of node features, $h = \{h_1, h_2, \ldots, h_N\}, h_{i,} \in R^F$, represents the total number of features for each node F, and N represents the total number of nodes. This layer generates a new set of node features, as the output. The weight matrix $W \in R^{F \times F}$ represents the weight-sharing linear transformation among nodes, and $a \in R^{2F}$ represents the weight vector of single-layer feedforward neural network. The weight vector is normalized using softmax activation function, and nonlinear characteristics are produced using the *LeakyRelu* function, as given in Equation (6.13). After obtaining the normalized attention coefficient $a_{i,j}$, it is used to calculate the linear combination of corresponding node features as each node's final output eigenvector h', using the formula in Equation (6.14):

$$h_i^{'} = \sigma\left(\sum_{j \in Ni} \alpha_{ij} Wh_j\right) \tag{6.14}$$

The activation function $\sigma(.)$ is employed similarly as the previous *LeakyRelu* function to enhance nonlinearity.

GAT uses multiple attention mechanisms to stabilize the network's learning process, referred to as multi-head attention. Specifically, K independent attention mechanisms are used to calculate each node's hidden state vectors, concatenated to obtain the final output. The calculation formula for multi-head attention in GAT is expressed as follows:

$$h_i^{'} = \|_{k=1}^{K} \sigma\left(\sum_{j \in Ni} \alpha_{ij} W^k h_j\right) \tag{6.15}$$

In Equation (6.15), the symbol $\|$ denotes the serial symbol, α_{ij}^k represents the normalized attention coefficient obtained from the *k-th* attention mechanism, and W^k represents the weight matrix for input linear transformation in the *k-th* attention mechanism. It should be noted that when using multiple attention mechanisms in the final output layer of GAT, corresponding to the final output $h_i^{'}$ will contain $K \cdot F$' eigenvectors. To address this, we use the average method to combine the eigenvectors, as shown in the following formula:

$$h_i^{'} = \sigma\left(\frac{1}{k} \sum_{k=1}^{K} \sum_{j \in N_i} \alpha_{ij}^k W^k h_j\right) \tag{6.16}$$

The average method in GAT is used to calculate the final output $h_i^{'}$ of each node. Each $h_i^{'}$ contains $F^{'}$ fused feature vectors, which can effectively aggregate the features of nodes and reduce computation for node classification in the graph.

6.3.2.3 GraphSAGE

GraphSAGE is a powerful algorithm designed to work with graph data. This algorithm learns to represent each node in a graph by aggregating information from its neighbors. GraphSAGE can be trained through supervised learning tasks, such as node classification, by minimizing the loss function that measures the difference between predicted and true labels of nodes in the graph. This approach allows GraphSAGE to effectively classify nodes in the graph and produce high-quality embeddings of each node for downstream tasks.

In GraphSAGE, a node's feature representation is learned by aggregating the features of its neighboring nodes. Given a graph $G = (V, E)$, where V is the set of nodes and E is the set of edges, the algorithm first samples the adjacent nodes of each node and then aggregates their feature sets using an aggregation function (Equation 6.17). This aggregation function can be a mean or max pooling operation or a more complex function such as an LSTM (long short-term memory) neural network. The node's own feature vector is also included in this aggregation process. The final output is a learned feature representation of each node in the graph. This approach allows GraphSAGE to scale large graphs while still learning expressive node embeddings.

$$h_{\mathrm{N}}^{k} = AGGREGATE_{K}\left(\left\{h_{u}^{k-1}, \forall u \in \mathrm{N}(v)\right\}\right) \tag{6.17}$$

At this stage, the node feature vector h_{N}^{k} encompasses both the feature information and the neighbor information of its adjacent nodes. h_{N}^{k-1} is a sample of the neighboring nodes, as some nodes in certain cases may have an extensive number of neighbors, reaching even up to 1 million or 10 million (such as a popular blogger with millions of followers). Since the adjacent nodes themselves form an unordered set, the sampling validity is not a concern. GraphSAGE typically employs a fixed number of samples, although it can also utilize a variable number depending on the specific problem. The formula has three types of aggregation functions: the mean aggregation function, the pool aggregation function, and the LSTM aggregation function. The formula is as follows:

$$\mathrm{Mean}: \mathrm{AGG} = \sum_{u \in \mathrm{N}(v)} \frac{h_{u}^{k-1}}{|\mathrm{N}(v)|} \tag{6.18}$$

$$\mathrm{Pool}: AGG = \gamma\left(\left\{Qh_{u}^{k-1}, \forall u \in \mathrm{N}(v)\right\}\right. \tag{6.19}$$

To capture the interdependent information between nodes on both ends of an edge, we consider using the node embeddings of the two adjacent nodes to represent the features of the edge. The edge features can be obtained through vector concatenation, average pooling, maximum pooling, or summation of the node embeddings. The concatenation operation can better capture the information of both nodes, and thus, we combine the aggregated information with the central node information to obtain a more informative feature representation.

$$\mathrm{CONCAT}\left(h_v^{k-1}, h_{\mathrm{N}(v)}^k\right) \tag{6.20}$$

And then embed it with the following formula.

$$h_v^k = \sigma\left(\mathrm{W}^k \cdot \mathrm{CONCAT}\left(h_v^{k-1}, h_{\mathrm{N}(v)}^k\right)\right) \tag{6.21}$$

The activation function σ and weight matrix W^k form a single-layer neural network. Although a multilayer neural network can also be used, a single-layer neural network is preferable for achieving optimal results [24]. Each node in the diagram performs the aforementioned calculations, acquiring information about its neighbors and structure. Subsequently, the next round of aggregation and embedding is carried out. Through this process, each node can integrate information from further away, and the number of cycles determines the range of integration. After each round of calculations, the resulting features must be normalized, which can be achieved with the following formula:

$$h_v^k = h_v^k / \| h_v^k \|_2 \ .\forall v \in V \tag{6.22}$$

After applying the calculation above method, a vector containing information on adjacent nodes up to a certain depth and the structure of these nodes can be obtained for each node. This vector represents the final embedding of the node. The probability of each class can be calculated using the softmax function based on the node embedding:

$$\mathrm{Z}_{\mathrm{j}} = \mathrm{soft\,max}\left(h_v^k\right) \tag{6.23}$$

The cross-entropy loss function is used in this model to measure the difference between the predicted class probabilities and the true class labels. The formula for the cross-entropy loss is:

$$\mathrm{loss} = -\sum\nolimits_{c=1}^{|L|} y_c \log\left(z_c\right) \tag{6.24}$$

6.3.3 Evaluation Metrics

Various evaluation metrics have been employed to evaluate the proposed framework's effectiveness. Among them, the commonly used metrics are accuracy, precision, recall, and F1 score, which are based on four variables:

- True Positive (TP) represents the number of attack samples in medium-sized IoT network traffic that the model has accurately identified as attack activity.
- True Negative (TN) refers to the total number of benign samples in medium-sized IoT network traffic that have been correctly identified as benign activity by the model.
- False Positive (FP) refers to the total count of benign samples in medium-sized IoT network traffic incorrectly detected as attack activity by the model.
- False Negative (FN) represents the total count of attack samples in a medium-sized IoT network incorrectly identified as normal actions by the model.

Accuracy (ACC): The model's efficiency is evaluated using the accuracy metric, which is defined as the ratio of correct predictions (true positive and true negative) to the total number of predictions.

$$\mathrm{ACC} = \frac{TP + TN}{TP + FP + TN + FN} \tag{6.25}$$

Precision (PRE): It is defined as the total number of positive activities predicated as positive to the number of predictions defined as attacks.

$$\mathrm{PRE} = \frac{TP}{TP + FP} \tag{6.26}$$

Recall (REC): REC determines the number of correct positive predictions made out of all positive predictions that could have been made.

$$\mathrm{REC} = \frac{TP}{TP + FN} \tag{6.27}$$

F1 score (F1): F1 score determines the weighted average of PRE and RE.

$$\mathrm{F1} = 2 * \frac{\mathrm{REC} * \mathrm{PRE}}{\mathrm{REC} + \mathrm{PRE}} \tag{6.28}$$

6.4 RESULTS AND ANALYSIS

This experiment evaluates the effectiveness of implementing GNN algorithms in detecting abnormal IoT traffic caused by malware utilizing the

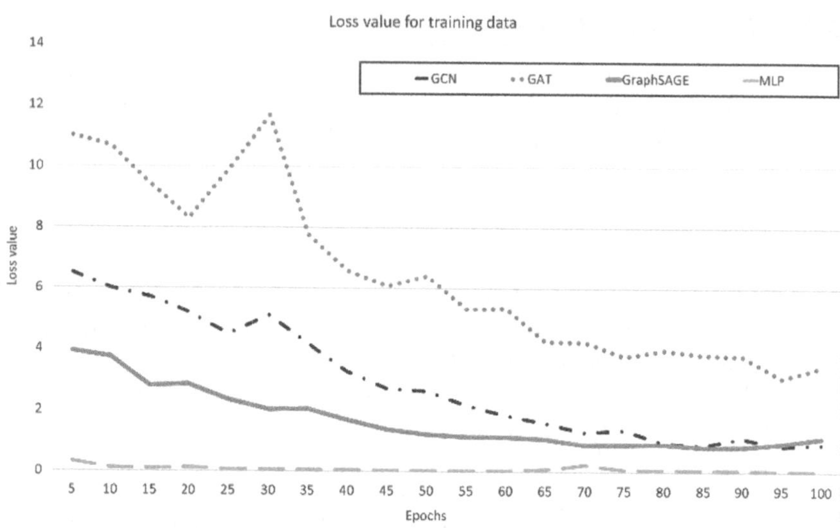

Figure 6.3 Loss value for training data of algorithms.

MedBIoT dataset. The dataset is divided into three parts: training, validation, and test data, with a ratio of 8:1:1. Binary classification assesses the efficiency of deploying GNN algorithms in the MedBIoT dataset.

Figure 6.3 illustrates the loss value obtained while training the model with GCN, GAT, GraphSAGE, and MLP algorithms. The results indicate that the best MLP algorithm reaches a loss value threshold of 0.045. In contrast, the GNN algorithms, particularly GCN and GraphSAGE, exhibit a good loss value and converge quite quickly, achieving convergence at epoch = 80.

The accuracy of the validation dataset for each epoch is presented in Figure 6.4. The results demonstrate that using the GCN algorithm yields a relatively high accuracy rate of approximately 96%. In comparison, using the MLP algorithm produces a higher accuracy rate of 99%. These findings suggest that leveraging the graph structure in the MedBIoT dataset can yield acceptable results, even when using traditional machine-learning approaches.

The results in Table 6.2 indicate that all four algorithms exhibit high performance in classifying IoT botnet network traffic, with F1 scores above 0.95 and high precision and recall scores.

When looking at F1 scores, the MLP algorithm achieved the highest score of 0.998, while the GCN algorithm had the lowest score of 0.961. However, all four algorithms exhibited good performance, demonstrating their ability to classify IoT botnet network traffic effectively.

In terms of precision, the GAT algorithm exhibited the highest score of 0.986, while the GCN algorithm had the lowest score of 0.954. Nonetheless, all four algorithms achieved high precision scores, indicating their ability to classify malware traffic with a low false positive rate accurately.

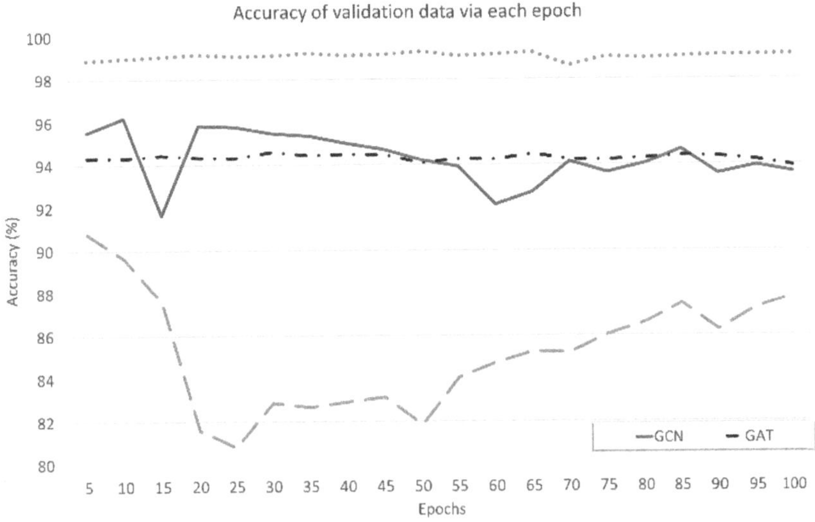

Figure 6.4 Accuracy of validation data via each epoch of algorithms.

Table 6.2 Comparison Table of Measures between Algorithms

Metrics	*GCN*	*GAT*	*GraphSAGE*	*MLP*
F1	0.961	0.988	0.974	0.998
Precision	0.954	0.986	0.969	0.986
Recall	0.969	0.991	0.979	0.991
Accuracy	0.974	0.992	0.983	0.992

Regarding recall, the GAT algorithm achieved the highest score of 0.991, while the GCN algorithm had the lowest score of 0.969. However, all four algorithms exhibited high recall scores, indicating their ability to detect malware traffic with a low false negative rate effectively.

Finally, in terms of accuracy, both the GAT and MLP algorithms achieved the highest score of 0.992, while the GCN and GraphSAGE algorithms scored 0.974 and 0.983, respectively. In general, all four algorithms demonstrated high accuracy in classifying IoT botnet network traffic.

The results indicate the effectiveness of utilizing GNN models, particularly GAT and GraphSAGE, for classifying IoT botnet network traffic, with high performance across all evaluation metrics. These findings provide valuable insights for future research in developing more efficient and accurate classification techniques for IoT network security.

The training time is an important factor to consider when selecting a model for classification tasks, mainly when dealing with large datasets or limited computational resources. The results in Figure 6.5 show that the

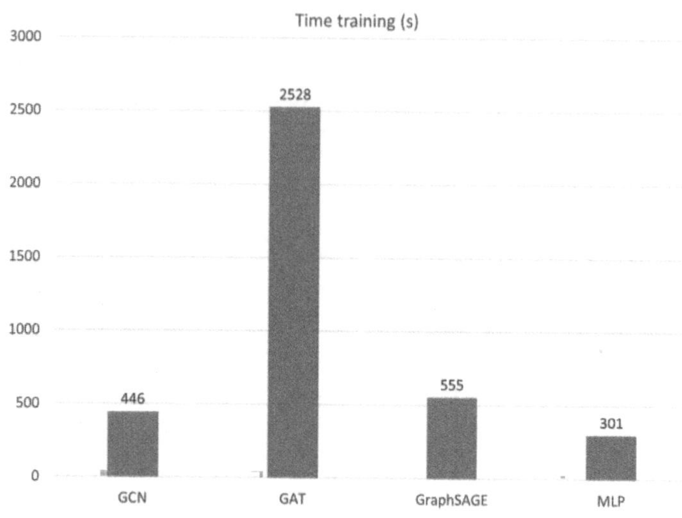

Figure 6.5 Time training of algorithms.

MLP algorithm had the shortest training time. The GCN model had a relatively short training time, while the GraphSAGE algorithm took slightly longer. On the other hand, the GAT model had a significantly longer training time.

These results suggest that, regarding training time, the MLP algorithm may be a more suitable choice for scenarios where speed is a critical factor. However, it is important to note that training time and accuracy are not the only factors to consider when selecting a classification algorithm. Various application-specific considerations and limitations, such as the size and complexity of the dataset, the availability of computational resources, and the required level of interpretability, may also influence the selection of an appropriate algorithm.

GNN models, such as GAT and GraphSAGE, are generally recognized as well-suited for capturing graphs' structural information. This property can be particularly advantageous for IoT botnet traffic classification. In certain scenarios, these models may have advantages over traditional machine learning algorithms such as MLP.

While the training time results did not show that the GAT and GraphSAGE algorithms had higher accuracy than the MLP algorithm, these models may achieve higher accuracy on different datasets or in various application domains. Therefore, the choice of the algorithm should be based on a thorough evaluation of multiple factors, including accuracy and training time, the specific characteristics of the dataset, and the application requirements.

6.5 CONCLUSION AND FUTURE WORK

In this chapter, we investigated the effectiveness of various GNN models for IoT botnet traffic classification. Our findings demonstrate that GNN-based approaches have the potential to be an effective and efficient solution for IoT botnet traffic classification.

GNN models have a notable advantage in that they can natively handle graph-structured data, which makes them highly suitable for analyzing the complex, dynamic, and irregular topologies that are characteristic of IoT networks. Additionally, GNN models effectively capture complex relationships within network traffic data, enabling the identification of patterns and anomalies associated with IoT malware. Combining local and global information in graphs enables GNN models to identify malware activities at different levels of locality. Furthermore, some GNN models are designed to be scalable to large graphs, a crucial property for analyzing extensive IoT networks. Finally, GNN models can be robust to imperfect data, maintaining performance in real-world IoT networks with noisy or incomplete information.

Our experiments also show that GNN models are robust and can generalize well to unseen data. However, challenges still need to be addressed in future work, such as the need for more diverse and comprehensive datasets to improve the performance and generalizability of GNN-based models. Additionally, the impact of different GNN architectures and hyperparameters on IoT botnet traffic classification performance could be explored. Furthermore, the interpretability of GNN-based approaches remains an important area of future research.

The findings of this research can contribute to improving the security and resilience of IoT devices and the broader digital infrastructure. Ultimately, developing more advanced techniques for classifying IoT malware traffic can help enhance our understanding of the emerging threats facing IoT ecosystems and their potential mitigation strategies.

ACKNOWLEDGMENT

This research is funded by the University of Danang under project number T2022-ĐHĐN-07.

REFERENCES

1. Bushelenkov, S., Paramonov, A., Muthanna, A., El-Latif, A. A. A., Koucheryavy, A., Alfarraj, O.,. . . Ateya, A. A. (2023). Multi-Story building model for efficient IoT network design. *Mathematics*, 11(6), 1403.
2. Osama, M., Ateya, A. A., Sayed, M. S., Hammad, M., Pławiak, P., Abd El-Latif, A. A., & Elsayed, R. A. (2023). Internet of medical things and healthcare

4.0: Trends, requirements, challenges, and research directions. *Sensors*, 23(17), 7435.

3. Sadhu, P. K., Yanambaka, V. P., & Abdelgawad, A. (2022). Internet of Things: Security and solutions survey. *Sensors*, 22(19), 7433.
4. Tahaei, H., Afifi, F., Asemi, A., Zaki, F., & Anuar, N. B. (2020). The rise of traffic classification in IoT networks: A survey. *Journal of Network and Computer Applications*, 154, 102538.
5. Do, P. H., Dinh, T. D., Le, D. T., Myrova, L., & Kirichek, R. (2021, October). An efficient feature extraction method for attack classification in IoT networks. In *2021 13th International Congress on Ultra Modern Telecommunications and Control Systems and Workshops (ICUMT)* (pp. 194–199). IEEE.
6. Pokhrel, S., Abbas, R., & Aryal, B. (2021). IoT security: Botnet detection in IoT using machine learning. *arXiv preprint* arXiv:2104.02231.
7. Hammad, M., ElAffendi, M., Ateya, A. A., & Abd El-Latif, A. A. (2023). Efficient brain tumor detection with lightweight end-to-end deep learning model. *Cancers*, 15(10), 2837.
8. Bendiab, G., Shiaeles, S., Alruban, A., & Kolokotronis, N. (2020, June). IoT malware network traffic classification using visual representation and deep learning. In *2020 6th IEEE Conference on Network Softwarization (NetSoft)* (pp. 444–449). IEEE.
9. Marín, G., Caasas, P., & Capdehourat, G. (2021). Deepmal-deep learning models for malware traffic detection and classification. In *Data Science–Analytics and Applications: Proceedings of the 3rd International Data Science Conference–iDSC2020* (pp. 105–112). Springer Fachmedien Wiesbaden.
10. Zhang, B., Li, J., Chen, C., Lee, K., & Lee, I. (2022). A practical botnet traffic detection system using GNN. In *Cyberspace Safety and Security: 13th International Symposium, CSS 2021, Virtual Event, November 9–11, 2021, Proceedings 13* (pp. 66–78). Springer International Publishing.
11. Ji, X., & Meng, Q. (2020, August). Traffic classification based on graph convolutional network. In *2020 IEEE International Conference on Advances in Electrical Engineering and Computer Applications (AEECA)* (pp. 596–601). IEEE.
12. Pang, B., Fu, Y., Ren, S., Wang, Y., Liao, Q., & Jia, Y. (2021). CGNN: Traffic classification with graph neural network. *arXiv preprint* arXiv:2110.09726.
13. Busch, J., Kocheturov, A., Tresp, V., & Seidl, T. (2021, July). Nf-gnn: Network flow graph neural networks for malware detection and classification. *ACM*. In *33rd International Conference on Scientific and Statistical Database Management* (pp. 121–132).
14. Liu, T., Li, Z., Long, H., & Bilal, A. (2023). NT-GNN: Network traffic graph for 5G mobile IoT android malware detection. *Electronics*, 12(4), 789.
15. Huoh, T. L., Luo, Y., Li, P., & Zhang, T. (2022). Flow-based encrypted network traffic classification with graph neural networks. *IEEE Transactions on Network and Service Management*. 20(2), 1224-1237.
16. Herath, J. D., Wakodikar, P. P., Yang, P., & Yan, G. (2022, June). CFGExplainer: Explaining graph neural network-based malware classification from control flow graphs. In *2022 52nd Annual IEEE/IFIP International Conference on Dependable Systems and Networks (DSN)* (pp. 172–184). IEEE.
17. Dvorak, S., Prochazka, P., & Bajer, L. (2022, April). GNN-based malicious network entities identification in large-scale network data. In *NOMS 2022–2022 IEEE/IFIP Network Operations and Management Symposium* (pp. 1–4). IEEE.

18. Pujol-Perich, D., Suarez-Varela, J., Cabellos-Aparicio, A., & Barlet-Ros, P. (2022). Unveiling the potential of graph neural networks for robust intrusion detection. *ACM SIGMETRICS Performance Evaluation Review*, 49(4), 111–117.
19. Guerra-Manzanares, A ., et al. (2020). MedBIoT: Generation of an IoT botnet dataset in a medium-sized IoT network. *In ICISSP (pp. 207-218).*
20. Mahfouz, A., Abuhussein, A., Venugopal, D., & Shiva, S. (2020). Ensemble classifiers for network intrusion detection using a novel network attack dataset. *Future Internet*, 12(11), 180.
21. Ji, X., & Meng, Q. (2020). Traffic classification based on graph convolutional network. In *2020 IEEE International Conference on Advances in Electrical Engineering and Computer Applications (AEECA)*. IEEE.
22. Pham, T.-D., Ho, T.-L., Truong-Huu, T., Cao, T.-D., & Truong, H.-L. (2021). Mappgraph: Mobile-app classification on encrypted network traffic using deep graph convolution neural networks. *In Proceedings of the 37th Annual Computer Security Applications Conference (pp. 1025-1038).*
23. Xiao, L., Wu, X., & Wang, G. (2019). Social network analysis based on graph SAGE. *2019 12th International Symposium on Computational Intelligence and Design (ISCID)*. Vol. 2. IEEE.
24. Kipf, T. N., & Welling, M. (2017). Semi-supervised classification with graph convolutional network. *France:ICLR*, 1–14.

Chapter 7

Addressing Unique Cybersecurity Challenges in Telehealth and Remote Physiologic Monitoring

Uzma Jafar and Hafiz Adnan Hussain

7.1 INTRODUCTION

In the wake of the global pandemic, the healthcare sector has experienced a significant shift toward digitalization, characterized by the rapid adoption of telehealth and remote physiologic monitoring (RPM) as illustrated in Figure 7.1. Telehealth, delivering healthcare services through telecommunications technology, has become essential for providing continuous, accessible, cost-effective care [1]. This transformation was prompted by the need to minimize physical contact, alleviate strain on healthcare facilities, and extend care to remote or underserved regions. RPM, a subset of telehealth, involves using digital technologies to capture and monitor medical data from patients remotely. This data is then transmitted electronically for assessment and recommendations by healthcare providers. Particularly beneficial for chronic disease management, post-operative care, and elderly care, RPM ensures timely medical attention while allowing patients to remain in the comfort of their homes [2]. These technologies have revolutionized the patient–provider relationship and redefined healthcare delivery. Telehealth and RPM, with their real-time health monitoring, personalized care, and enhanced patient engagement, are integral components of the modern healthcare ecosystem [3]. However, this digital transformation has introduced unique cybersecurity challenges. The reliance on digital platforms and IoT devices for health monitoring and transmission raises concerns about data security, privacy, and compliance with regulatory standards. Key challenges encompass data vulnerability, where protected health information (PHI) becomes a prime target for cyberattacks, especially during transmission across networks [4]. Additionally, the integrity of RPM devices, from wearable health monitors to implanted devices, is susceptible to hacking, leading to inaccurate data reporting or malicious tampering. Privacy concerns arise with the shift to home-based telehealth, questioning patient privacy in shared living spaces and unauthorized use or exposure of PHI [5]. Compliance with healthcare regulations such as Health Insurance Portability and Accountability Act (HIPAA) in the United States and General Data

 DOI: 10.1201/9781003470038-7

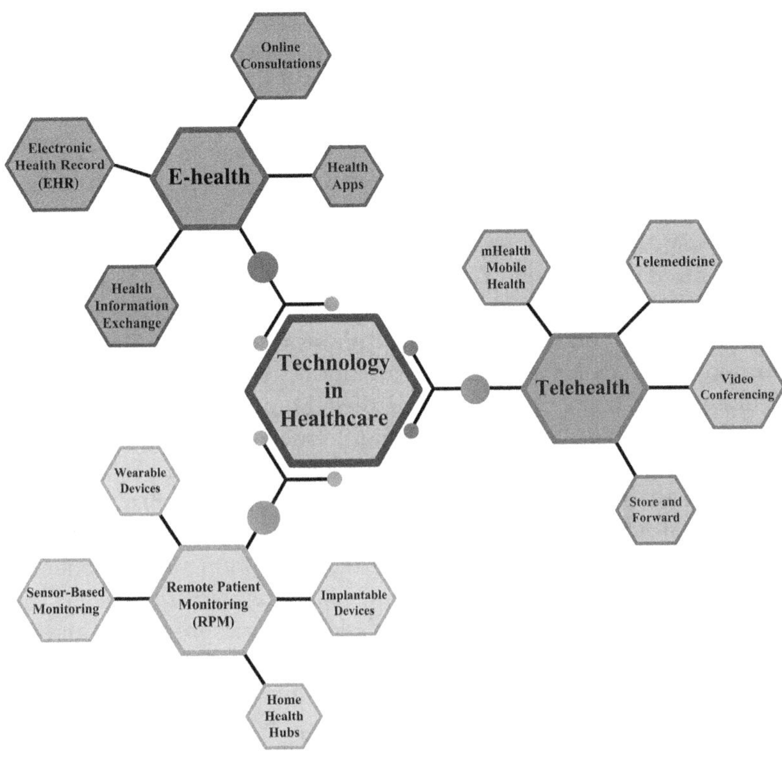

Figure 7.1 Revolutionizing healthcare, a visual exploration of technology integration—from e-health to telehealth and remote physiologic monitoring (RPM).

Protection Regulation (GDPR) in Europe becomes more challenging as data crosses multiple digital platforms and geographic boundaries [6].

Telehealth and RPM have emerged as critical components of contemporary healthcare, transforming the landscape of medical service delivery, especially in the post-COVID-19 era. Integrating telehealth and RPM into routine healthcare practices has improved access to care and enhanced the continuity and quality of healthcare services, particularly for chronic conditions like hypertension, diabetes, and cardiovascular diseases [7]. The application of RPM in telehealth leverages the IoT, enabling devices to record vital health data remotely, including body temperature, blood pressure, heart rate, oxygen saturation, and blood sugar levels. The adoption of RPM has been driven by advancements in medical technology, growing awareness among providers and patients, and the ability to manage and prevent severe complications in remote locations [8]. The demand for telehealth services, including RPM, has surged, as reflected by the projected $39 billion patient monitoring devices market [9]. This growth is attributed to the increasing prevalence of chronic diseases, rising demand for continuous monitoring, and legislative changes. Moreover, the healthcare industry's focus on artificial intelligence (AI) and machine learning (ML) is expected to enhance interactions between healthcare providers and patients, especially in RPM [10].

The healthcare landscape is undergoing a profound transformation, with telehealth and RPM emerging as powerful tools that reshape how healthcare is delivered, accessed, and experienced. The ability to remotely monitor and provide care to patients has not only increased accessibility but also revolutionized the concept of patient-centered healthcare [11] as illustrated in Figure 7.2. Telehealth and RPM have shattered traditional barriers, offering healthcare beyond the confines of physical spaces. Patients now have the opportunity to receive medical attention, consultations, and continuous monitoring from the comfort of their homes, eliminating geographical distances as impediments. Integrating connected devices, wearables, and smart technologies enables real-time tracking of vital signs, ensuring proactive healthcare interventions and personalized treatment plans [12]. These technological advancements have made RPM devices more compact, less invasive, and easier to use, accelerating their adoption among patients and practitioners. Figure 7.3 presents the detailed architecture of RPM, which comprises "data collection and transmission," "data processing and accessibility," and "healthcare provider and patient interaction." However, the increasing reliance on telehealth and RPM raises significant cybersecurity concerns. Patient data's safekeeping, integrity, and confidentiality are paramount, given the sensitive nature of the information transmitted and stored. Cybersecurity measures are crucial to protect against data breaches and ensure the privacy and security of patient information in the telehealth context [13].

Amidst this revolutionary shift, the allure of telehealth and RPM is accompanied by an imperative to address unprecedented cybersecurity challenges. The digitization of healthcare processes and the exchange of sensitive patient information over networks have opened new avenues for cyber threats. Securing these technologies against data breaches, unauthorized access, and malicious attacks is crucial [14]. This chapter provides an in-depth analysis of the relationship between telehealth, RPM, and cybersecurity. It addresses the unique challenges that arise from the convergence of healthcare and digital technologies and emphasizes the importance of safeguarding patient data to sustain the momentum of telehealth and RPM adoption. The primary objective of this chapter is to analyze the risks associated with telehealth and RPM and propose effective strategies to mitigate them. It involves examining the nature of cyber threats, understanding the vulnerabilities of digital health systems, and assessing the impact of such threats on patients and healthcare providers. To achieve this objective, this chapter covers the background of telehealth and RPM, the methodologies employed to understand cybersecurity challenges, specific vulnerabilities, proposed solutions, and the future trajectory of these transformative healthcare technologies. It also

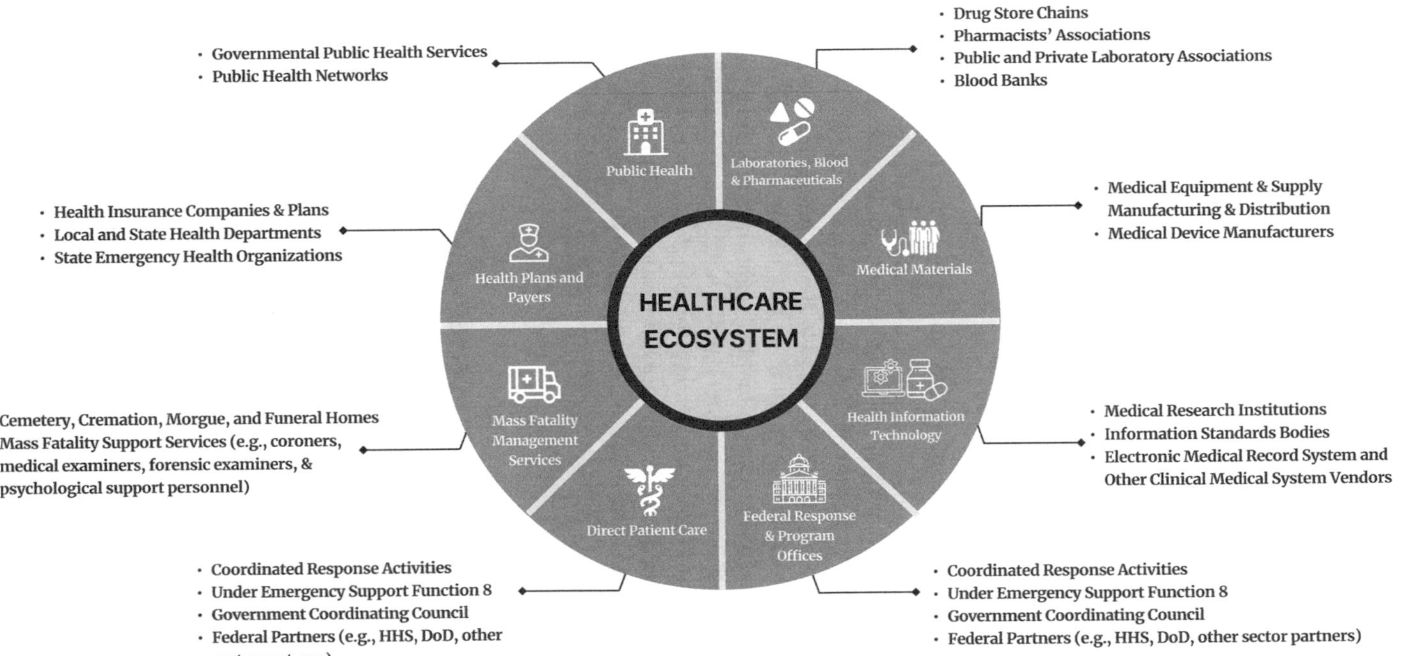

Figure 7.2 Healthcare ecosystem interconnected sectors focused on patient-centric care.

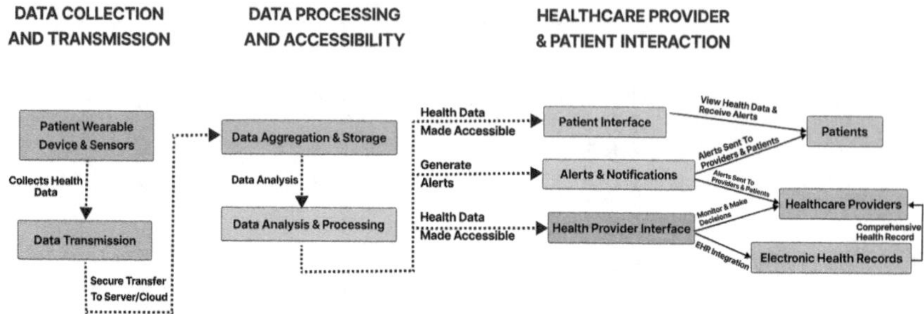

Figure 7.3 Remote physiologic monitoring architecture.

explores technological solutions like encryption and secure data transmission protocols, policy measures, and compliance strategies.

Furthermore, this chapter highlights the importance of cybersecurity awareness and training among healthcare professionals and patients. This is critical to ensure a proactive approach to developing robust cybersecurity measures aligned with these technologies' dynamic and evolving nature. In conclusion, this chapter offers valuable insights and guidance for healthcare organizations, technology providers, policymakers, and patients, contributing to the safer and more secure adoption of telehealth and RPM technologies in the evolving digital healthcare landscape. By addressing these aspects, this chapter aims to contribute to a deeper understanding of how cybersecurity can be seamlessly integrated into telehealth and RPM, ensuring a secure and resilient healthcare future.

7.2 THE EVOLUTION OF TELEMEDICINE AND TELEHEALTH

Throughout history, humans have developed various means to communicate over long distances, including smoke signals, drums, and carrier pigeons. In the realm of healthcare, access to high-quality medical care was traditionally restricted to the wealthy, and others relied on intermediaries to communicate their symptoms and receive diagnoses and treatment plans [15]. The advent of telecommunications began with the discovery of electricity in the 19th century, leading to wired communication and initial ideas of telehealth. During the American Civil War, telegraphs were used to send lists of casualties and provide medical updates to soldiers [16]. The telephone, a more straightforward communication tool than the telegraph, gradually allowed the public to access this technology. The first recorded instance of a telehealth consultation can be traced back to Alexander Graham Bell in 1876 [17], when he sought assistance from his assistant, Mr. Watson, after an acid spill. *The Lancet* reported a case in 1879 where a doctor successfully diagnosed a child over the telephone at night, highlighting the potential of remote patient care to reduce unnecessary home visits [18].

In subsequent years, telemedicine emerged as a recognized field, with early efforts focused on transmitting two-way television and audio signals for communication. In the 1940s, radiographic images were transmitted over telephone circuits in Pennsylvania [19]. The late 1950s and early 1960s marked the first uses of telemedicine to transmit videos, images, and complex medical data. The University of Nebraska pioneered real-time video telemedicine consultations with neurological examinations in 1959, and telepsychiatry followed soon after NASA's space missions underscored the necessity of telemedicine for astronaut monitoring, leading to its integration into spacecraft and spacesuits [20]. Initially, telemedicine projects focused on providing healthcare access in rural areas and addressing medical emergencies [21]. Radiology became the first specialty to fully embrace telemedicine in the 1980s, advancing from the digital storage of medical images *Picture Archiving and Communication System* (PACS) to remote access for radiologists [22]. Table 7.1 summarizes the key milestones in the evolution of telehealth services.

The early phases of telemedicine were marked by large, complex projects requiring specialized staff and organizational changes. Rapid technological advancements and the push for standardization often rendered these systems outdated [23]. The advent of broadband Internet and mobile networks like 4G and 5G facilitated the growth of telemedicine [24]. Advancements in storage, standardization, security, and application development, alongside the rise of cloud computing, have revolutionized telemedicine. The use of personal computing devices has significantly reduced costs and simplified operations [25]. As telemedicine continues to advance, it's important to compare traditional patient monitoring methods with RPM. Table 7.2 provides an in-depth analysis of these two approaches, focusing on cost-effectiveness,

Table 7.1 Key Milestones in the Evolution of Telehealth Services

Year	*Milestone*
1960s	Early experiments with telehealth (closed-circuit television for medical consultations)
1970s	First interactive telemedicine system (University of Nebraska)
1980s	Widespread adoption of personal computers and digital communication
1996	Health Insurance Portability and Accountability Act (HIPAA).
2000s	Rise of smartphones and mobile health applications
2010	Introduction of 4G technology, enhancing telehealth capabilities
2020	COVID-19 pandemic leads to unprecedented spike in telehealth adoption

Table 7.2 Comparison of Benefits—Traditional Patient Monitoring vs. RPM

Aspect	*Traditional Patient Monitoring*	*RPM*
Cost	Often incurs higher costs due to in-person visits and hospital stays.	Reduces costs by minimizing the need for physical visits and hospitalization.
Accessibility	Limited to clinical settings; challenging for patients in remote areas or with mobility issues.	Enhances access to care, especially for patients in remote locations or with mobility challenges.
Patient engagement	Patient engagement is typically limited to in-person visits.	Promotes active patient participation through continuous monitoring and digital communication.
Effectiveness in chronic disease management	Can be less effective due to infrequent monitoring and follow-ups.	Improves chronic disease management through regular monitoring and timely interventions.

accessibility, patient engagement, and effectiveness in chronic disease management. This table is intended to help healthcare professionals and stakeholders understand the practical benefits and improved outcomes of RPM, which sets a new standard for patient care continuity. Nevertheless, telemedicine has become increasingly routine in various fields, driven by a focus on caring for the aged and infirm. However, it still needs to meet its initial goal of vastly improving healthcare access for remote and rural populations.

7.3 EXISTING WORK

The widespread adoption of digital technologies has led to many aspects of life going online, including commerce, social connections, business, industry, and unfortunately, criminal activities [26, 27]. Recent reports mentioned that cybercrime is becoming more frequent and severe, with predictions that it was generated $6 trillion in revenue in 2021, up from $3 trillion in 2015 [28]. Cybercrime is on track to overtake traditional crime in terms of volume and cost [29]. It is clear that cybercrime is profitable and carries low risks, as perpetrators can launch attacks from anywhere in the world [19]. Cybercrime, like traditional crime, follows a three-step model known as the crime triangle [30]. This model states that for cybercrime to occur, three factors must be present: a victim, a motive, and an opportunity. The victim is the target of the attack, the motive drives the criminal to commit the crime, and the opportunity is the vulnerable system or network that the attacker exploits. Other models used to explain cybercrime include the Routine Activity Theory [31] and the Fraud Triangle [32]. These models also consider similar factors to describe crimes, but some replace the victim with the attacker's means, which is part of the opportunity. Zeadally et al. [33] conducted a comprehensive review of literature on security threats to Electronic Health Systems (E-Health). They found that telecommunication technologies used in E-Health applications are vulnerable to sophisticated cyberattacks. Recent breaches in various segments of E-Health have been related to security and privacy concerns. As a result, they stressed the need for researchers to address these security challenges. Ida et al. [8] explored security aspects within IoT and Cloud Computing, with a particular focus on E-Health systems. They identified disparities between IoT systems and their inherent vulnerabilities in the E-Health context. They also examined vulnerabilities within IoT in a cloud environment, proposing innovative solutions to safeguard health information. Garg and Brewer [1] conducted a systematic analysis of security issues in Telemedicine. Their research focused on physical security, legal implications, policies, and standards within this domain. One important finding was the impact of system reliability and availability on life-critical systems. They also highlighted the importance of maintaining system usability without sacrificing security. In network communication, Kompara and Holbl [34] examined security challenges associated with body sensor networks. Their research identified potential attacks that could compromise intra-body area.

7.4 WHY HEALTHCARE ORGANIZATIONS ARE THE BIGGEST TARGET FOR CYBERSECURITY ATTACKS

Healthcare systems are facing increasing cybersecurity threats due to the integration of medical information systems with IoT devices and other hardware and software components. These elements often lack adequate cyber protection and are connected with external components that access sensitive patient data [33]. The COVID-19 pandemic has further escalated the risk with the surge in usage of these technologies. Cyber attackers target healthcare organizations for various reasons, including the high value of personal health data on the black market. The abundance of patient information in health records presents opportunities for data misuse, such as identity theft and fraudulent activities involving insurance companies. Healthcare institutions are also prone to pay substantial amounts to attackers to release critical patient data and maintain uninterrupted health services [35]. The potential consequences of service unavailability or inaccurate patient data are severe. Privacy regulations like HIPAA impose hefty fines for violations related to privacy, security, breach notifications, and electronic health transactions [36]. Compliance with regulations like GDPR necessitates proactive measures by healthcare actors to prevent data breaches or service disruptions. In 2021, as summarized in Table 7.3, healthcare institutions and their associated businesses experienced a series of cyberattacks and

Table 7.3 Major Cyberattacks on Healthcare Organizations in 2021

Covered Organization	*Number of Individuals Affected*	*Breach Cause*
Florida Healthy Kids Corporation	3,500,000	Hosting patch failure
20/20 Eye Care Network Inc.	3,253,822	Insider wrongdoing
Forefront Dermatology S.C.	2,413,553	Information technology (IT) network hacked
CaptureRx	1,656,569	Ransomware
Eskenazi Health	1,515,918	IP spoofing
The Kroger Co.	1,474,284	Third-party file transfer failure
St. Joseph's/Candler Hospital	1,400,000	Ransomware
University Medical Center Southern Nevada	1,300,000	REvil ransomware
American Anesthesiology Inc.	1,269,074	Third-party phishing incident
PracticeFirst	1,210,688	Ransomware

unauthorized access to healthcare data. In April of that year, Reproductive Biology Associates and their affiliate, my Egg Bank North America, fell victim to a cyberattack [37]. The breach enabled hackers to access sensitive personal information, including medical details and social security numbers, of approximately 38,000 patients [19]. Cybercriminal groups are largely behind these attacks in the healthcare sector, such as the infamous REvil ransomware group, which was implicated in the data breach at the University Medical Center Southern Nevada in August 2021, impacting around 1.3 million individuals [38].

The targeting of healthcare organizations by cyber attackers can be understood by examining the unique characteristics and resources of these entities, leading to the identification of key vulnerabilities. Medical devices designed for specific medical functions may lack robust cybersecurity features and are vulnerable to cyber threats [39]. Attackers can exploit these devices as gateways into the system, potentially controlling them and endangering patient lives. Inadequate cybersecurity knowledge among medical staff, who are typically untrained in recognizing and responding to cyber threats, is another primary concern. Ensuring a secure computer network that is user-friendly is essential. Moreover, healthcare organizations are often connected to numerous devices and hardware components, and external access through personal devices further compromises cybersecurity [14]. The necessity of immediate and accessible health information sharing, especially in emergency services, requires security procedures that do not hinder timely patient care [40]. Limited budgets for security mechanisms in smaller healthcare organizations contrast with larger organizations that, despite having more resources, are more appealing targets due to extensive patient data. Using outdated technologies that do not meet modern security standards is also a significant issue [41]. Discontinuation of updates for cost-saving reasons leaves technologies vulnerable over time, but network-level security enhancements can prevent further access to patient data by attackers.

7.5 CYBERSECURITY CHALLENGES IN TELEHEALTH AND RPM

Security challenges in the healthcare sector can result in significant financial costs and, more importantly, endanger lives. This emphasizes the need to prevent security breaches. The primary goal of cybersecurity in e-health, telemedicine, and RPM is to protect medical data and ensure the confidentiality of patient informations [42]. E-health systems face various risks of data breaches, including internal or malicious attacks, loss or theft of devices, and mistakes made by healthcare staff. Before discussing solutions, it is crucial to recognize the prevalent cyber threats that target e-health, telemedicine, and RPM systems. Ransomware and other malware types pose a serious threat to healthcare systems, potentially leading to dire consequences, including loss of life [43]. Recent years have seen an escalation in the frequency and severity of cyberattacks in the healthcare industry. Notable incidents include a major data breach in 2023 summarized in Table 7.4, where over 900,000 healthcare records were compromised due to a network server hack [44]. This is part of a trend observed since 2014, where the healthcare sector has been continually targeted, affecting millions of patients. Healthcare data is particularly valuable to cybercriminals due to the difficulty in altering personal information such as social security numbers and birthdates. In contrast, credit cards can be easily cancelled [45]. The financial implications are significant, with stolen healthcare records fetching high prices on the dark web, far surpassing the value of credit card information. The high value of healthcare data, combined with often inadequate encryption practices, has led to a surge in system breaches [46].

These breaches extend beyond financial losses, enabling illegal activities such as the unauthorized purchase of drugs or medical equipment, and obtaining medical care under false pretenses. The impact of these breaches is broad, affecting not just the financial health of institutions but also the physical and mental well-being of individuals involved [58]. In 2022, 49.6 million Americans were impacted by healthcare data breaches, and the average cost of a healthcare data breach was a staggering $10.10 million, marking the highest increase in cost-per-breach across industries [59]. This

Table 7.4 Summary of Significant Healthcare Data Breaches in 2023

Organization	*Number of Individuals Affected*	*Type of Incident*	*Month Reported*	*Sources*
CompleteCare Health Network	313,973	Ransomware attack	December	[47]
Health Alliance Hospital	264,197	Hacking incident	December	[47]
HCA Healthcare	11 million	Data theft from external storage	July	[48, 49]
PJ&A	8.95 million	Unauthorized network access	November	[50]
MCNA	8.8 million	Data viewed/ copied in cyberattack	May	[51]
Welltok	8.5 million	MOVEit file transfer tool breach	November	[49]
PharMerica Corporation	5.8 million	Cyberattack	March	[52]
Health EC	4.4 million	Cyberattack	December	[53]
Reventics	4.2 million	System breach	Not specified	[49]
Colorado Dept. of Health Care Policy & Financing	4 million	MOVEit transfer hacking incident	Not specified	[54]
Regal Medical Group	3.4 million	Ransomware attack	Not specified	[55]
CareSource	3.1 million	MOVEit breach	July	[56]
Cerebral, Inc.	3.1 million	Impermissible disclosure	Not specified	[57]

trend underlines the critical need for improved cybersecurity measures in the healthcare sector to protect sensitive patient data and mitigate the risks of future attacks.

7.5.1 Recent Developments and Statistical Overview

The healthcare industry has been facing a growing cybersecurity crisis for several years now. Since 2009, there have been over 2,100 reported data breaches, making it the industry that is targeted the most by cyberattacks [60]. This trend has become especially noticeable in recent years. Between 2017 and 2021, ransomware attacks on healthcare entities increased fourfold, resulting in enormous cybersecurity spending of about $65 billion during this period. In 2020, the global healthcare industry incurred staggering costs exceeding $6 trillion due to cyberattacks [61]. As we move into 2021, the frequency and severity of these breaches continue to increase. On average, around 59 data breaches were reported each month, with a total of 710 breaches recorded throughout the year. Notable incidents included a phishing attack at the Florida Healthy Kids Corporation that impacted 3.5 million individuals, and a breach at Forefront Dermatology that affected over 2.5 million people. The financial impact of these breaches was significant, with the healthcare industry incurring costs of $25 billion in 2021 alone. Each healthcare data record breach had the highest cost across all industries at $408 [62]. Despite a slight decrease in the number of data breaches reported in 2023 compared to previous years, the extent of the damage continued to grow. By October 2023, although the number of reported breaches was lower than the 12-month average, the exposed or impermissibly disclosed healthcare records had surged dramatically, with over 82.6 million records affected. By mid-November, this number had exceeded 100 million. Hacking remained the primary cause of these breaches, highlighting the persistent and evolving challenges in healthcare cybersecurity [63]. According to Verizon, 76% of healthcare data breaches in 2022 were caused by basic web application attacks, miscellaneous errors, and system intrusions. 61% of breaches were external, and 39% were internal. According to Security Intelligence, hacking caused 80% of healthcare data breaches in 2022. According to Stanford University, roughly 88% of data breaches are caused by employee mistakes [64]. Table 7.5 summarizes the statistics indicating a rapidly evolving and increasingly challenging cybersecurity landscape in healthcare, emphasizing the critical need for robust security measures and awareness in this sector.

7.5.2 Data Breaches in Healthcare Services Including Telehealth and RPM

A data breach occurs when an unauthorized person gains access to, copies, transmits, views, steals, or uses sensitive, protected, or confidential data. This type of breach can include various types of information such as financial information like credit card or bank account numbers, Personally Identifiable Information (PII), personal health information, corporate trade secrets, or intellectual property. Typically, these types of breaches involve the exposure of unstructured data such as files, documents, and other sensitive materials. Patient records are highly attractive to criminals because they contain personal data like names, addresses, dates of birth, social security numbers, bank and credit card details, medication histories, treatment and surgery details, insurance information, and more. The abundance of information contained in these records can cause significant harm to individuals, as criminals may either sell the data or use it to carry out targeted attacks. To document incidents involving the breach of PHI, the US Department of

Table 7.5 Summary of Healthcare Data Breaches from 2020 to 2022: A Retrospective View on the Trends and Significant Incidents in Healthcare Provider (HPH) and Protected Health Information (PHI) Breaches [65]

Year	*Total Number of Breaches*	*Number of Healthcare Provider (HPH) Breaches*	*Number of Protected Health Information (PHI) Breaches*	*Notes*
2020	2,354	560	12	Maze was the first ransomware gang to adopt double extortion in 2020. By the end of the year, at least 17 other groups had followed suit.
2021	2,323	1,203	Unknown	One cyberattack targeted a provider maintaining over 600 locations. The attack resulted in a cost of over $110 million to HPH.
2022	2,421	290	17	This year, only hospitals were monitored for cyberattacks instead of other HPH. Unfortunately, there was an incident where a computer system responsible for calculating medication dosage was attacked. This resulted in a 3-year-old patient receiving an excessive amount of pain medicine.

Health and Human Services (HHS) keeps a breach portal. According to the HHS breach portal in 2019, data breaches affected 27 million people in the United States. The portal also provides information on the top breaches [62]. As per Health Insurance Portability and Accountability Act (HIPAA) 2023 was a particularly bad year for healthcare data breaches, as depicted in Figure 7.4, with complaints and losses over the last five years. Between January 1, 2023, and October 31, 2023, more than 82.6 million healthcare records were exposed or impermissibly disclosed, compared to 45 million records in 2021 and 51.9 million records in 2022. As of November 17, 2023, more than 100 million records have been breached [66]. Table 7.6 lists the top breaches in terms of the number of people affected.

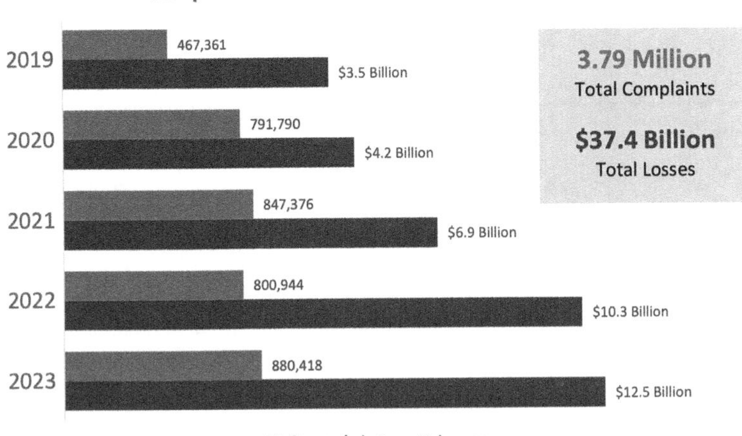

Figure 7.4 Chart includes yearly and aggregate data for complaints and losses over the years 2018 to 2022. Over that time, IC3 received a total of 3.26 million complaints, reporting a loss of $27.6 billion [based on 68].

Table 7.6 Top Breaches in 2023 by the Number of Individuals Affected in the United States

Name of Covered Entity	*Covered Entity Type*	*Individuals Affected*	*Cause of breach*
Postmeds, Inc. (TruePill)	Healthcare provider	2,364,359	Hacking incident (details not disclosed)
Western Washington Medical Group	Healthcare provider	350,863	Hacking incident (details not disclosed)
Greater Rochester Independent Practice Association, Inc.	Healthcare provider	279,156	Hacking incident (details not disclosed)
Radius Global Solutions	Business associate	135,742	Hacking incident—MoveIT transfer vulnerability exploited
Dakota Eye Institute	Healthcare provider	107,143	Hacking incident (details not disclosed)
Walmart, Inc. Associates Health and Welfare Plan	Health plan	85,952	Hacking incident (details not disclosed)

(Continued)

Table 7.6 (Continued) Top Breaches in 2023 by the Number of Individuals Affected in the United States

Name of Covered Entity	*Covered Entity Type*	*Individuals Affected*	*Cause of breach*
Westat, Inc.	Business associate	50,065	Hacking incident—MoveIT transfer vulnerability exploited
Brooklyn Premier Orthopedics	Healthcare provider	48,459	Hacking incident (details not disclosed)
PeakMed	Healthcare provider	27,800	Hacking incident (compromised credentials)
Hospital & Medical Foundation of Paris, Inc.	Healthcare provider	16,598	Hacking incident (details not disclosed)
Fredericksburg Foot & Ankle Center, PLC	Healthcare provider	14,912	Hacking incident (details not disclosed)
Cadence Bank	Business associate	13,862	Hacking incident—MoveIT transfer vulnerability exploited
Peerstar LLC	Healthcare provider	11,438	Hacking incident (details not disclosed)
Atlas Healthcare CT	Healthcare provider	10,831	Hacking incident (details not disclosed)

Verizon has recently published its Data Breach Investigation report for 2023. In this report, Verizon analyzed approximately 16,312 security incidents that occurred across different sectors, out of which over 5,199 were data breaches. Healthcare was found to be involved in just under 525 of these security incidents, with over 436 confirmed data disclosures [67]. Further details about healthcare-related data can be found in Table 7.7.

7.5.2.1 Types of Breaches

As per Verizon, the majority of healthcare data breaches in 2023 were caused by hacking and IT incidents, accounting for 74% of the total breaches. Unauthorized access and disclosure of health records were also significant, constituting 21% of the breaches. Other causes like theft, loss, and improper disposal of data, while less prevalent, still contributed to the overall cybersecurity threats faced by the healthcare industry [67]. Table 7.8 categorizes the types of data breaches in the healthcare sector by their prevalence,

Table 7.7 Summary of Healthcare Data Breach Characteristics and Details in 2023

Category	*Details*
Frequency	525 incidents, 436 with confirmed data disclosure
Top patterns	System intrusion, basic web application attacks and miscellaneous errors represent 68% of breaches
Threat actors	External (66%), internal (35%), multiple (2%) (breaches)
Actor motives	Financial (98%), espionage (2%), fun (1%), ideology (1%) (breaches)
Data compromised	Personal (67%), medical (54%), credentials (36%), other (17%) (breaches)
What is the same?	The top three patterns remain the same, although the order has changed. Internal actors making mistakes continue to trouble this sector.

Table 7.8 Distribution of Healthcare Data Breaches in 2023

Type of Breach	*Percentage of Total Breaches*
Hacking/IT incident	74%
Unauthorized access/disclosure	21%
Theft	3%
Loss	1%
Improper disposal	1%

illustrating the dominant role of hacking/IT incidents and the significance of unauthorized access/disclosure, along with other breach types like theft, loss, and improper disposal.

7.5.3 Impersonation Attacks

Hackers, hacktivists, and cybercriminals often use deception attacks to gain unauthorized access to sensitive personal information and data stored in computer systems. These attackers can exploit security system weaknesses, bypass authentication processes, or use stolen identity credentials or passwords to assume a false identity. In e-health, these attacks can come from insiders such as medical personnel or external sources, as illustrated in Figure 7.5. Once these intruders breach the e-health system, they gain complete control over the patient records and confidential data. They can either erase or alter data, including network settings [69].

Deception attacks pose a more significant threat to medical applications that rely on wireless sensor networks. If the network is compromised by a Denial of Service (DoS) attack, it can cause significant disruptions to healthcare applications, making them unavailable. These attacks can also target implantable or

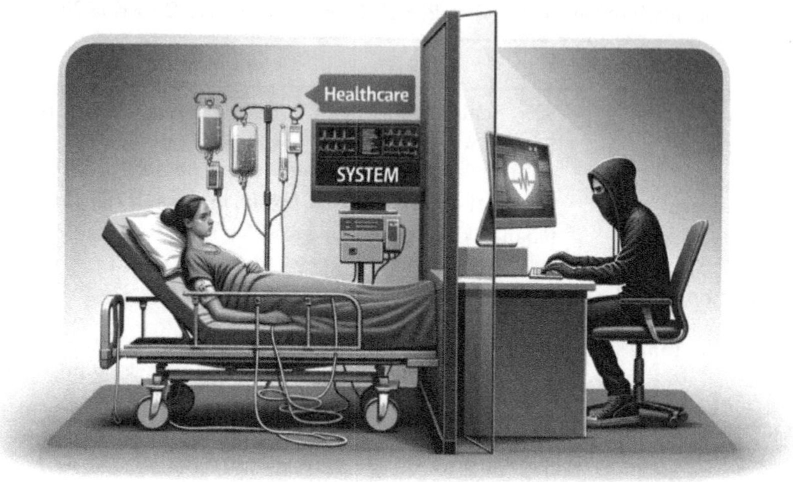

Figure 7.5 Cybersecurity in healthcare protecting vulnerable patients from digital predators.

wearable medical devices. For example, a compromised cardiac monitor could display incorrect patient readings, resulting in incorrect medical decisions, such as medication dosages [70]. Moreover, deception attacks can intercept patients' physiological data, leading to replay threats where outdated treatment instructions are repeatedly sent to the healthcare application, causing either under or over-treatment. As health applications rely on the most recent data from medical sensor networks, the implications of deception attacks can be particularly severe for e-health and telemedicine systems.

7.5.4 Ransomware Attacks

Cybercriminals have found ransomware to be a profitable method of exploiting healthcare data and records. Ransomware is a type of malware that encrypts user data with a key only known to the hacker, locking users out of their data. The user is then faced with a ransom demand, and failure to pay can lead to permanent data access denial or public data release. In the healthcare industry, attackers target healthcare provider records, as well as entire hospital databases [71]. Since this type of attack's emergence in 2016, the healthcare industry has seen significant data corruption and damage. Ransomware trends in 2024 have shown a diversification in the types of ransomware used, with a sharp increase in ransom demands. In 2023, ransomware affected 66% of organizations, and attacks have increased by 85% since 2020. The total global cost of ransomware was expected to exceed $30 billion in 2023. Notably, for large enterprises in 2022, the average total cost of a ransomware breach was $4.54 million [72]. Ransomware attacks often start via email, with about 75% of attacks in organizations with more than 250 employees initiated this way. Moreover, ransomware's threat to mobile devices is expanding, with over 10 million people having lost money and data to ransomware targeting Android users. Ransomware as a Service (RaaS) has also grown, allowing cybercriminals to use sophisticated tools to launch widespread attacks [73].

These statistics and trends underline the escalating threat ransomware poses, particularly in sectors like healthcare, where the impact can be devastating both financially and in terms of patient care and data security. Cybercriminals have increasingly turned to ransomware as a lucrative method of exploiting healthcare data and records. Ransomware, a form of malware, locks users out of their data by encrypting it with a key only known to the hacker. The user is then faced with a ransom demand; failure to pay can lead to permanent data access denial or public data release [74]. In the healthcare sector, attackers target records of healthcare providers and even entire hospital databases. Since the emergence of this type of attack around 2016, the healthcare industry has seen significant data corruption and damage. Emsisoft's reports the total annual ransomware attacks in United States in 2022 and their impact on healthcare is shown in Table 7.5.

7.5.5 Injection Attacks

Injection attacks, especially SQL injections, pose a significant threat to web security. They enable attackers to send harmful SQL queries through web applications to manipulate databases, leading to unauthorized access, data manipulation, or theft. SQL injections are dangerous because even inexperienced attackers can use simple tools to exploit system vulnerabilities and gain control. In the field of telehealth and RPM, security concerns are even more magnified. With the rapid adoption of telehealth technologies due to the COVID-19 pandemic, the risks to patient data have increased, especially through web-based applications used in telehealth services. The use of these applications has surged, drawing attention from cybercriminals. In early 2020, researchers noticed a significant increase in dark web and deep web mentions of top telehealth companies, indicating a higher risk to patient data.

Financially, cyberattacks can be very costly to healthcare companies. As per Figure 7.6 in 2022, healthcare data breaches averaged a cost of $10.10 million, an increase from $9.23 million in 2021 [59]. It was the highest increase in cost-per-breach compared to other industries. Healthcare records are especially valuable due to the sensitive and unchangeable personal details they contain, making them a frequent target for attackers. Furthermore, the healthcare industry has seen a significant investment in cybersecurity measures, with Anthem investing $260 million following a massive data breach that affected 78.8 million people [75]. However, despite such investments, 81% of telehealth providers are concerned about data leakage, with more

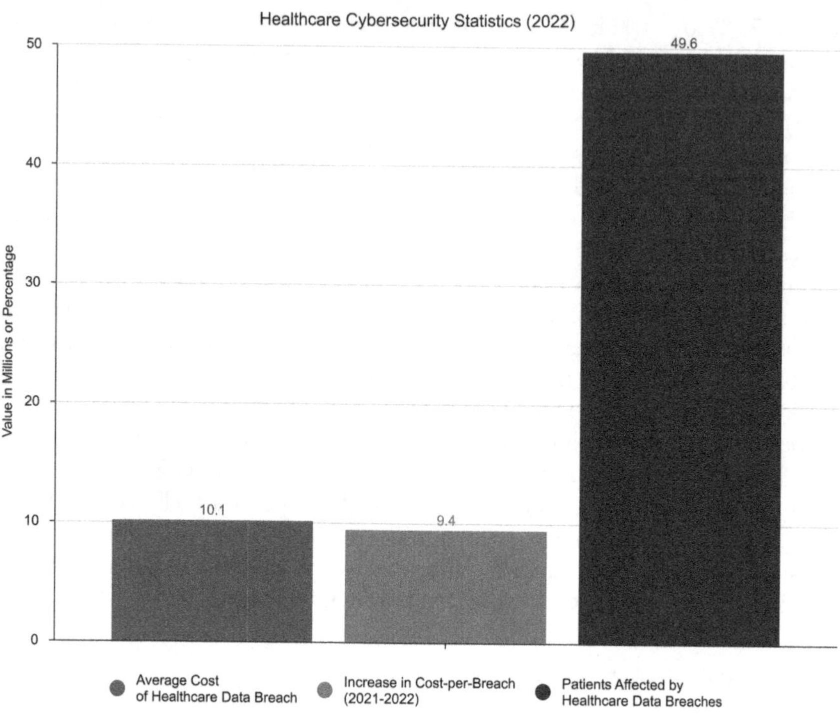

Figure 7.6 A bar chart analysis of healthcare data breach costs and impact in 2022.

than half reporting that patients have refused telehealth services due to data security and privacy worries. The rapid shift to telehealth has brought new challenges in securing patient data and maintaining privacy. The statistics and trends indicate that while the healthcare sector is increasingly aware of and investing in cybersecurity, the complexity and frequency of attacks continue to pose significant threats. The industry is engaged in a cyber-arms race, with the effectiveness of new security measures continually tested by the evolving tactics of cybercriminals.

7.5.6 Healthcare Cloud Systems Attacks

Digital health platforms often use a mix of cloud environments to store patient medical records. Unfortunately, these systems are vulnerable to security breaches from two primary sources. Internal breaches can occur when individuals with authorized cloud access exploit user permissions to modify or replace data stored within the cloud infrastructure. On the other hand, external breaches are executed by individuals without authorized access using social engineering tactics and existing security weaknesses within the cloud system to intercept or compromise data during transmission. Recent statistics show that cybersecurity incidents in cloud-based services, including those used for e-health, are increasing. In 2022, there was a significant rise in internal and external cyber threats targeting the healthcare sector [33]. Cybersecurity measures have had to evolve quickly to counter these threats, especially as healthcare providers continue to adapt to the growing use of telehealth services. It expanded the potential attack surface for cybercriminals. The increased reliance on RPM and other digital health technologies underscores the need for robust, multi-layered security protocols to protect sensitive health data against the evolving landscape of cyber threats.

7.5.7 Dark Web

The dark web is an online space where cybercriminals can trade stolen credit card details, login credentials, and proprietary content like Netflix's software. It is also a platform for illegal services such as phishing attacks or RaaS. Unfortunately, there is a growing demand for medical information on dark web sites, showing that it is more valuable than other personal data such as credit card numbers. Health insurance records can be sold for up to $20 each, compared to $7.50 for a credit card record [39]. Healthcare organizations are increasingly targeted by advanced hacking techniques like remote access Trojans and phishing schemes. This trend suggests that healthcare entities are lagging in cybersecurity advancements compared to other sectors, making them more vulnerable to cyberattacks. Cybercriminals prefer the dark web because it maintains anonymity, making it a hotbed for illegal transactions involving healthcare data. With the ongoing COVID-19 vaccine distribution, there has been a surge in the demand for health related data such as vaccination records and COVID-19 test outcomes on the dark web. Pfizer and BioNTech have reported that documents related to their vaccine development were illegally obtained from the European Medicines Agency (EMA), altered, and then disseminated on the dark web [14]. Such incidents not only compromise the integrity of sensitive information but also pose a significant risk to the vaccine supply chain, which could hinder vaccine distribution efforts.

7.5.8 Attack on Medical Devices in the Age of Telehealth and RPM

Implantable and wearable medical devices are essential for patient healthcare but are increasingly vulnerable to cyberattacks, which can pose serious health risks. These devices are used for monitoring, diagnosis, and treatment, and their connectivity and reliance on electronic systems make them susceptible to security breaches. For instance, an insulin pump that monitors glucose levels can be compromised using publicly available information such as radio chip specifications. An attacker can gain access to the device's control mechanisms by intercepting its wireless communications and reverse-engineering the protocol [76]. Such breaches can lead to erroneous readings or unauthorized adjustments in insulin dosage, potentially leading to severe health consequences like hyperglycemia or even death. In recent years, there has been a significant increase in cybersecurity incidents targeting healthcare systems, including RPM and telehealth services. Notable cyber threats to healthcare occurred in 2022, emphasizing the need for enhanced security measures. The expansion of telehealth services has further amplified these risks, as many healthcare providers rapidly adopted these technologies, needing more time to implement robust cybersecurity defenses. This shift has exposed vulnerabilities in internal and external network infrastructures, leading to increased data breaches and attacks on healthcare devices [77]. The vulnerabilities of medical devices to cyberattacks underscore the critical importance of strengthening cybersecurity protocols in healthcare. It includes ensuring secure communication channels, regular software updates, and stringent access controls to protect sensitive patient data and the functionality of life-sustaining medical devices.

7.5.8.1 IoT-Connected Medical Devices

The advancement of technology and the rise of the IoT have brought new possibilities for the healthcare industry. However, it has also given rise to a number of challenges, including the need for healthcare organizations to protect themselves against cyberattacks. With the increasing number of sophisticated cyber threats targeting healthcare networks, it is more important than ever for these organizations to be vigilant and take necessary measures to safeguard patient data. IT professionals face a complex task in monitoring the security status, location, and usage of each IoT device [78]. It is crucial to determine which devices are connected to the network, their activities, locations, and current status. Managing IoT devices can be difficult due to a lack of centralized control, which raises questions about how to effectively manage these devices without clear visibility of their operations and locations. According to a report, investment in Internet-connected medical devices is expected to increase at a Compound Annual Growth Rate (CAGR) of 29.5% until 2028 [79]. In a typical hospital room, there are around 15 to 20 connected medical devices, such as patient monitors, ventilators, and IV pumps. While these Internet of Medical Things (IoMT) devices are critical for patient care, they also pose significant security vulnerabilities [80].

7.5.8.2 mHealth and Telehealth Technologies

The rise of remote healthcare delivery has led to an increase in the use of Mobile Health (mHealth) and Telehealth technologies. These technologies have revolutionized healthcare by providing patients with more avenues for accessing care. However, this increased accessibility has also raised concerns about data breaches. According to the US Department of Health and Human Services (HHS) Office for Civil Rights (OCR), nearly 1,500 data breaches were recorded in 2017, with 35% of these breaches involving mobile devices or portable media. To ensure the success of Telehealth, it is essential to address significant privacy and security concerns [81]. For instance, sensors designed for detecting safety issues or medical emergencies may unintentionally expose confidential information about personal household activities. The trust of providers and patients in telehealth solutions depends on the data and technology being secure and private. To achieve this, key practices include implementing strong authentication procedures, end-to-end encryption, suitable technical controls, and following established best practices for data security.

7.5.9 Attacks on Home Network

Telemedicine solutions involve linking remote medical devices with central healthcare systems through a patient's personal network. It can include various connections like Wi-Fi, Local Area Network (LAN), or cellular networks like 4G and 5G. Patients can use telemedicine devices such as blood glucose meters, body fat gauges, blood testing kits, and blood pressure monitors to transmit health information from their homes or offices to the healthcare provider's telemedicine system. General Purpose Operating System (GPOS) embedded devices can also communicate with telemedicine systems. However, integrating personal networks with telemedicine systems can lead to security vulnerabilities, particularly the "Man-in-the-middle" (MITM) attack [77]. This type of attack involves an unauthorized entity intercepting the communication between the patient's device and the healthcare system. Recent data reveals that the risk of cyberattacks has increased significantly, especially since the COVID-19 pandemic led to the rapid expansion of telehealth and RPM services. In 2022, there was a notable rise in cybersecurity incidents targeting telehealth services, highlighting the urgent need for enhanced security measures in these systems. The increased adoption of telehealth has exposed existing vulnerabilities in network security, emphasizing the importance of robust encryption, secure communication protocols, and continuous monitoring of network activities to safeguard patient data and the integrity of telemedicine services.

7.5.10 Attacks on Public Networks in RPM and Telehealth

Telehealth services rely on standard Internet services to remotely connect patients with healthcare providers. However, this involves transmitting sensitive medical information and prescriptions over publicly accessible networks, which can make them vulnerable to security threats, especially through exploiting telemedicine system vulnerabilities. Unauthorized interception and modifications of the transmitted data are among the risks associated with public network attacks. Recent data and statistics have shown that the risks associated with public network attacks have increased significantly with the surge RPM and telehealth, particularly during the COVID-19 pandemic.

7.5.11 Attacks through End User's Negligence

There is a significant vulnerability in telehealth and RPM that comes from the patients themselves, who often lack cybersecurity awareness. They may misuse applications or set easily guessable passwords, which can inadvertently invite cyber threats such as data breaches, phishing, and various software attacks. Recent statistics underline the gravity of this issue. In 2023, a study revealed that a substantial percentage of telehealth and RPM users employed weak or repetitive passwords, significantly increasing the risk of unauthorized access [82]. Moreover, after the rapid expansion of telehealth services in 2020, security breaches caused by patient actions have increased. This trend has led to a call for more rigorous patient education on cybersecurity best practices, as well as the development of more secure and user-friendly authentication methods in telehealth applications.

7.5.12 Lack of Funding and Insufficient Staffing in IT Departments

The healthcare industry has made significant strides in recent years by adopting new technologies to improve patient care and outcomes. However, with these technological advancements, the threat of cyberattacks has also increased. Healthcare organizations are faced with multiple priorities, including integrating new technologies, adapting to evolving payment models, and complying with new regulatory standards, all while working with limited resources. Unfortunately, only 55% of healthcare organizations have fewer than 10 full-time employees dedicated to IT security, in contrast to 24% in other industries. This is alarming, given that over 90% of healthcare organizations now use cloud or hybrid environments—higher than the 82% in other sectors [83]. The shortage of staff in the face of increasing reliance on complex IT environments presents a significant risk. Cybersecurity professionals in the healthcare industry have already identified the shortage of IT staff as a significant issue. Most IT departments are overburdened with day-to-day responsibilities, leaving them little time to improve their security infrastructure. They often find themselves reacting to issues instead of proactively enhancing their systems. Many of their tasks, such as ticket creation, could be automated, and this further exacerbates the situation.

7.5.13 Lack of Employee's Security Training

In today's world, where data breaches have become increasingly common, it is crucial for employees to be able to identify suspicious emails, secure devices containing sensitive information, and more. Unfortunately, many healthcare providers have not adequately educated their staff on essential IT security principles. Security analysts have pointed out that most security breaches in healthcare are non-malicious. Research conducted by the Ponemon Institute reveals that there has been a rise in incidents caused by insider threats over the last two years. For example, the number of credential thefts has nearly doubled since 2020. The most common cause of insider threats is the carelessness or negligence of employees, although all three insider threat profiles have experienced an increase. Research indicates that 56% of incidents organizations report are due to employee negligence. The average cost to remediate an incident annually is $6.6 million. The cost of an insider threat can vary depending on the incident type, primarily due to the activities required following an incident. These activities include monitoring, surveillance, investigation, escalation, incident response, containment, ex-post analysis, and remediation [84]. However, with 91% of cyberattacks starting with an email and 24% of physicians unable to distinguish phishing emails, the risk of a breach is high. Therefore, it is crucial to train employees to identify potentially harmful emails. Additionally, employees should be educated on the importance of robust password practices and other security measures, such as avoiding leaving laptops or mobile devices unattended in public spaces.

7.6 MITIGATE CYBERSECURITY THREATS IN TELEHEALTH AND RPM

National standardization organizations are responsible for developing national standards and contributing to the creation of international standards by incorporating best practices. These standards, along with various guidelines and recommendations, are voluntarily adopted by organizations. These practices and objectives are usually related to operational development, which represents proactive strategies. In the realm of cybersecurity, following these practices helps users to improve the reliability, continuity, quality, risk management, and preparedness of an organization's operations, which can include managing and administering cybersecurity or the technical development, maintenance, or usage of information systems, information networks, and ICT services [85]. Many organizations, including hospitals, often take a reactive approach to their cybersecurity measures. This reactive approach involves immediate actions and swift decision-making in response to a cyberattack. By following best practices, hospitals can shift toward proactive cybersecurity methodologies rather than reactive responses.

The National Institute of Standards and Technology (NIST) Framework for Improving Critical Infrastructure Cybersecurity provides a common language for understanding, managing, and communicating cybersecurity risks to both internal and external stakeholders. It facilitates the identification and prioritization of actions for mitigating cybersecurity risks and serves as a means for coordinating policy, business, and technological strategies for risk management. The framework can be applied organization-wide or focused specifically on delivering critical services [86]. Its core comprises a set of activities for achieving specific cybersecurity outcomes, with guidance provided for accomplishing these outcomes. The NIST framework outlines various cybersecurity measures including:

(1) Identifying and managing cybersecurity risks related to systems, personnel, assets, data, and capabilities.
(2) Implementing safeguards for critical service delivery.
(3) Detecting cybersecurity incidents.
(4) Responding to such incidents.
(5) Maintaining resilience and restoring services affected by cybersecurity incidents.

The major activities involved in cybersecurity are divided into review groups such as "access control" or "identification processes." These review groups have subcategories that are further broken down into technical sections and/or management activities. The US Health Care Industry Cybersecurity Task Force collected information from stakeholders and experts across the healthcare sector and identified six key imperatives for improving security in the healthcare industry [87]. The imperatives are as follows:

(1) Define and simplify leadership, governance, and expectations for cybersecurity.
(2) Increase the security and resilience of medical devices and health IT.
(3) Develop the capacity of the healthcare workforce to prioritize cybersecurity awareness and technical capabilities.
(4) Improve cybersecurity education and awareness to enhance the readiness of the healthcare industry.
(5) Identify mechanisms to protect research and development efforts and intellectual property from attacks and exposure.
(6) Enhance information sharing of cybersecurity threats, risks, and mitigations within the healthcare industry.

Including defining leadership and governance in cybersecurity, bolstering the security of medical devices and health IT, developing workforce capacity for cybersecurity, enhancing industry preparedness through awareness and education, protecting research and intellectual property, and improving the sharing of cybersecurity threats and mitigations. Healthcare organizations often struggle with outdated systems, which are vulnerable to numerous cybersecurity threats and lack modern countermeasures [88]. Key cybersecurity measures include:

(1) Network segmentation
(2) Monitoring and intrusion detection
(3) Robust encryption
(4) Access control
(5) Authentication

Clinicians usually use a single-factor authentication method, such as a username and password, to access various computer systems in hospitals. This method is susceptible to cyberattacks due to potential password weaknesses and vulnerability to external threats. NIST SP 800–6355 proposes alternatives to password-based user authentication, including physical tokens or biometrics. In addition, medical devices must be assured for their integrity from both bioengineering and cybersecurity perspectives. It includes authenticating the provider operating the device and accurately identifying the patient authorized for the treatment [86]. Communication between the devices and other healthcare technologies should also be authenticated. However, many hospitals still follow a reactive approach to information security, primarily responding post-incident. Given the high importance of trustworthiness in healthcare, avoiding incidents is crucial because security breaches can compromise both personal health information and patient safety should be well-prepared for potential security incidents with concrete response and recovery plans. The healthcare industry must extend its cybersecurity outreach to all healthcare workforce members through workshops, meetings, conferences, and exercises [61]. Cybersecurity education programs should be developed for decision-makers and executives, emphasizing the importance of cybersecurity as a top management responsibility. Establishing a thorough baseline for trust between patients, clinicians, technologies, processes, and institutions is critical in this holistic cybersecurity strategy.

The rapid advancement in technology requires secure data exchange in various sectors, especially in healthcare. Server security, which includes tools and processes, is critical in protecting vital assets and data within a company's servers. Since servers are central to an organization's IT infrastructure and allow multiple users to access data and functions remotely, they are prime targets for cybercriminals. To create a secure environment, implementing patches in the server's Operating System (OS) is necessary to prevent hackers from exploiting vulnerabilities. An active firewall is crucial for defending against suspicious network traffic, and strict user access controls significantly reduce the risk of security breaches [56]. However, outdated firmware and drivers can lead to significant business losses. The rise of e-health and telehealth has led healthcare organizations to adopt private cloud networks for improved security in data and workload management.

It requires IT professionals to develop robust network designs that comply with privacy standards like HIPAA and governance, risk, and compliance (GRC) frameworks. Obtaining Service Organization Control (SOC) 1 and SOC 2 certifications ensures data security and integrity, which is crucial for operational safety [89].

Healthcare practices have evolved to mitigate potential risks, with solutions addressing specific aspects of the problem. For example, Derriford Hospital's plastic surgery department demonstrated the effectiveness of the store-and-forward telemedicine approach in managing e-health challenges. Similarly, telemedicine has been advocated to improve healthcare quality. The HIPAA of 1996 is instrumental in addressing security issues in telemedicine. Healthcare organizations typically implement foundational security measures such as firewalls, antivirus programs, and VPNs. Advanced security measures, such as Security Information and Event Management (SIEM) and Network Access Control (NAC), are increasingly being adopted to enhance cybersecurity defenses [90]. This integrated approach is crucial for maintaining a secure and efficient digital healthcare environment.

7.6.1 Planning for Legacy System Upgradation

In healthcare, every application, system, patient monitoring devices and technological device will eventually become outdated. To manage this issue, health systems should develop a plan to transition outdated devices until they can be upgraded or replaced. Hardware and software that have reached their end-of-life should not remain within the corporate network, as they are at high risk for cyberattacks. Healthcare organizations should be vigilant about the expiration dates of support for their systems and proactively plan for the replacement of obsolete software and devices. It is crucial to keep all software updated, regardless of the technology systems in use [91]. Healthcare organizations use a variety of software across different departments, with each software performing specific functions. Software developers release updates regularly to address weaknesses and close loopholes found in earlier versions. Ensuring that all software is consistently updated is essential not only for optimal performance but also for safeguarding against cyber threats. Outdated software is a prime target for cybercriminals exploiting known vulnerabilities. When new software updates are available, developers usually notify all users. It is the responsibility of IT administrators to regularly update all software and OS across the organization. This practice is essential to maintain robust IT system security and network defense.

7.6.2 Perform Regular Audits

Audit procedures involve examining how well a healthcare organization adheres to established security standards. This process involves assessing the physical setup of the system, the procedures used to manage information, user behavior, and software security. Regularly performing audits is essential for identifying security issues and weaknesses in the system, establishing a baseline for security to use as a benchmark for future audits, complying with internal and external security regulations, and recognizing redundant resources. Additionally, it helps to ensure that any new or modified information entered into the system is done so by an authorized user and that system access is granted only after identity verification. During an audit, system administrators must confirm that two-factor authentication is implemented, ensure that all users use strong passwords and update them regularly, and review access permissions to ensure that former employees cannot access sensitive data.

7.6.3 Authentication and Access Control

Authentication and access control are critical components of ensuring the security of telehealth systems. Robust authentication methods need to be implemented to ensure that only authorized individuals can gain access. It involves multiple layers of security measures to prevent unauthorized access. One of the primary methods of authentication is multi-factor authentication (MFA). MFA requires users to provide two or more verification factors to gain access. These factors can include something the user knows (such as a password), something the user has (such as a security token or a mobile device), and something the user is (such as a fingerprint or facial recognition). MFA adds an extra layer of security beyond just a username and password. Another advanced method of authentication is biometric verification. This method utilizes unique biological traits of individuals, such as fingerprints, retina scans, voice recognition, or facial recognition. Biometric verification leverages the uniqueness of these biological characteristics, making it extremely difficult for unauthorized users to mimic or replicate. In addition to these methods, it's essential to use unique user IDs and passwords. Passwords should be strong, complex, and regularly updated [92]. They should be a combination of letters, numbers, and special characters, and not easily guessable information like common words or birthdays. Regularly updating passwords helps in mitigating risks associated with password leaks or breaches. Furthermore, access control should be strictly enforced. It means setting permissions and privileges for each user based on their role and necessity of access. For instance, a healthcare provider might have access to a wider range of patient data compared to administrative staff. Regular audits and reviews of these access privileges are also necessary to ensure that they are always up to date and align with the current roles and responsibilities of the users.

7.6.4 Validate and Isolate Backups

Having a remote backup system is a critical aspect of data security management. This type of backup is separated from other backups and is inaccessible from the user-interface level. By implementing such an isolated backup system, security breaches can be mitigated, particularly in the case of ransomware attacks. Ransomware is a type of cyberattack that encrypts files on a hard drive quickly and spreads to other devices within the network. Local backups alone are insufficient in protecting systems and networks from these types of attacks, which is why remote and isolated backups are very important. If data is compromised, having a remote backup available allows organizations to quickly restore their data [93]. Creating a remote backup involves transferring data backups to remote servers within an isolated network, which are accessed sporadically. It is vital to periodically validate and update these backups to ensure their integrity and relevance. This practice enhances data security and also helps ensure the continuity of organizational operations in the face of cyber threats.

7.6.5 Improve Your VPN Encryption

In today's digital age, privacy and security are top concerns for both individuals and businesses alike. One technology that has gained widespread adoption in recent years is Virtual Private Network (VPN), which enables the creation of a private network using public Internet infrastructure. Essentially, a VPN encrypts your Internet connection, making it virtually impossible for anyone to track or monitor your online activities, Figure 7.7 illustrates the VPN security enhancement in details. When it comes to healthcare institutions, safeguarding network details is of utmost importance due to the highly sensitive nature of the data that is transmitted and received. By utilizing a VPN, you can rest assured that your network is completely secure and protected against potential attackers who may try to intercept or monitor your data [94]. This is because the encryption process of a VPN involves disguising your data as it travels through its safe channels, making

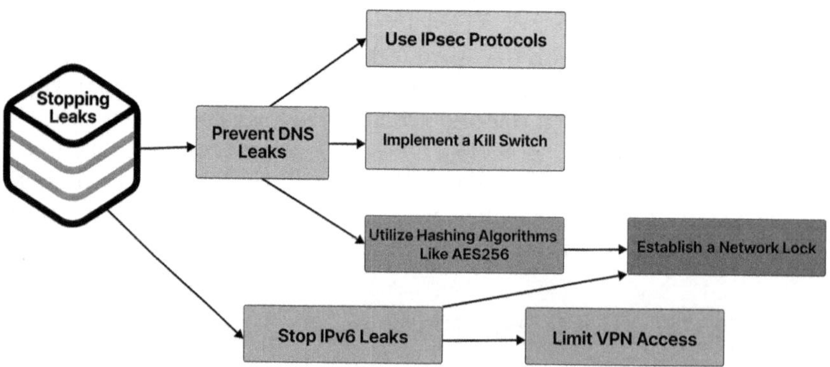

Figure 7.7 VPN security enhancements.

it impossible for anyone to access or decipher it. As a result, healthcare institutions can maintain the highest levels of confidentiality and privacy while ensuring that their network remains secure and protected at all times.

7.6.6 Upgrade Your Security with Effective Endpoint Detection and Response (EDR) Tools

As operations go digital, cybersecurity threats get more complex. To avoid these attacks, advanced security measures are needed to detect and respond to potential threats. Endpoint detection and response (EDR) technology, enhanced system visibility, and network segmentation are some of the most effective ways to protect your network from security threats. EDR technology functions as an alarm system, notifying security teams of any potentially malicious activities or security threats. It enables rapid investigation and neutralization of threats at various endpoints, such as employee workstations, cloud systems, servers, and mobile or IoT devices. One of the most significant benefits of using EDR tools is that they collect and analyze data from endpoints, providing valuable insights into the processes being executed, endpoint communications, and user login activities. Robust EDR tools are essential for detecting and responding to any unusual or suspicious activities as they occur [95]. By leveraging EDR technology, security teams can enhance the overall security posture of their network, ensuring that their organization is protected against cyber threats. Categorization of top EDR tools is illustrated in Figure 7.8.

7.6.7 Migrating to a Virtual Server

Adopting cloud technology for data storage has led to substantial growth in the cloud-based deployment category, with an increase of 158.74% [96]. Organizations can choose between on-site and off-site servers or work with

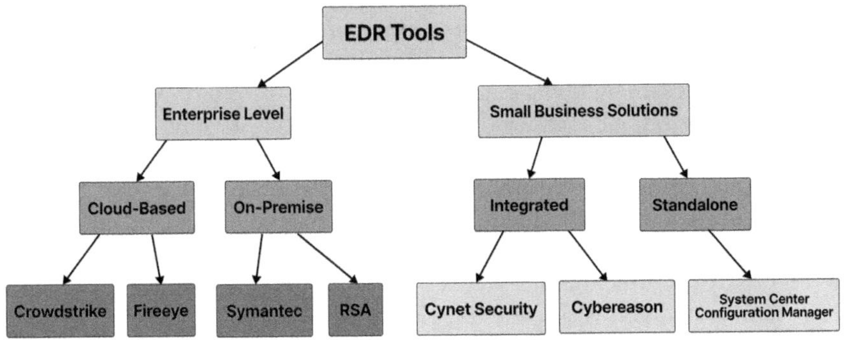

Figure 7.8 Categorization of top EDR tools.

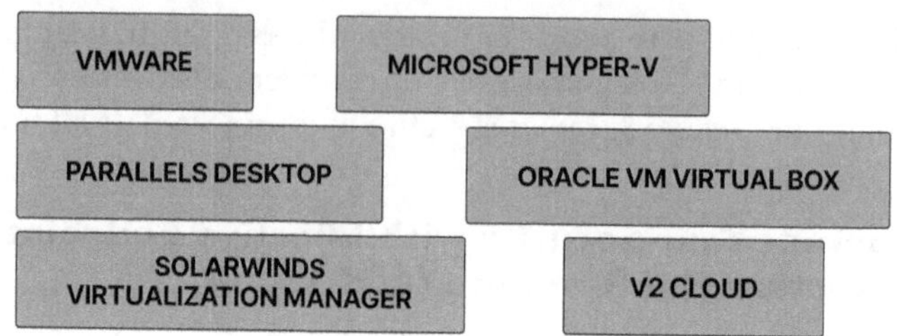

Figure 7.9 Virtualization software options for server migration to virtual server.

cloud service providers based on their needs. Virtual servers, which share hardware and software resources with other OS, emulate the functionality of physical servers. This setup enables the establishment of multiple virtual servers on a single physical server, improving resource allocation and utilization. Virtual servers provide several benefits, such as hardware independence, mobility/failover options, and enhanced disaster recovery capabilities.

For healthcare organizations, transitioning to a virtual server infrastructure is crucial due to its numerous advantages in addressing security concerns. These advantages include the ability to prioritize critical network traffic, enhance network agility, and reduce the workload on IT departments. Healthcare organizations can adopt virtual server technology through industry-standard hypervisors (virtualization software). Hypervisors facilitate the creation and management of virtual servers, providing a scalable and secure platform for healthcare data and systems. Its move to virtual servers is a strategic decision to strengthen data security, enhance system resilience, and ensure consistent uptime in healthcare operations. Figure 7.9 presents some virtualization software options for server migration to virtual servers.

7.6.8 Implementing Two-Factor Authentication

Multi-factor authentication (MFA), also known as two-factor authentication (2FA), is a widely adopted security protocol used by companies to authenticate access to their systems. This protocol is designed to ensure that only authorized individuals can access sensitive information by requiring users to confirm their identity through multiple factors such as passwords, security tokens, biometric data, or personal identification numbers (PINs). Within the healthcare industry, the implementation of two-factor authentication is crucial for compliance with HIPAA regulations and to protect patient, employee, and organizational data [37]. MFA adds an extra layer of security to healthcare IT systems by ensuring that access is granted only to authenticated and verified users. Healthcare organizations can choose to develop their in-house systems or integrate existing pre-constructed tools

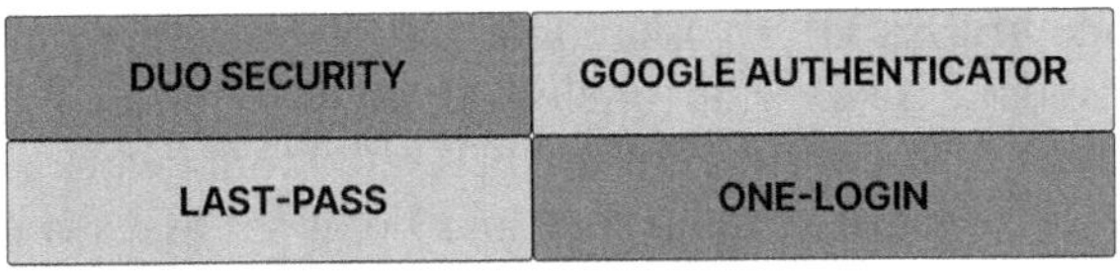

DUO SECURITY	GOOGLE AUTHENTICATOR
LAST-PASS	ONE-LOGIN

Figure 7.10 Essential tools for two-factor authentication.

to incorporate two-factor authentication. These tools may include smart cards, USB tokens, biometric scanners, or mobile authenticator applications. Regardless of the method, the integration of 2FA is an essential step toward enhancing security and safeguarding sensitive healthcare data. Figure 7.10 illustrates some essential 2FA tools.

7.6.9 Industry 4.0 and AI in Healthcare, Enhancing Care, and Cybersecurity

The technological revolution is creating new opportunities for growth and transformation across various sectors. In healthcare and pharmaceuticals, advanced technology is increasingly recognized as essential for improving patient care. AI is a prime example of Industry 4.0 technologies. AI can process and learn from the extensive data prevalent in healthcare, opening up a range of possibilities. Cyber-physical systems, which are used in various applications such as industrial control systems and critical infrastructure, generate, process, and exchange substantial amounts of data that are both security-sensitive and privacy-sensitive. It makes them vulnerable to cyberattacks. The healthcare sector is undergoing a transformation due to Industry 4.0 and its associated technologies, such as the IoT, Cloud and Fog Computing, and Big Data, which are pushing it toward Healthcare 4.0. Industry 4.0 integrates automation, manufacturing, and smart machines, encompassing digitization, IoT, interconnected networks, human supervision, Supervisory Control and Data Acquisition (SCADA) systems, automation robots, valves, sensors, actuators, PLC systems, communication protocols, and cybersecurity [10]. AI is crucial in clinical decision-making, digital information sharing in hospitals, and the development of robust cybersecurity in healthcare environments. AI is defined as machine-exhibited intelligence, encompassing systems that perceive their environment and act to maximize success. It includes cognitive computing, which relies on Deep Learning (DL), ML, natural language processing, and other technologies.

AI and robotics are increasingly integral in healthcare, enhancing expertise and disseminating it widely. Cognitive systems, by learning from top experts, provide increasingly precise responses over time, eventually surpassing human accuracy [42]. AI facilitates outsourced comprehension with advancements, utilizes DL to assimilate collective information, employing digital sensor data to develop intelligent advisors and assistants. A key aspect of cybersecurity solutions is an integrated framework of key security capabilities, with security intelligence and analytics at its core. It involves the analysis of security data from various IT environment aspects, coupled with external information sources, to comprehend threats and attacks. The security infrastructure employs an interconnected network of security capabilities for intelligent detection and response to cyberattacks. IBM's integrated cybersecurity solution is an example of this concept, where analytics is central, providing visibility and defense unattainable by singular security solutions. The MIT Computer Science and Artificial Intelligence Laboratory (CSAIL) and PatternEx have developed an AI2 platform for predicting cyberattacks. This platform has demonstrated significant accuracy improvements in attack detection, achieved by applying clustering algorithms and unsupervised ML to data, followed by confirmation of real attacks by analysts. The inclusion of these results into the platform's models for subsequent datasets enables continual learning and model generation, enhancing the speed and accuracy of cyberattack detection. In a notable application, doctors at the University of Tokyo used IBM Watson to diagnose a 60-year-old woman with a rare form of leukemia, which had previously been misidentified. In just 10 minutes, Watson analyzed the patient's genetic changes against a vast database of cancer research, providing an accurate diagnosis, treatment plan, and medication recommendations [97]. It exemplifies the transformative potential of AI in healthcare, offering precision and efficiency in diagnosis and treatment that was previously unattainable.

7.7 DISCUSSION

Cybersecurity risks are an omnipresent element in contemporary life, necessitating vigilant attention, particularly within healthcare organizations. These organizations are frequently targeted by cybercriminals due to their access to a diverse and valuable array of information, ranging from personal health records to financial data. The scale of a healthcare organization does not determine its vulnerability; rather, any information system handling patient records, integrating medical devices, or encompassing other subsystems is susceptible to cyber threats. Empirical evidence indicates that even the most fortified systems are not impervious to cyberattacks. There is a continuous evolution and sophistication in cyberattack strategies, placing an imperative on health institutions to prioritize investments in cybersecurity. It not only safeguards patient welfare but also upholds their fundamental role in health service provision. Historical data on cyberattacks against healthcare entities should inform the formulation of cybersecurity strategies in these organizations. Essential investment areas for enhancing a healthcare organization's cyber resilience summary is given below.

(1) Authentication and access control is crucial to verify user identities and ensure appropriate access privileges. Strong authentication methods need to be implemented.
(2) Network security to protecting the telehealth network infrastructure is vital. It involves implementing firewalls, intrusion detection systems, and security patches.
(3) Incident response and recovery to establish protocols to detect, respond to, and recover from cybersecurity incidents is essential. It includes having response plans, security audits, and disaster recovery mechanisms in place.
(4) Utilizing advanced encryption, regular data backups, and access controls are key strategies to manage data breaches.
(5) Implementing anti-ransomware tools, frequent data backups, and incident response plans are critical to mitigate the risks posed by ransomware.
(6) Training employees to recognize phishing attempts and using email filters can help prevent phishing attacks.
(7) Implementing strict access controls, regularly monitoring user activities, and training employees are necessary to address insider threats.
(8) Regular software updates, anti-malware tools, and network security measures are essential for combating malware.
(9) Securing IoT devices with passwords, conducting regular software updates, and implementing network segmentation can protect against vulnerabilities in IoT devices.
(10) The US Health Care Industry Cybersecurity Task Force recommends defining and simplifying leadership governance for cybersecurity, enhancing the security of medical devices and health IT, developing workforce capacity for cybersecurity, increasing industry readiness through cybersecurity education and awareness, protecting research and development, and improving information sharing of cybersecurity threats within the healthcare industry.
(11) Take additional measures like network segmentation, monitoring and intrusion detection, robust encryption, access control, and authentication are also key components of a comprehensive cybersecurity strategy.
(12) Employee readiness for cyber threats through awareness and cyber hygiene.
(13) Identification of vulnerabilities through risk assessments and ongoing monitoring.
(14) Development of a response strategy encompassing training, preparedness, and communication.

Table 7.9 Cybersecurity Threats in Telehealth and RPM with Corresponding Mitigation Strategies

Cybersecurity Threat	*Mitigation Strategy*
Data breaches	Use of advanced encryption, regular data backups, and access controls
Ransomware	Implementation of anti-ransomware tools, frequent data backups, and incident response plans
Phishing attacks	Employee training on recognizing phishing attempts, use of email filters
Insider threats	Strict access controls, regular monitoring of user activities, employee training
Malware	Regular software updates, anti-malware tools, network security measures
Unsecured IoT devices	Securing IoT devices with passwords, regular software updates, network segmentation

Promising best practices in combating cyber threats involve understanding the organization's assets and preparing for the inevitability of an attack. It includes categorizing resources as critical infrastructure, creating data backups, and formulating a system backup strategy. Regular expert assessments of cybersecurity risks and constant monitoring are crucial. It may include implementing basic cyber protection at the network level, continuous employee training, and routine system vulnerability tests. Furthermore, reinforcing employee knowledge and skills through ongoing training in cyberattack prevention, recognition, and incident reporting is vital. Establishing downtime procedures and ensuring resource availability for swift organizational response during disruptions is also critical. Maintaining external backups of essential information and fostering effective coordination and communication with various stakeholders are key strategies. Recognizing vulnerabilities in all devices and technologies used within the organization and ensuring suppliers adhere to cybersecurity standards is essential. Finally, establishing and perpetually enhancing a cybersecurity culture within the organization, including regular checks of cyber hygiene practices and realistic simulations of cyber threats, is paramount. Communication protocols with patients and staff in the event of cyber incidents should prioritize brand protection and risk mitigation, aligning with law enforcement recommendations.

7.8 FURTHER RECOMMENDATIONS

To prevent future data breaches and avoid the financial burdens they bring, healthcare facilities must adopt the use of specialized and skilled third-party

IT and infrastructure service providers, rather than relying on traditional managed service providers (MSPs). These providers can handle the complex cloud and IT management tasks, allowing companies to focus on their core competency. In today's constantly evolving tech landscape, new "as a service" providers are emerging daily, and choosing the right agency can be crucial to business success. Here are a few types of providers to consider:

(1) **Managed Communication Services:** This kind of service provider is responsible for implementing and overseeing a comprehensive unified communications infrastructure that includes messaging software, VoIP (Voice over Internet Protocol), and mobile data services, along with email and video conferencing solutions. A well-designed communication system, whether it is hosted or on-premise, can empower you to communicate efficiently, particularly if you have remote offices and mobile users. With a single solution that manages your business communications effectively and economically, you can streamline your operations and enhance your productivity.
(2) **Managed Cloud Infrastructure:** Managed Cloud infrastructure services offer a reliable and secure way of moving your company's operations from a traditional data center to a flexible and highly available cloud environment. These services provide a range of essential solutions, including migration, configuration, optimization, security, and ongoing maintenance of your cloud resources and infrastructure. As a result, businesses can streamline their cloud networking, improve application interoperability, and simplify database management. By entrusting your cloud infrastructure, application stacks, and tools to these experts, you can enjoy the peace of mind that your business is running optimally and efficiently while avoiding the complexities of managing cloud infrastructure in-house. Plus, managed cloud services are typically delivered as a service for a fixed monthly fee, making them a cost-effective solution for businesses of all sizes.
(3) **Managed Networks and Infrastructure:** Modern businesses rely heavily on technology to streamline their operations and stay competitive. This is where IT infrastructure comes in. MSPs offer a wide range of IT infrastructure services to help businesses design, upgrade, and deploy systems that support their growth and success. These services cover everything from hardware and software to networks and data management. A good IT infrastructure MSP takes on the task of managing your entire network. They establish local area networks (LAN), wireless access points (WAPs), firewall solutions, and data backups to ensure your data is safe and secure. They also offer reporting and data analytics services, providing you with valuable insights into your business operations. By taking the responsibility for all network tasks, IT infrastructure MSPs allow you to focus on your core business while they ensure durability and uptime.

(4) **Managed Security Service Providers (MSSPs):** If you are looking for a comprehensive security solution for your organization, then look no further than a managed security service provider (MSSP). This service covers a wide range of security infrastructure needs, including anti-malware options and backup and disaster recovery (BDR) solutions. By partnering with an MSSP, you can rest assured that you will receive real-time alerts if any security incidents occur, and that your organization will be protected by a range of defensive measures such as firewalls, virtual private networks, data encryption, intrusion detection systems, authentication protocols, and more. An MSSP is the perfect catch-all solution for any organization looking for a reliable and comprehensive security service.
(5) **Managed Support Services:** This type of service is designed to offer round-the-clock technical assistance to businesses in need of help desk support. Typically, the staff comprises of experienced engineers and other skilled personnel who are available to provide assistance at any time, or during specific pre-agreed hours. While larger corporations may have the resources to manage such services internally, smaller businesses often lack the budget, expertise, or bandwidth to do so, and therefore opt to outsource their support desk to an MSP. It not only allows them to free up their in-house IT teams to focus on more critical, revenue-generating projects, but also enables them to benefit from the assurance of an iron-clad service level agreement, which significantly improves the overall user experience.
(6) **Data Center as a Service (DCaaS):** There are two types of data center services—one is known as Infrastructure as a Service (IaaS), which provides virtualized computing resources like servers, storage, and networking infrastructure to clients. The second type, called Data Center as a Service (DCaaS), involves the provision of physical data center infrastructure and facilities to clients. This type of service enables data center operators to run efficient data center controls and improve data center infrastructure planning and design. By outsourcing to a service provider, companies can avoid logistical and budgetary problems related to their on-site data centers. Data Center as a service provider often offers Data Center Infrastructure Management (DCIM) services, which help safeguard the performance and integrity of the core data center components. A competent DCIM team ensures that everything stays connected, from change management and capacity planning to software integration and data analysis and reporting. This way, businesses can focus on their core operations without worrying about the technical aspects of their data center infrastructure.

Healthcare organizations face numerous options for enhancing system and network security and managing potential threats. However, the level of expertise required to mitigate these threats often necessitates the involvement of professional services. Assigning the task of system security management to an external agency relieves internal teams from the burden of data and network security, allowing them to focus on medical-related tasks. Based on our analysis of the approach used to manage cybersecurity in the healthcare industry, we highly recommend the adoption of specialized data center infrastructure management and application migration support tailored to meet healthcare needs. These strategies are crucial in combating data breaches through advanced structures with enhanced security levels and training in best practices. We strongly advise healthcare organizations to prioritize the following key elements when managing their cybersecurity: uplink, firewall, switches, hosts, VMs configuration, and storage. These elements play a critical role in handling sensitive data like personal health information records and tackling challenges in database environmental architecture, scalability, data volume, complexity, and decentralization management. Furthermore, we recommend the adoption of a well-defined system architecture that contributes to improved data quality, information governance, and data management. Healthcare organizations should consider working with IT and engineering experts to develop efficient stacks that address critical database issues, including aspects like load balancing, platform production space, routing layer, data layer, hosting console, and platform system console for device configurations requiring high availability. Furthermore, we strongly recommend that healthcare organizations adopt a comprehensive approach to managing cybersecurity that prioritizes specialized data center infrastructure management and application migration support, as well as strategic planning and implementation of key elements and well-defined system architecture.

7.9 CONCLUSION

This chapter sheds light on the significance of addressing cybersecurity challenges that arise in the context of telehealth and RPM. As these technologies are becoming more integrated into healthcare delivery, the risks associated with cybersecurity also increase, threatening the privacy and safety of patient records. Therefore, it is crucial to adopt a vigilant and proactive approach to deal with these challenges. To combat these risks, this chapter proposes a multi-pronged strategy that emphasizes the continuous development and implementation of advanced cybersecurity technologies, which can detect and prevent attacks in real-time. Additionally, adapting healthcare policies to keep up with technological advancements is equally important to establish a secure and reliable healthcare infrastructure. Moreover, this chapter highlighted the need for ongoing training and education for healthcare professionals and patients to recognize and mitigate cybersecurity risks effectively. It includes educating patients on how to protect their personal information, such as passwords, and how to identify and report suspicious emails or messages. Healthcare professionals must also be trained to handle sensitive data, follow secure protocols, and identify potential vulnerabilities in the system. Ultimately, ensuring the security and efficacy of telehealth and RPM services is vital in maintaining patient trust and upholding the standards of modern healthcare in an increasingly digital world. An effective cybersecurity strategy can help healthcare organizations prevent data breaches, safeguard sensitive patient information, and maintain the confidentiality and integrity of healthcare services.

REFERENCES

1. V. Garg and J. Brewer, "Telemedicine security: A systematic review," *Journal of Diabetes Science and Technology*, vol. 5, no. 3, pp. 768–777, 2011.
2. O. Ali, A. G. Hajduczok, and J. P. Boehmer, "Remote physiologic monitoring for heart failure," *Current Cardiology Reports*, vol. 22, pp. 1–10, 2020.
3. F. Tettey, S. K. Parupelli, and S. Desai, "A review of biomedical devices: classification, regulatory guidelines, human factors, software as a medical device, and cybersecurity," *Biomedical Materials & Devices*, pp. 1–26, 2023.
4. A. Dimitrievski, T. Loncar-Turukalo, and V. Trajkovik, "Securing patient information in connected healthcare systems in the age of pervasive data collection," in *2023 IEEE International Mediterranean Conference on Communications and Networking (MeditCom)*. IEEE, 2023, pp. 29–33.
5. HIPAA, "HIPAA privacy rule and disclosures of information relating to reproductive health care," 2022. [Online]. Available: https://www.hhs.gov/hipaa/for-professionals/privacy/guidance/phi-reproductive-health/index.html.
6. HIPAA, "Resource for health care providers on educating patients about privacy and security risks to protected health information when using remote communication technologies for telehealth," 2023. [Online]. Available: https://www.hhs.gov/hipaa/for-professionals/privacy/guidance/resource-health-care-providers-educating-patients/index.html.
7. M. S. Jalali, A. Landman, and W. J. Gordon, "Telemedicine, privacy, and information security in the age of COVID-19," *Journal of the American Medical Informatics Association*, vol. 28, no. 3, pp. 671–672, 2021.
8. I. B. Ida, A. Jemai, and A. Loukil, "A survey on security of IoT in the context of eHealth and clouds," in *2016 11th International Design & Test Symposium (IDT)*. IEEE, 2016, pp. 25–30.
9. G. M. Insights, "Patient monitoring devices market size by product (cardiac monitoring devices, neuromonitoring devices, anesthesia monitor, hemodynamic monitoring devices, fetal and neonatal monitoring, multiparameter devices), type, end-use & forecast, 2020–2027," 2024. [Online]. Available: https://www.gminsights.com/industry-analysis/patient-monitoring-devices-market.
10. S. Dilek, H. Çakır, and M. Aydın, "Applications of artificial intelligence techniques to combating cyber crimes: A review," *arXiv preprint* arXiv:1502.03552, 2015.
11. A. Esther Omolara, A. Jantan, O. I. Abiodun, H. Arshad, K. V. Dada, and E. Emmanuel, "HoneyDetails: A prototype for ensuring patient's information privacy and thwarting electronic health record threats based on decoys," *Health Informatics Journal*, vol. 26, no. 3, pp. 2083–2104, 2020.

12. D. M. Dhabarde, M. P. Maske, J. R. Baheti, and H. V. Shahare, "A telehealthcare system for diagnosis and treatment of patients during a pandemic," in *Handbook of Research on Artificial Intelligence and Soft Computing Techniques in Personalized Healthcare Services*. Apple Academic Press, 2024, pp. 279–299.
13. A. Hummelholm, "E-health systems in digital environments," in *Proceedings of the European Conference on Information Warfare and Security*. Academic Conferences International, 2019.
14. M. Hasib, *Cybersecurity in Healthcare: A National Study of HIPAA Implementation*. Tomorrow's Strategy Today, 2022.
15. M. Martin-Khan, S. Freeman, K. Adam, and G. Betkus, "The evolution of telehealth," *Mobile e-Health*, pp. 173–198, 2017.
16. M. J. Field, "Telemedicine: A guide to assessing telecommunications for health care," 1996.
17. S. H. Aronson, "The Lancet on the telephone 1876–1975," *Medical History*, vol. 21, no. 1, pp. 69–87, 1977.
18. R. L. Bashshur and G. W. Shannon, *History of Telemedicine: Evolution, Context, and Transformation*. Mary Ann Liebert, Inc., Publishers, 2009.
19. M. Alawida, A. E. Omolara, O. I. Abiodun, and M. Al-Rajab, "A deeper look into cybersecurity issues in the wake of Covid-19: A survey," *Journal of King Saud University-Computer and Information Sciences, vol. 34*, no. 10, pp. 8176-8206, 2022.
20. J. A. Greene, *The Doctor Who Wasn't There: Technology, History, and the Limits of Telehealth*. University of Chicago Press, 2022.
21. R. L. Bashshur, E. A. Krupinski, J. H. Thrall, and N. Bashshur, "The empirical foundations of teleradiology and related applications: A review of the evidence," *Telemedicine and e-Health*, vol. 22, no. 11, pp. 868–898, 2016.
22. A. Vladzymyrskyy, M. Jordanova, and F. Lievens, "A century of telemedicine: Curatio Sine Distantia et Tempora," *Sofia, Bulgaria*, 2016.
23. S. Gogia, "Rationale, history, and basics of telehealth," in *Fundamentals of Telemedicine and Telehealth*. Elsevier, 2020, pp. 11–34.
24. R. S. Bakalar, "Telemedicine: its past, present and future," in *Healthcare Information Management Systems: Cases, Strategies, and Solutions*. Springer, 2022, pp. 149–160.
25. C. R. Doarn, "Technological advances making telemedicine and telepresence possible," *Telemedicine, Telehealth and Telepresence: Principles, Strategies, Applications, and New Directions*, pp. 257–271, 2021.
26. H. S. Lallie *et al.*, "Cyber security in the age of COVID-19: A timeline and analysis of cyber-crime and cyber-attacks during the pandemic," *Computers & Security*, vol. 105, p. 102248, 2021.
27. W. Auyporn, K. Piromsopa, and T. Chaiyawat, "Critical factors in cybersecurity for SMEs in technological innovation era," in *ISPIM Conference Proceedings*. The International Society for Professional Innovation Management (ISPIM), 2020, pp. 1–10.
28. F. Adeyoju, "Cybercrime and cybersecurity: FinTech's greatest challenges," *Available at SSRN 3486277*, 2019.
29. C. Netherlands, "Less traditional crime, more cybercrime," *Retrieved December*, vol. 15, p. 2022, 2020.

30. R. Khweiled, M. Jazzar, and D. Eleyan, "Cybercrimes during COVID-19 Pandemic," *International Journal of Information Engineering & Electronic Business*, vol. 13, no. 2, 2021.
31. M. Yar, "The novelty of 'cybercrime': An assessment in light of routine activity theory," *European Journal of Criminology*, vol. 2, no. 4, pp. 407–427, 2005.
32. D. R. Cressey, "Other people's money; a study of the social psychology of embezzlement," 1953.
33. S. Zeadally, J. T. Isaac, and Z. Baig, "Security attacks and solutions in electronic health (e-health) systems," *Journal of Medical Systems*, vol. 40, pp. 1–12, 2016.
34. M. Kompara and M. Hölbl, "Survey on security in intra-body area network communication," *Ad Hoc Networks*, vol. 70, pp. 23–43, 2018.
35. HHS.GOV, "Notification of enforcement discretion for telehealth remote communications during the COVID-19 nationwide public health emergency," 2021. [Online]. Available: https://www.hhs.gov/hipaa/for-professionals/special-topics/emergency-preparedness/notification-enforcement-discretion-telehealth/index.html.
36. B. Edwards, S. Hofmeyr, and S. Forrest, "Hype and heavy tails: A closer look at data breaches," *Journal of Cybersecurity*, vol. 2, no. 1, pp. 3–14, 2016.
37. T. H. Journal, "Healthcare industry has highest number of reported data breaches in 2021," *The HIPAA Journal*, 2021. [Online]. Available: https://www.hipaajournal.com/healthcare-industry-has-highest-number-of-reported-data-breaches-in-2021/.
38. K. Jercich, "Nevada hospital ransomware attack could affect data of 1.3M patients," 2021. [Online]. Available: https://www.healthcareitnews.com/news/nevada-hospital-ransomware-attack-could-affect-data-13m-patients.
39. N. A. Khan, S. N. Brohi, and N. Zaman, "Ten deadly cyber security threats amid COVID-19 pandemic," TechRxiv IEEE , *Authorea Preprints*, 2023.
40. S. Nifakos *et al.*, "Influence of human factors on cyber security within healthcare organisations: A systematic review," *Sensors*, vol. 21, no. 15, p. 5119, 2021.
41. A. J. Cartwright, "The elephant in the room: Cybersecurity in healthcare," *Journal of Clinical Monitoring and Computing*, pp. 1–10, 2023.
42. B. Kelly, C. Quinn, A. Lawlor, R. Killeen, and J. Burrell, "Cybersecurity in Healthcare," in *Trends of Artificial Intelligence and Big Data for E-Health*. Springer, 2023, pp. 213–231.
43. A. Garcia-Perez, J. G. Cegarra-Navarro, M. P. Sallos, E. Martinez-Caro, and A. Chinnaswamy, "Resilience in healthcare systems: Cyber security and digital transformation," *Technovation*, vol. 121, p. 102583, 2023.
44. T. Marjanov, M. Konstantinou, M. Jóźwiak, and D. Spagnuelo, "Data Security on the Ground: Investigating Technical and Legal Requirements under the GDPR," *Proceedings on Privacy Enhancing Technologies*, vol. 3, pp. 405–417, 2023.
45. K. T. Smith, L. M. Smith, M. Burger, and E. S. Boyle, "Cyber terrorism cases and stock market valuation effects," *Information & Computer Security*, 31 (4), 385-403, **2023**.
46. T. M. Dorn, *US Critical Infrastructure: Its Importance and Vulnerabilities to Cyber and Unmanned Systems*. Page Publishing Inc, 2023.
47. S. Alder, "December 2023 healthcare data breach report," 2024. [Online]. Available: https://www.hipaajournal.com/december-2023-healthcare-data-breach-report/.

48. R. Southwick, "These are the 11 biggest health data breaches of 2023," 2024. [Online]. Available: https://www.chiefhealthcareexecutive.com/view/these-are-the-11-biggest-health-data-breaches-of-2023.
49. N.Schwartz,"11millionpatientsmaybeaffectedinHCAdatatheft,"2023.[Online]. Available: https://www.beckershospitalreview.com/cybersecurity/11-million-patients-may-be-affected-in-hca-data-theft.html#:~:text=An%20unauthorized%20party%20stole%20patient,news%20release%20provided%20to%20Becker's.
50. Pj&A, "Pj&A yber Incident Notice," 2023. [Online]. Available: https://www.documentcloud.org/documents/24168644-pja-transcription-firm-data-breach-notice.
51. R. Southwick, "Data breaches are down, but number of people affected is rising," 2023. [Online]. Available: https://www.medicaleconomics.com/view/data-breaches-are-down-but-number-of-people-affected-is-rising.
52. B. Toulas, "Ransomware gang steals data of 5.8 million PharMerica patients," 2023. [Online]. Available: https://www.bleepingcomputer.com/news/security/ransomware-gang-steals-data-of-58-million-pharmerica-patients/.
53. M. Watch, "Console & Associates, P.C.: HealthEC reports data breach exposing social security numbers of 4.4 million patients at 17 healthcare providers," 2024. [Online]. Available: https://www.marketwatch.com/press-release/console-associates-p-c-healthec-reports-data-breach-exposing-social-security-numbers-of-4-4-million-patients-at-17-healthcare-providers-14fd69eb#:~:text=3%2C%202024-,MARLTON%2C%20N.J.%2C%20Jan.,the%20healthcare%20software%20company%20HealthEC.
54. S. Alder, "Records of 4 million coloradans compromised in MOVEit transfer attack," 2023. [Online]. Available: https://www.hipaajournal.com/records-of-4-million-coloradans-compromised-in-moveit-transfer-attack/.
55. R. Southwick, "California medical group discloses ransomware attack, more than 3 million affected," 2023. [Online]. Available: https://www.chiefhealthcareexecutive.com/view/california-medical-group-discloses-ransomware-attack-more-than-3-million-affected.
56. H. I. Security, "This year's largest healthcare data breaches," 2023. [Online]. Available: https://healthitsecurity.com/features/this-years-largest-healthcare-data-breaches.
57. S. Alder, "Pixel use results in impermissible disclosure of the PHI 3.1 million cerebral platform users," 2023. [Online]. Available: https://www.hipaajournal.com/cerebral-impermissible-disclosure-pixel-3170000/.
58. M. N. Sadiku, U. C. Chukwu, and J. O. Sadiku, "Cybersecurity in healthcare," *European Journal of Modern Medicine and Practice*, vol. 3, no. 6, pp. 22–29, 2023.
59. IBM, "Fight back against data breaches," 2023. [Online]. Available: https://www.ibm.com/reports/data-breach?mhsrc=ibmsearch_a&mhq=IBM%20Cost%20of%20data%20breach%20report%202021.
60. T. H. Journal, "Healthcare data breach statistics," *The HIPAA Journal*, 2023. [Online]. Available: https://www.hipaajournal.com/healthcare-data-breach-statistics/.
61. H. T. Neprash *et al.*, "Trends in ransomware attacks on US hospitals, clinics, and other health care delivery organizations, 2016–2021," (in eng),

JAMA Health Forum, vol. 3, no. 12, p. e224873, Dec 2 2022, doi: 10.1001/jamahealthforum.2022.4873.

62. ocrportal.hhs.gov, "Cases currently under investigation," 2024. [Online]. Available: https://ocrportal.hhs.gov/ocr/breach/breach_report.jsf.
63. F. H. Security, "Report on the state of cybersecurity in healthcare 2024," 2023. [Online]. Available: https://fortifiedhealthsecurity.com/wp-content/uploads/2024/01/Fortified_2024_Horizon-Report.pdf.
64. verizon, "Healthcare NAICS 62," 2022. [Online]. Available: https://www.verizon.com/business/resources/reports/dbir/2022/healthcare-data-breaches/.
65. HHS.GOV, "2022 healthcare cybersecurity year in review, and a 2023 look-ahead," 2023. [Online]. Available: https://www.hhs.gov/sites/default/files/2022-retrospective-and-2023-look-ahead.pdf.
66. S. Alder, "October 2023 healthcare data breach report," 2023. [Online]. Available: https://www.hipaajournal.com/october-2023-healthcare-data-breach-report/.
67. Verizon, "2023 data breach investigations report: Frequency and cost of social engineering attacks skyrocket," 2023. [Online]. Available: https://www.verizon.com/about/news/2023-data-breach-investigations-report.
68. F. B. o. Investigation, "Internet crime complaint center (IC3)," 2022. [Online]. Available: https://www.ic3.gov/.
69. A. I. Newaz, A. K. Sikder, M. A. Rahman, and A. S. Uluagac, "A survey on security and privacy issues in modern healthcare systems: Attacks and defenses," *ACM Transactions on Computing for Healthcare*, vol. 2, no. 3, pp. 1–44, 2021.
70. A. Wright, S. Aaron, and D. W. Bates, "The big phish: Cyberattacks against US healthcare systems," *Journal of General Internal Medicine*, vol. 31, pp. 1115–1118, 2016.
71. D. P. Paul III, N. Spence, N. Bhardwa, and C. D. PH, "Healthcare facilities: Another target for ransomware attacks," 2018.
72. P. D. Professor Stuart E. Madnick, "The continued threat to personal data: Key factors behind the 2023 increase," 2023. [Online]. Available: https://www.apple.com/newsroom/pdfs/The-Continued-Threat-to-Personal-Data-Key-Factors-Behind-the-2023-Increase.pdf.
73. N. Spence, D. P. Paul III, and A. Coustasse, "Ransomware in healthcare facilities: the future is now," 2017.
74. H. T. Neprash *et al.*, "Trends in ransomware attacks on US hospitals, clinics, and other health care delivery organizations, 2016–2021," *JAMA Health Forum*, vol. 3, no. 12: American Medical Association, pp. e224873-e224873, 2022.
75. C. D. o. Insurance, "Anthem data breach," 2021. [Online]. Available: https://www.insurance.ca.gov/0400-news/0100-press-releases/anthemcyberattack.cfm.
76. Z. Wenhua *et al.*, "A lightweight security model for ensuring patient privacy and confidentiality in telehealth applications," *Computers in Human Behavior*, p. 108134, 2024.
77. S. C. Sethuraman, V. Vijayakumar, and S. Walczak, "Cyber attacks on healthcare devices using unmanned aerial vehicles," *Journal of medical systems*, vol. 44, no. 1, p. 29, 2020.
78. R. K. Kodali, G. Swamy, and B. Lakshmi, "An implementation of IoT for healthcare," in *2015 IEEE Recent Advances in Intelligent Computational Systems (RAICS)*. IEEE, 2015, pp. 411–416.

79. N. Sharma, B. Allardyce, R. Rajkhowa, A. Adholeya, and R. Agrawal, "A substantial role of agro-textiles in agricultural applications," *Frontiers in Plant Science*, vol. 13, p. 895740, 2022.
80. S. Selvaraj and S. Sundaravaradhan, "Challenges and opportunities in IoT healthcare systems: A systematic review," *SN Applied Sciences*, vol. 2, no. 1, p. 139, 2020.
81. A. H. Seh *et al.*, "Healthcare data breaches: Insights and implications," *Healthcare*, vol. 8, no. 2: MDPI, p. 133, 2020.
82. P. Khatiwada, M. A. Fauzi, B. Yang, P. Yeng, J.-C. Lin, and L. Sun, "Threats and risk on using digital technologies for remote health care process," in *Proceedings of the 8th International Conference on Sustainable Information Engineering and Technology*, acm 2023, pp. 506–522.
83. M. Mehrtak *et al.*, "Security challenges and solutions using healthcare cloud computing," (in eng), *Journal of Medicine and Life*, vol. 14, no. 4, pp. 448–461, July–August 2021, doi: 10.25122/jml-2021-0100.
84. P. Institute, "2022 cost of insider threats global report," 2022. [Online]. Available: https://www.proofpoint.com/sites/default/files/threat-reports/pfpt-us-tr-the-cost-of-insider-threats-ponemon-report.pdf.
85. J. Pöyhönen, "Cyber security of an electric power system in critical infrastructure," in *Cyber Security: Critical Infrastructure Protection*. Springer, 2022, pp. 217–239.
86. M. Lehto, P. Neittaanmäki, J. Pöyhönen, and A. Hummelholm, "Cyber security in healthcare systems," in *Cyber Security: Critical Infrastructure Protection*. Springer, 2022, pp. 183–215.
87. P. H. Emergency, "Health care industry cybersecurity task force," 2017. [Online]. Available: https://www.phe.gov/preparedness/planning/cybertf/documents/report2017.pdf.
88. ENISA, "Cyber security and resilience for smart hospitals," 2016. [Online]. Available: https://www.enisa.europa.eu/publications/cyber-security-and-resilience-for-smart-hospitals.
89. P. Sikdar, *Strong Security Governance Through Integration and Automation: A Practical Guide to Building an Integrated GRC Framework for Your Organization*. CRC Press, 2021.
90. H. Meagher and L. L. Dhirani, "Cyber-resilience, principles, and practices," in *Cybersecurity Vigilance and Security Engineering of Internet of Everything*. Springer, 2023, pp. 57–74.
91. Z. Irani, R. M. Abril, V. Weerakkody, A. Omar, and U. Sivarajah, "The impact of legacy systems on digital transformation in European public administration: Lesson learned from a multi case analysis," *Government Information Quarterly*, vol. 40, no. 1, p. 101784, 2023.
92. P. K. Dhillon and S. Kalra, "Multi-factor user authentication scheme for IoT-based healthcare services," *Journal of Reliable Intelligent Environments*, vol. 4, pp. 141–160, 2018.
93. A. Tahir *et al.*, "A systematic review on cloud storage mechanisms concerning e-healthcare systems," *Sensors*, vol. 20, no. 18, p. 5392, 2020.
94. M. B. Younes and N. N. El-Emam, "Information security and data management for IoT smart healthcare," in *Intelligent Internet of Things for Smart Healthcare Systems*. CRC Press, 2023, pp. 69–80.

95. S. Rangaraju, "Secure by intelligence: Enhancing products with AI-driven security measures," *EPH-International Journal of Science and Engineering*, vol. 9, no. 3, pp. 36–41, 2023.
96. P. Harbor, "2021 data breach for trend report," 2021. [Online]. Available: https://protectedharbor.com/healthcare-data-trend-report/.
97. IBM, "What is cybersecurity?" 2023. [Online]. Available: https://www.ibm.com/topics/cybersecurity.

Chapter 8

Optimum Transportation Scheme for Healthcare Supply Chain Management

Lokesh Sakamuri, Sai Chandana Thiruvuru, Rohit Gupta Kunala, Siva Swetha Vennapusa, Kartheek Pusala, Vijay Ramasamy, Amirtharjan R and Padmapriya Pravinkumar

8.1 RELATED WORK AND BACKGROUND

Most individuals require blood at some time either for themselves or for their loved ones. In fact, every two seconds, someone needs a blood transfusion to fight cancer, recover from surgery and survive a horrible accident. Without a safe, dependable blood supply chain, many medical miracles that are taken for granted would be impossible. Blood is required in most situations, but fewer than 1 in 20 people regularly donate blood; volunteers or donors can give blood at hospitals, blood centres and blood camps.

The healthcare sector has a major impact on blood supply chain management. Blood donation is an important operation sequence to fulfil the blood platelet requirements. Blood platelet is a component of the blood that is majorly used for blood clotting, which is used in the treatment of cancer, trauma, dengue, platelet dysfunction, bone marrow transplants, low blood platelets level and so on. As these blood platelets have a lower life span, hospitals in healthcare sector must get the blood platelets as per their requirement. Generally, blood platelets are collected in two different ways; one is the traditional method of collection, and the other is the Apheresis method. In the traditional method, the donors give blood in blood facility units which take a few hours to separate the blood platelets from the blood. The Apheresis method is different from the traditional one; at the time of collection, the platelets are directly separated from the other blood, which is time-saving but costly compared to the traditional one.

The next step in healthcare supply chain management is transporting the blood platelets from blood facility units to the blood centre, as shown in Figure 8.1. The blood centre not only stores the platelets but also performs several tests on the platelets to validate them as per the demands and requirements of the hospitals. The major obstacle in the platelets supply chain is the blood platelets' decaying nature and lower life span. According to the national health services, blood and transplant authority single donation can benefit either three adults or 12 children.

According to the World Health Organization (WHO), blood units required by the health sector are fulfilled by blood collection from one percent of the

DOI: 10.1201/9781003470038-8

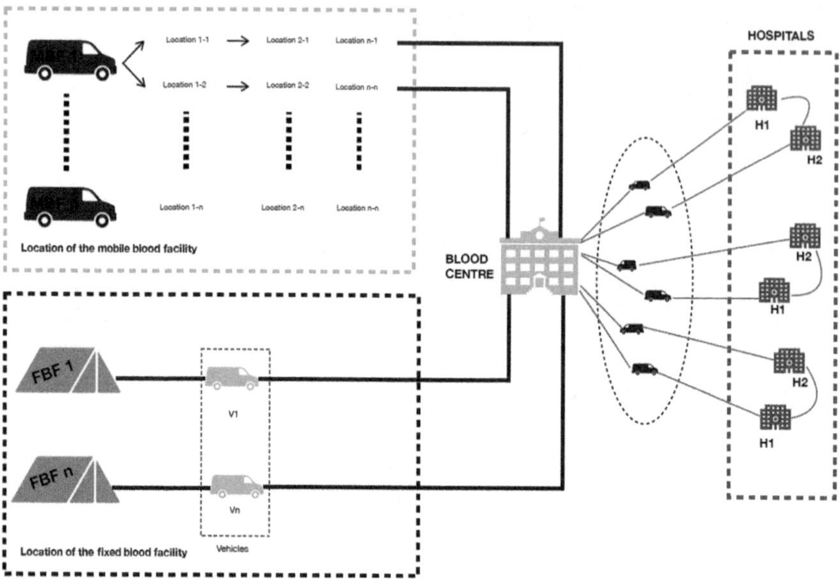

Figure 8.1 Supply chain network of platelets.

whole population. In India, approximately 14.56 million units of blood are required for clinical purposes [1]. Figure 8.2 provides the statistics about the amount of blood collected. Still, the quantity of blood units collected doesn't reach the clinical evaluation of the blood requirement in India.

To meet this requirement, more donors should be ready for blood donation. Blood wastage should be avoided by adopting supply chain management (SCM) practices in the health sector to ensure blood is used before it decays.

SCM can be carried out by creating awareness about the significance of blood donation and supply. The required amount of blood units can be supplied to the hospitals by locating an optimal location for the fixed blood facility closer to the locations of the donors based on their choice and by providing an optimum path for the mobile blood facility to ensure hospitals are getting the required blood units in a short time without blood wastage.

8.1.1 Blood Facility Centres

The blood facility units gather blood from donors at shorter distances are considered and transferred to a blood centre. If the blood facility units are absent, donors should donate their blood to the blood centres. Blood facility units are of two categories. They are fixed blood facility (FBF) and mobile blood facility (MBF).

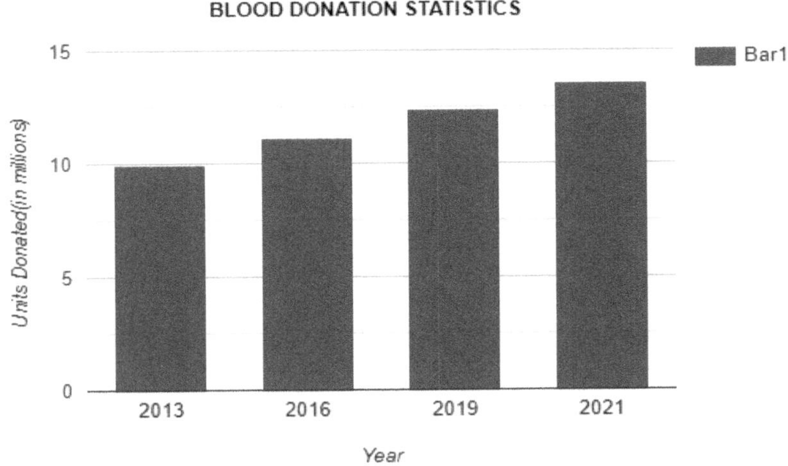

Figure 8.2 Blood donation statistics in India [based on 1].

8.1.1.1 Fixed Blood Facility

The blood facility unit is arranged closer to the location of multiple donors. First, the donors reach this fixed blood facility unit to donate their blood; later, it is transported to the blood centre for further processing.

8.1.1.2 Mobile Blood Facility

A vehicle travels to the donor location in the mobile blood facility unit. It collects the blood from donors covering multiple locations and transports it to the blood centre for processing.

8.1.1.3 Blood Centre

Blood collected in the blood facility units is deposited in the blood centre. Further, based on the demands and requirements of various hospitals, various tests are performed on the platelets, stored in the inventory and distributed to the hospitals, as shown in Figure 8.3.

8.2 INTRODUCTION

Low cost and efficient energy can be achieved by finding an optimum supply chain for blood platelets. The optimum supply chain can be found by generating an optimum path for MBF and finding an optimum location for FBF. W. J. Guerrero et al. [2] studied the articles published in 2005 related to

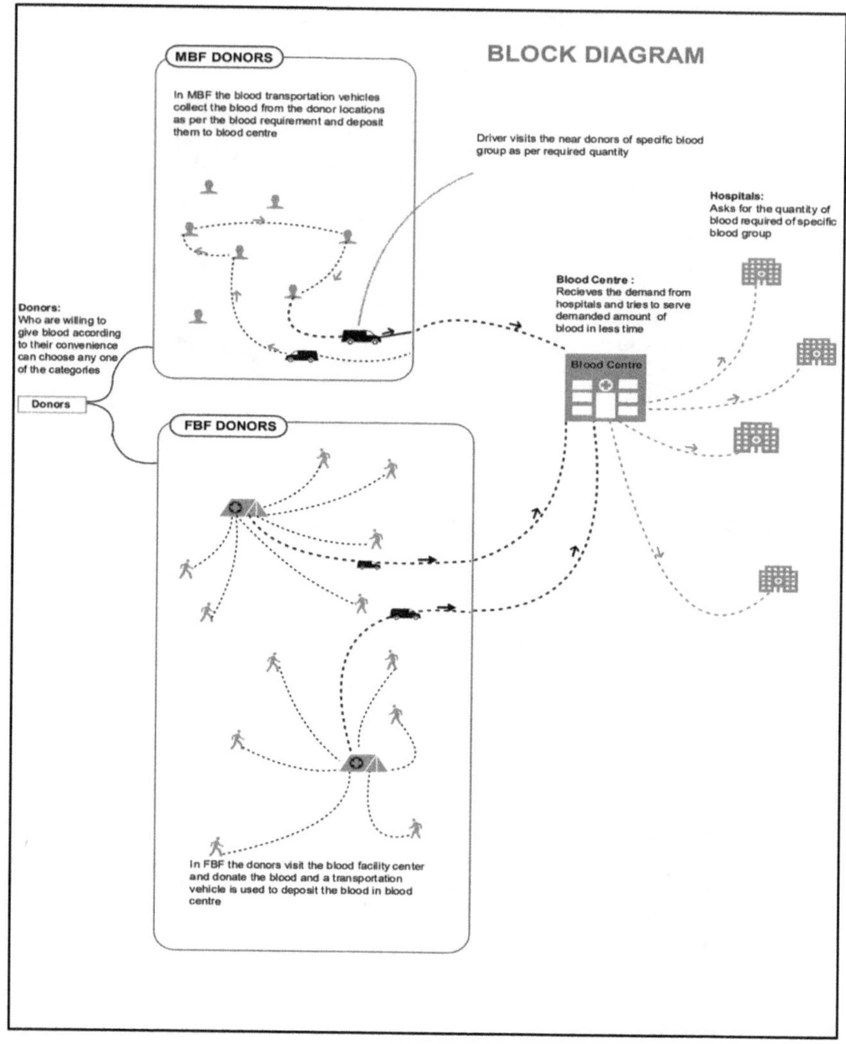

Figure 8.3 Block representation of the proposed optimum SCM to handle blood platelets.

the blood supply chain. They studied around 104 articles. The papers were classified based on the algorithms, characteristics of the blood supply chain and planning. B. Zahiri et al. [3] addressed a distribution network design. For designing a cost-efficient network which makes decisions considering the optimal locations. Hadi Mokhtari et al. [4] studied the healthcare supply chain of blood platelets; considering the equipment used for transportation, they proposed a closed-loop supply chain.

Mohammad et al. [5] designed a blood supply chain network by proposing a new mathematical model. Different transportation types are considered in this model for transporting the blood between blood donor groups, blood collection facilities, laboratories, blood centres and hospitals. Masoud Rabbani et al. [6] created a solution to produce platelets by proposing two models. In the first model, the location of mobile facilities was studied. Hamed Nozari et al. [7] designed a blood supply chain network modelled by considering platelets' lifetime. They provided an objective function to minimise the cost of the whole supply chain. Finally, Sule Itir Satoglu et al. [8] proposed a mathematical model that determines the location of mobile facilities to collect the blood during each period in a natural catastrophe and supply the blood required to the hospitals in the disaster region.

Ayad Hendalianpour et al. [9] proposed a mathematical model to curtail the cost of maintaining the inventory levels, the necessity of the supply capacity, and the shortage of blood by introducing the transportation of the product between the blood centres. Mohammad Reza Ghatreh Samani et al. [10] introduced a programming modular approach to reduce the costs required to maintain an inventory. Multiple costs are included in a supply chain. Saeed Yaghoubi et al. [11] proposed a model to curtail the costs involving diffusion and scarcity. The platelets are collected based on the age that the class of the patient requires to improve the transfusion of platelets in the clinical points. Hadis Derikvand et al. [12] proposed a random probabilistic distribution programming model where the objectives are used to reduce the diffusion and scarcity costs involved in the supply chain and to improve the interrelation between the hospitals.

Milad Abolghasemian et al. [13] proposed a linear programming approach where the objectives of the collection of blood units should be augmented and reduce the time dealing with the transportation of the mobile blood facility vehicles and aerial vehicles to transfer the blood to the demand points. R. Tavakkoli-Moghaddam et al. [14] considered blood groups, facility centres and the expiration of donated blood to develop a blood supply chain network. They proposed a model to curtail the cost required to sustain the supply chain and the inimical effects caused by transportation between the blood facilities. The cessation date of the blood and type of blood groups is considered. Platelets required for several patients suffering from various diseases were focused on by Saeed Yaghoubi et al. [15]. Mir Saman Pishvaee et al. [16] designed a blood supply chain network considering blood group comparability. A mathematical model is developed for the total cost minimisation and maximisation of unsatisfied demand.

A model was developed by Mohammad Reza Ghatreh Samani et al. [17] to design an integrated blood supply chain for disaster relief. That model accounts for the uncertain demands, irregular supply, perishability of blood products and shortage avoidance, and this model concentrates on three major issues: efficiency, responsiveness and effectiveness. Saeed Yaghoubi et al. [18] formulated a problem of RBC under uncertain supply and demand. The proposed model application is investigated with a case study. The objective was mainly to minimise the total costs such as transportation, transshipment, substitution and inventory. Masoud Rabbani et al. [19] proposed a strategy to deal with uncertainties. The issue of transferring blood products from neighbourhood blood banks to demand locations, such as hospital blood banks. The requirement of blood platelets in India and the necessity of SCM are the healthcare industry's requirements to prevent unnecessary emergencies [1, 20–22]. Table 8.1 compares the available literature with the proposed optimisation model.

Table 8.1 Comparison of the Proposed Model with Available Literature [2–19]

Literature	*Highlights*	*Limitations*
1	A brief overview of around 104 articles published from 2005 to 2014 related to the blood supply chain was highlighted.	It does not propose any method to achieve an optimum blood supply chain.
14	The model was proposed to create awareness about blood donation among the public.	It does not consider the cost into account for creating awareness.
2, 5, 9, 16 and 17	Proposed a model to make decisions for optimal locations and routing, and it is cost-effective.	Does not consider the lifetime of blood platelets and the unused blood samples.
3, 4, 8, 12 and 13	Proposed a model to curtail the cost required to sustain the supply chain.	Does not consider optimal locations for blood facilities.
6, 10, 11 and 18	Considered platelet's lifetime and provided an objective function to minimise cost.	Does not provide any registration choice for donors.
7 and 15	An optimum path was generated between the donor locations under uncertain conditions.	It does not provide an effective algorithm for optimal locations, and costs were not taken into account.
Proposed Model A website is created to get the details of donors and hospitals and to show the locations of donors and hospitals on Google maps.	The optimum location for FBF is found, and optimum path for MBF is generated. The details of registered donors under either FBF or MBF are displayed in the blood centre web page table format.	An acknowledgement can be sent to the registered donors regarding the optimum location for FBF donors and the appropriate time of transportation vehicle arrival to the MBF donors.

The highlights of the proposed model are:

- Optimum location from locations of registered FBF donors is calculated so that it is near to all the registered FBF donors.
- Optimal path from the locations of registered MBF donors is generated so that the blood transportation vehicle can visit all the MBF donors within the optimum time.
- Optimal location is calculated by sorting a 2D array which is obtained by calculating the distances between every FBF donor location.
- Optimal path is generated using the nearest neighbour algorithm.
- The generated path is displayed in the MBF map using Google Application Program Interface (API).
- The path generated between the blood centre and the registered hospital is displayed in the hospital map using Google API.
- The locations of registered donors and hospitals are marked on the maps using separate markers.
- The details of registered donors and hospitals are stored and displayed.

8.3 SYSTEM REQUIREMENTS

The implementation of the suggested website complies with Microsoft Windows 11 on a laptop with an x64-based PC which uses AMD Ryzen 5 4500U from the 11th generation with 8 GB RAM. VS Code version 1.67.2, Node.js version 16.13.0, and NPM version 6.14.15 were used. Similarly, react JS with the version of 18.1.0 along with internal packages like react-dom with version of 18.1.0, react-router-dom with version of 6.3.0, react-hook-form with version of 7.30.0, react-scripts with version of 5.0.1, react-select with version of 5.3.1, react-table with version of 7.7.0 and react-typed with version of 1.2.0 are utilised. Additionally, Material UI with version 5.6.4, material-ui/core with version of 4.12.4, material-ui/icons with version of 4.11.3, mui/icons-material with version of 5.8.0 with other internal packages like mui/x-data-grid-pro, mui/x-data-grid-generator and mui/data-grid with version of 5.10.0 are used. Google Maps API, react-google-maps version 2.11.8 has been used for the proposed model.

8.4 METHODOLOGY

In the platelets supply chain, hospitals request the amount of blood under a specific blood group to the blood centre. Along with quantity, the blood centre must collect basic details like hospital name, location and age. After getting the demand from the hospital, the blood centre will search for donors.

Hence, donors play a crucial role in platelet supply chain management. Donors need to notify the blood centre before donating their platelets. Basic details like first name, last name, age, blood group, mobile number, location and facility choice of donors need to be collected to proceed further. After getting the details from both the hospitals and donors, the details need to be stored.

8.4.1 Modelling of the Blood Platelet SCM

In this platelet supply chain, the hospitals will raise demands primarily by broaching the required blood quantity. The blood centre will collect the blood after receiving the respective demands from the hospitals.

The blood is collected from the fixed and mobile blood facilities and deposited in the blood centre. The blood can be collected from the blood centre itself. The total blood collected and deposited in the blood centre can be calculated using the following expressions:

$$\mathrm{F} = \sum_{i=1}^{N1} Q_i; \quad \mathrm{M} = \sum_{i=1}^{N2} Q_i; \quad \mathrm{B} = \sum_{i=1}^{N3} Q_i$$

where

Q_i = Quantity of blood collected from the ith donor
F = Amount of blood collected in fixed blood facility
N1 = Number of donors registered under fixed blood facility
M = Amount of blood collected in mobile blood facility
N2 = Number of donors registered under mobile blood facility
B = Amount of blood collected in blood Centre
N3 = Number of donors registered under blood Centre

The total amount of blood collected by the blood centre can be determined using

$$\mathrm{T} = \mathrm{F} + \mathrm{M} + \mathrm{B}$$

T = Total amount of blood deposited in the blood centre

After the collection of blood from the fixed blood facility, it should be deposited in the blood centre. To accomplish this necessity, transportation vehicles are to be used for depositing the blood.

The process of determining the optimal location for a fixed blood facility implicitly includes the transportation cost, as finding the optimal location involves finding the distances between the locations.

$$\mathrm{Fc} = \sum_{i=1}^{N} d_i * C$$

where

F_C = Transportation cost from fixed blood facilities to the blood centre
N = Number of fixed blood facilities
d_i = Distance between ith fixed blood facility and the blood centre
C = Cost of fuel per kilometre

Determining the optimal location and optimal path involves calculating the distances between each and every location, for which two different graph algorithms are utilised A*, and Dijkstra algorithms are used to determine the minuscule distance between the locations. Finding the optimal path for the mobile blood facility also includes the transportation costs, as determining the optimal path again involves the calculation of distances between the locations. The transportation cost for a mobile blood facility to reach the blood centre can be found using

$$\mathrm{Mc} = \sum_{i=1}^{N2+1} d_i * \mathrm{C}$$

where

F_C = Transportation cost for mobile blood facility to reach the blood centre
di = Distance between ith location and $(i-1)$th location in the route
N_2 = Number of donors registered under mobile blood facility
C = Cost of fuel per kilometre

After collecting and depositing blood in the blood centre, blood is to be delivered to the hospitals as per their demands. To transport the blood, multiple routes will be determined where each route will be including multiple hospitals. The transportation cost for delivering the required blood to hospitals through multiple routes can be found using

$$\mathrm{Hc} = \sum_{i=0}^{R} \sum_{j=1}^{Ni+1} d_j * \mathrm{C}$$

where

H_C = Total transportation cost for depositing blood from the blood centre to the hospitals
R = Number of routes
Ni = Number of hospitals in the ith route
d_1 = Distance between blood centre and the first hospital in the route
dj = Distance between jth and $(j-1)$th hospitals
d_{N^i+1} = Distance between the last hospital on the route and the blood centre
C = Cost of fuel per kilometre

8.4.2 Case Study

In the proposed model, the Nellore district from Andhra Pradesh is chosen with one fixed blood facility, one mobile blood facility, one blood centre, 10 hospitals, 15 donor locations and three blood transportation vehicles as shown in Table 8.2.

In the Nellore district, 10 hospitals were taken into consideration. The locations of the selected hospitals are shown in Table 8.3, along with their latitudes and longitudes.

Table 8.2 Data Considered in Case Study

FBF	*MBF*	*BC*	*Hospitals*	*Donor Locations*	*Vehicles*
1	1	1	10	15	3

Table 8.3 Hospital Locations with Its Latitude and Longitude

Hospital Name and Location	*Latitude*	*Longitude*
Vijaya Hospital, Pogathota	14.4490	79.9832
KIMS Hospital, Ambedkar Nagar	14.4344	79.9682
Apollo Hospitals, Ramji Nagar	14.4383	79.9926
Narayana Hospital, Chinthareddy Palem	14.4464	79.9830
Vijaya Care Hospital, Rama Murthy Palem	14.4521	79.9878
Rainbow Super Speciality Hospital, Brindavan Colony	14.4520	79.9859
Simhapuri Hospital, Balaji Nagar	14.4481	79.9953
Lotus Hospital, Pogathota	14.4486	79.9847
St. Joseph Hospital, Santhapet	14.4576	79.9830
Jayabharath Hospital, Somasekhara Puram	14.4450	79.9832

In the same way, 15 locations were selected as donor locations as shown in Table 8.4. The locations were shown in the above table along with their latitudes and longitudes. One location is selected for blood centre along with donor and hospital locations. The location is shown in Table 8.5 along with its latitude and longitude.

Donors may be under FBF or MBF based on their choice. For the donors under FBF, an optimal location based on their locations must be determined. Then, all FBF donors must assemble to donate their blood in that optimal location. And for the donors under MBF, an optimal path must be generated based on their locations. The blood transportation vehicle needs to follow the optimal path and collect the blood from MBF donors and deposit in the blood centre.

8.4.3 Optimum Location

The methods used to find optimal location and optimal path are not the same. Hence, two different approaches must be followed to determine the optimal path and location.

8.4.3.1 Optimal Location for FBF

After getting the locations of FBF donors, the distance between every location needs to be calculated and those distances were taken into a matrix format. After estimating the distances, sorting is performed to determine the

Table 8.4 Donor Locations with Their Latitude and Longitude

Donor Location	*Latitude*	*Longitude*
Chemudugunta	14.3777	79.9291
Kakutur	14.3605	799291
Kumkumpudi	14.3785	79.9137
Padarupalli	14.3993	79.9626
Kallurpalli Rural	14.3805	79.9584
Golagamudi	14.3519	79.9759
Kanuparthipadu	14.3819	79.9920
Sportello Presto	14.4136	79.9861
Ambapuram	14.4163	79.9221
Akkacheruvupadu	14.4390	79.9165
Ogurupadu	14.4337	79.9317
Vengalrao Nagar	14.4172	79.9445
Kottur	14.4107	79.9438
Ayyappa Swamy Temple	14.4030	79.9500
Ganga Bhavani Temple, Kanuparthipadu	14.3932	79.9823

Table 8.5 Blood Centre Location

Blood Centre Location	*Latitude*	*Longitude*
Vedayapalem	14.4155	79.9587

optimal location. The matrix needs to be sorted in both row and column to finalise the optimal location.

Considering A, B, C and D as FBF donor locations, the distances between each and every location (Figures 8.4–8.7) are calculated and shown in Table 8.6.

To begin with, the distances in each row are sorted and every value of each row is compared to each value of the next row. If the next row value is lesser than the current row, then rows need to be swapped. When a row gets swapped, then row-wise sorting again starts from the first row.

Now the first column shows the optimal locations order-wise. So the first location in the column will be the optimal location. Hence C is the optimal location for the considered scenario, as shown in Table 8.7.

8.4.3.2 Optimal Path for MBF

For MBF, a path needs to be found to collect the blood from MBF donors in optimal time. To satisfy this criterion, an optimum path needs to be found. The number of possible paths will increase as will the number of donor locations.

Number of possible paths = ${}^{n}P_{n}$, where n is the number of MBF donors

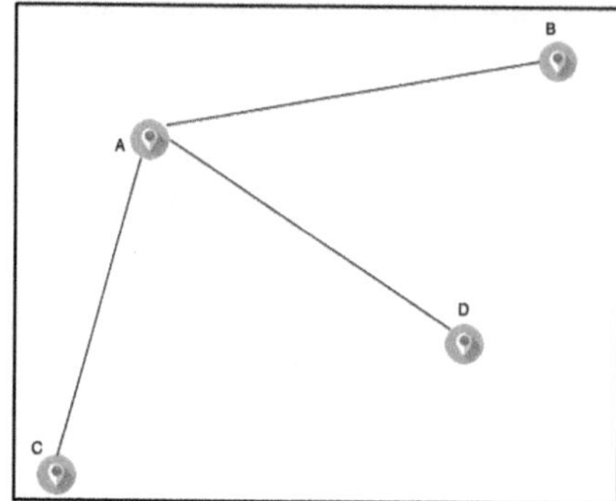

Figure 8.4 Distances of other locations from A.

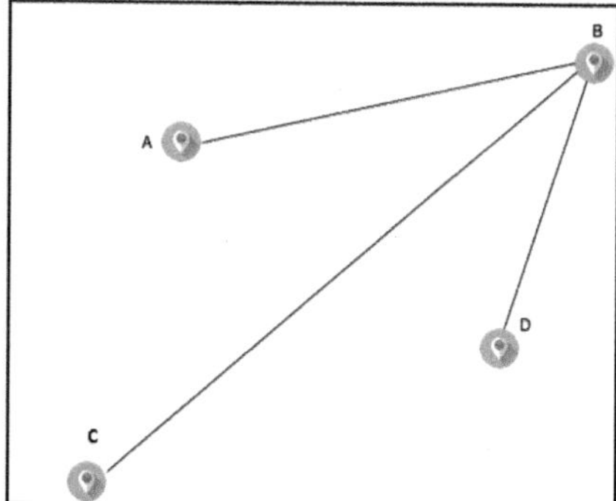

Figure 8.5 Distances of other locations from B.

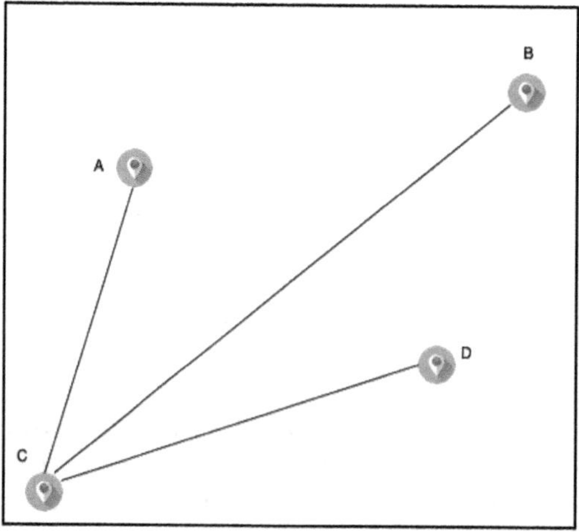

Figure 8.6 Distances of other locations from C.

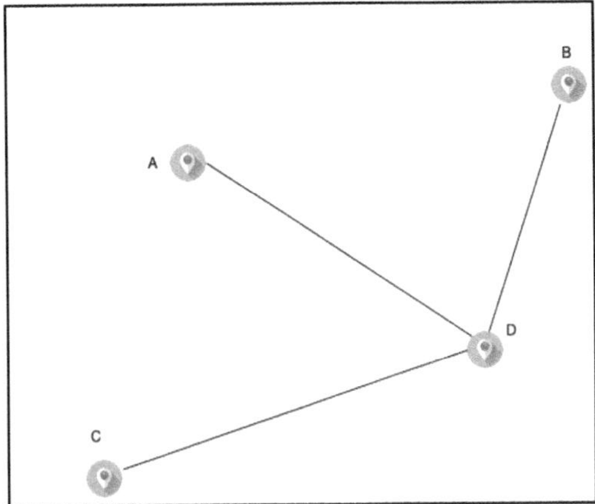

Figure 8.7 Distances of other locations from D.

Table 8.6 Distance Matrix of Locations ABCD

Locations	*A*	*B*	*C*	*D*
A	0	7472	1756	4062
B	7484	0	5803	7288
C	1756	5790	0	2380
D	4057	7295	2375	0

Table 8.7 Optimal Location Matrix

C	0	1756	2380	5790
A	0	1756	4062	7472
D	0	2375	4057	7295
B	0	5803	7288	7484

For example, if there are four MBF donors, then there would be 24 ($^4P_4$) possible paths. A distance matrix is found for the registered MBF donors, and the blood centre is considered the starting point, and then the nearest location among the four is chosen as the next arriving point.

As shown in Figure 8.8, the nearest location to A (blood centre) is the location which is at a distance of 1562 m and it is denoted as B. Hence, the blood transportation vehicle will visit that first and collect the blood from the donor. Now, the vehicle is at B; the nearest location from B is at a distance of 1650 m which is marked as C. In the same way, this process continues until all the MBF donors are covered. Then, finally, the blood transportation vehicle will deposit the blood at the blood centre as shown in Figures 8.9, 8.10 and 8.11. Figure 8.12 shows the final optimal path the

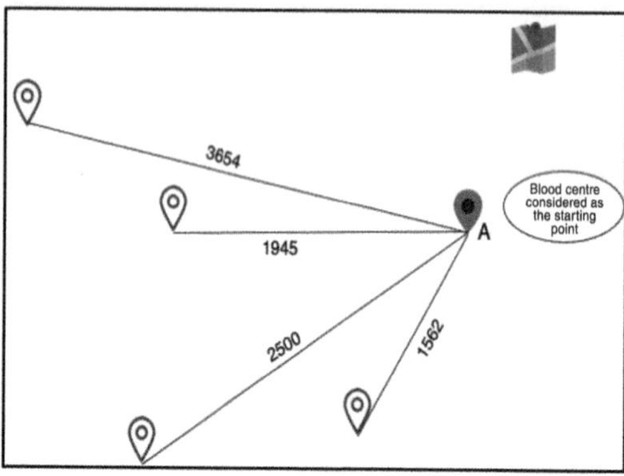

Figure 8.8 Distances from MBF locations to BC.

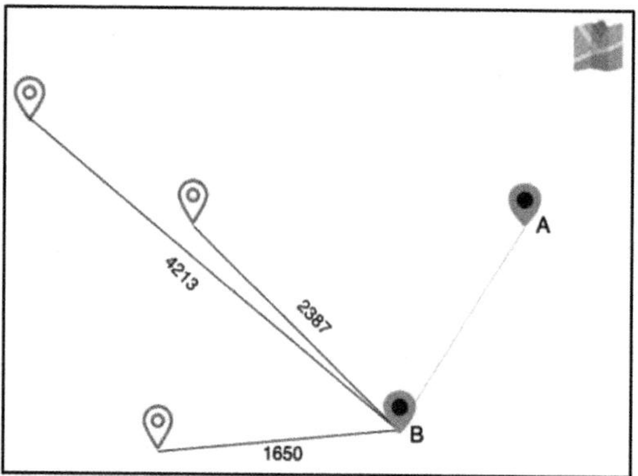

Figure 8.9 Path from A to B.

blood transportation vehicle needs to follow to collect the blood from MBF donors in the optimum time.

8.5 RESULTS AND DISCUSSION

The proposed methodology has been implemented using technologies like react, maps and UI material. To get the requirements like donor details and hospital details, a web page would be more convenient where users can register and view many details about the blood donation irrespective of their location.

A donor will know the location of FBF, and the transportation vehicle operator will know the path of MBF and the path of the registered hospitals from the blood centre. For designing the website's frontend, react framework, HTML, CSS and material ui are used, and for backend design, python flask framework has been utilised.

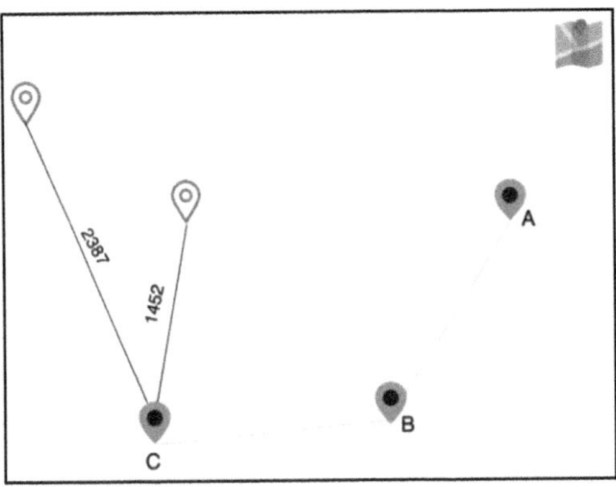

Figure 8.10 Path from B to C.

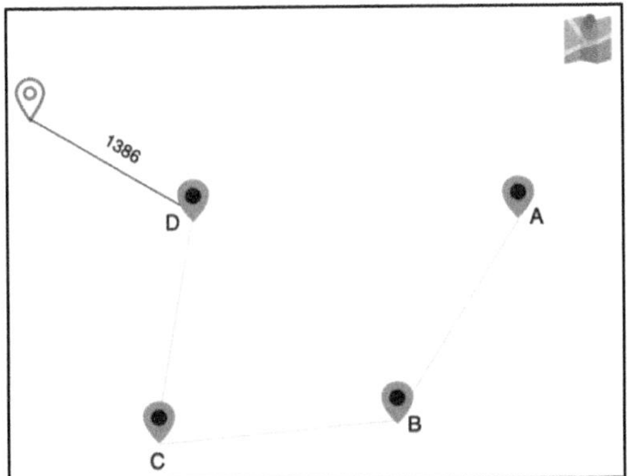

Figure 8.11 Path from C to D.

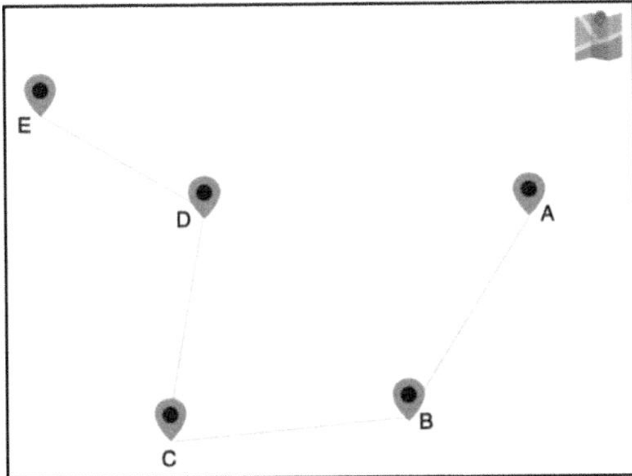

Figure 8.12 Optimal path for MBF locations.

The name of the website is Offer Life. When a user visits the website, the home page is visible for the user and the main parts of the home page are about, maps for users, navigations for donor registration, hospital registration, blood centre details and related FAQ's as shown in Figures 8.13–8.15, respectively. The proposed methodology and the code is uploaded in GITHUB: https://github.com/rohitkunala/bloodcenter.

8.5.1 Registration Pages

There are mainly two registration pages created in the website: One is for donor registration and another is for hospital registration.

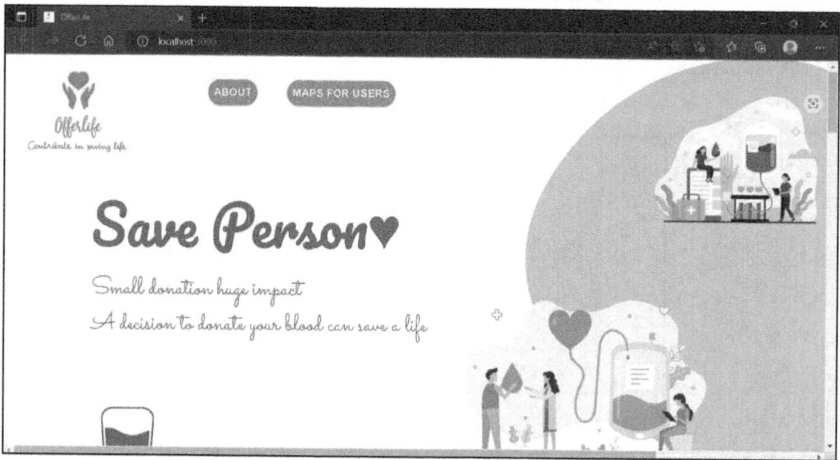

Figure 8.13 Home page of the website for platelet SCM.

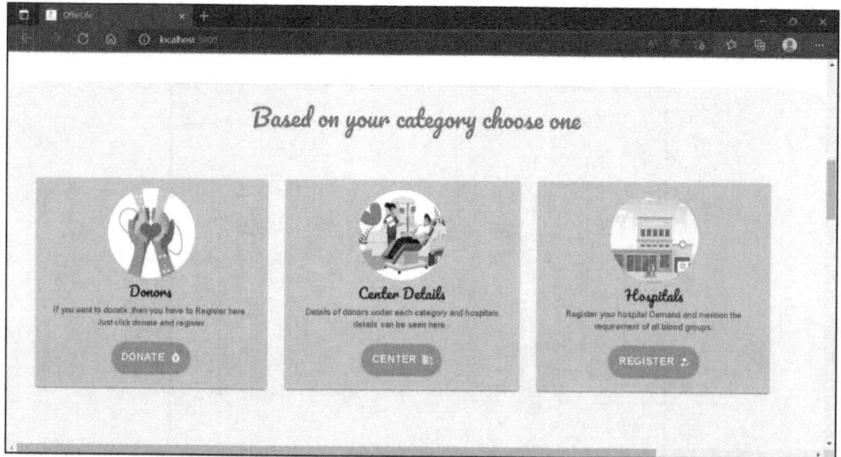

Figure 8.14 Category selection page at Offer Life.

8.5.1.1 Donor Registration

When a user clicks on the donate button on home page, the user will be redirected to donor registration page as shown in Figure 8.16. When a donor clicks on register button after giving all the necessary required details, a backend call will be sent, and the details are stored.

8.5.1.2 Hospital Registration

When a hospital clicks on the register button on home page, the user will be redirected to hospital demand registration page as shown in Figure 8.17.

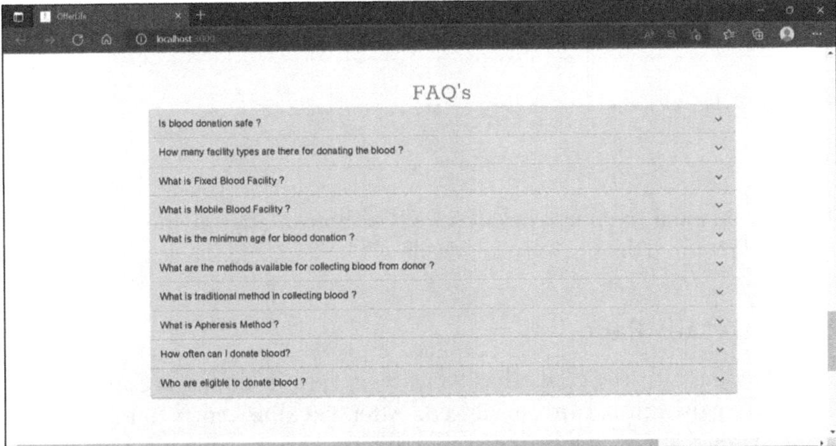

Figure 8.15 FAQ's related to blood donation.

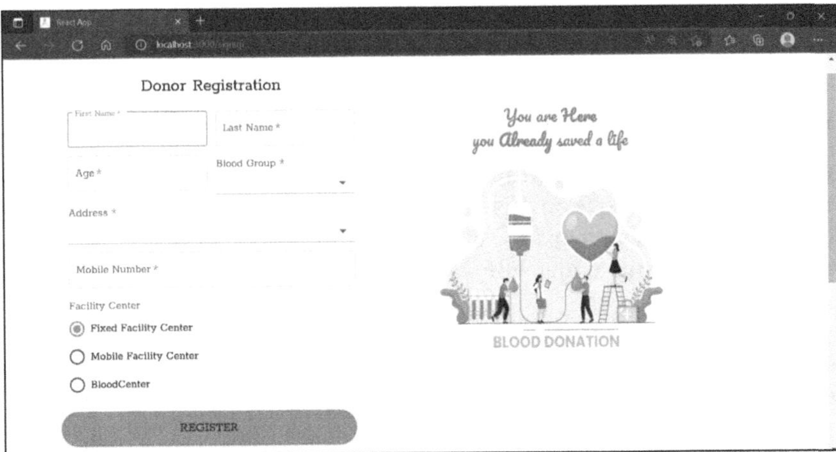

Figure 8.16 Donor registration page created in website.

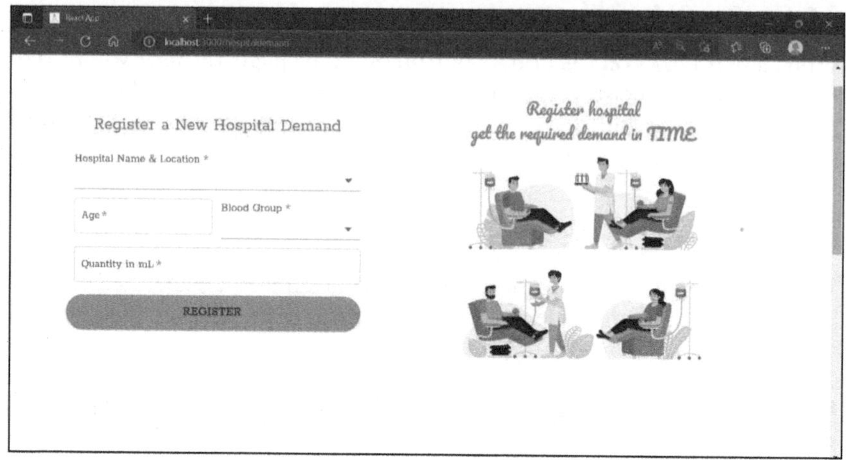

Figure 8.17 Hospital registration page created at the website.

When a hospital member clicks on register button after giving all the necessary and required details, a backend call will be sent, and the details are stored.

8.5.2 Details Page

In this page, all the details that were registered in donor registration and hospital registration can be viewed. After clicking centre button on the home page, the user will be redirected to blood centre subpage. On this subpage, four cards and one demand button regarding the registrations of both donors and hospitals can be viewed.

As there are three facility choices on the donor registration page, three cards are created to view the details of each category, and the last card is used to view all the details together, as shown in Figure 8.18.

8.5.3 Google Maps for Users

Google Maps for users is created to view the locations of donors and hospitals. When a user clicks on this button, the user is redirected to another web page which displays maps for FBF, MBF and hospitals. When the donors register their details under FBF category, their details are stored as shown in Figure 8.19.

The locations of the registered donors will be marked on the map. It is shown in Figure 8.20. From these locations, the distance between each and every location is calculated. Finally, it is displayed in a table as shown in

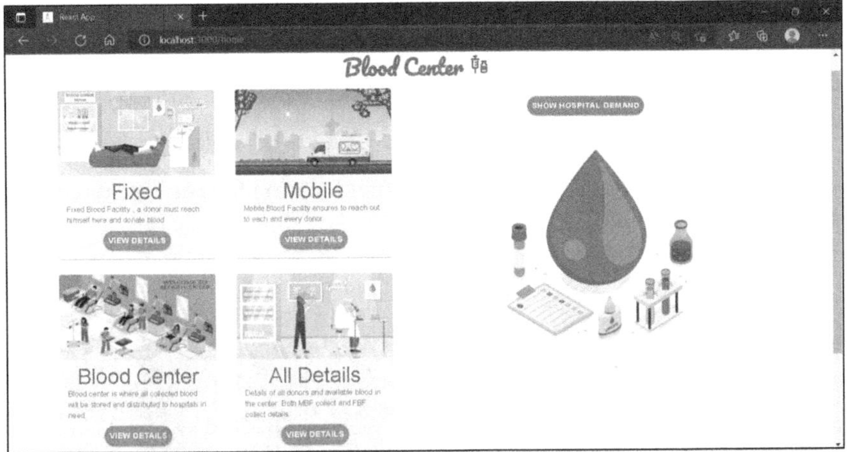

Figure 8.18 Collective user interface page.

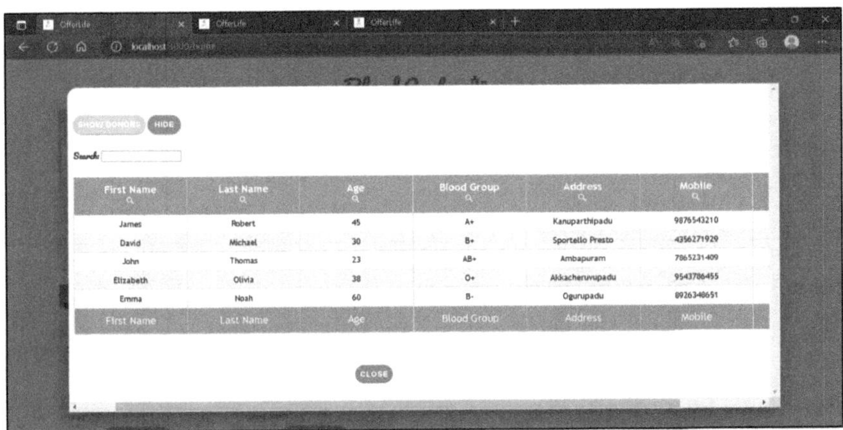

Figure 8.19 FBF donor details.

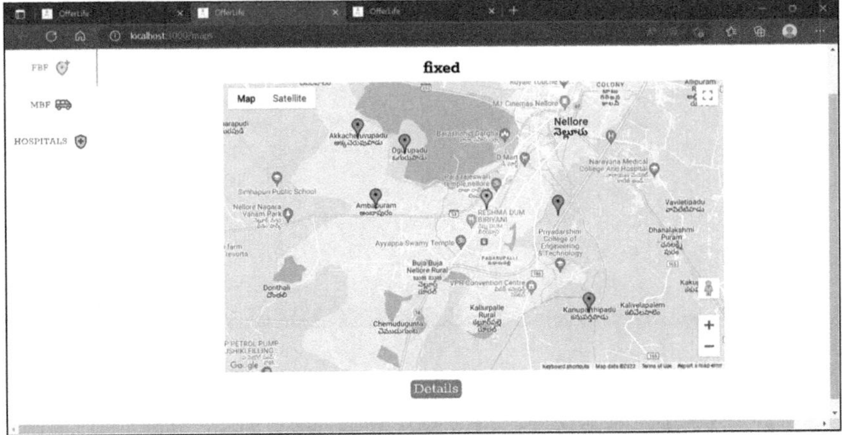

Figure 8.20 FBF locations on Google Map.

Figure 8.21. After getting the distance table, row-wise and column-wise sorting is done to know the optimised distance.

After final sorting, the location in the first column is the optimal location as shown in Figure 8.22. Hence, the optimal location for the registered FBF donor is Ogurupadu.

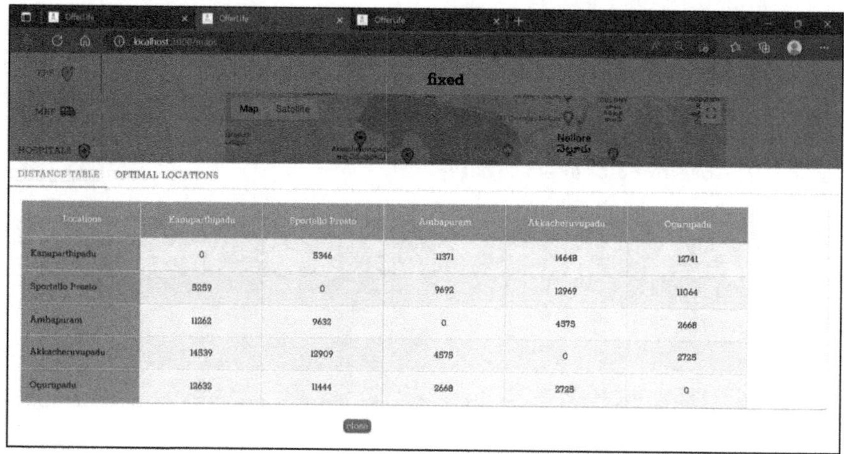

Locations	Kanuparthipadu	Sportello Presto	Ambapuram	Akkacheruvupadu	Ogurupadu
Kanuparthipadu	0	5346	11371	14648	12741
Sportello Presto	5259	0	9692	12969	11064
Ambapuram	11262	9632	0	4575	2668
Akkacheruvupadu	14539	12909	4575	0	2725
Ogurupadu	12632	11444	2668	2725	0

Figure 8.21 FBF distance at various locations.

fixed

Map Satellite

DISTANCE TABLE OPTIMAL LOCATIONS

Optimal Location for fixed facility center : Ogurupadu

Ogurupadu	0	2668	2725	11444	13074
Ambapuram	0	2668	4575	9632	11262
Akkacheruvupadu	0	2725	4575	12909	14981
Sportello Presto	0	5259	9692	11064	12971
Kanuparthipadu	0	5346	11371	12741	14649

close

Figure 8.22 FBF optimal Location.

When the donors register their details under MBF category, their details are stored in a table format as shown in Figure 8.23.

The locations of the registered donors will be marked in the map, and it is shown in Figure 8.24; using these locations, the distance between each and every location is calculated, and it is displayed as distance table as shown in Figure 8.25.

As discussed in the methodology, the blood centre is the starting point marked as A, and the nearest location is found and marked as B. Similarly,

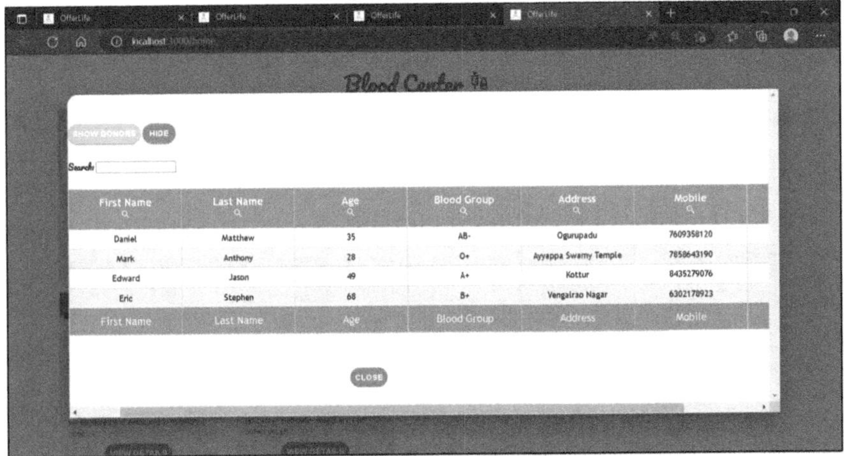

First Name	Last Name	Age	Blood Group	Address	Mobile
Daniel	Matthew	35	AB-	Ogurupadu	7609358120
Mark	Anthony	28	O+	Ayyappa Swamy Temple	7858643190
Edward	Jason	49	A+	Kottur	8435279076
Eric	Stephen	68	B+	Vengalrao Nagar	6302178923
First Name	Last Name	Age	Blood Group	Address	Mobile

Figure 8.23 MBF donor details at website.

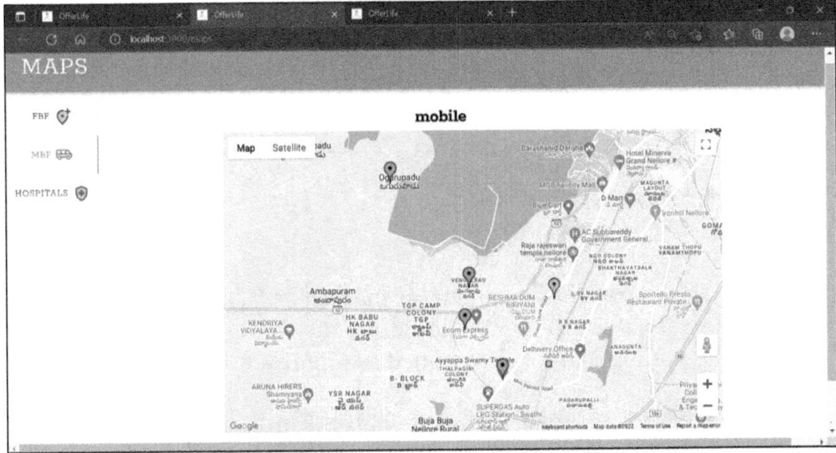

Figure 8.24 MBF locations on Google Map.

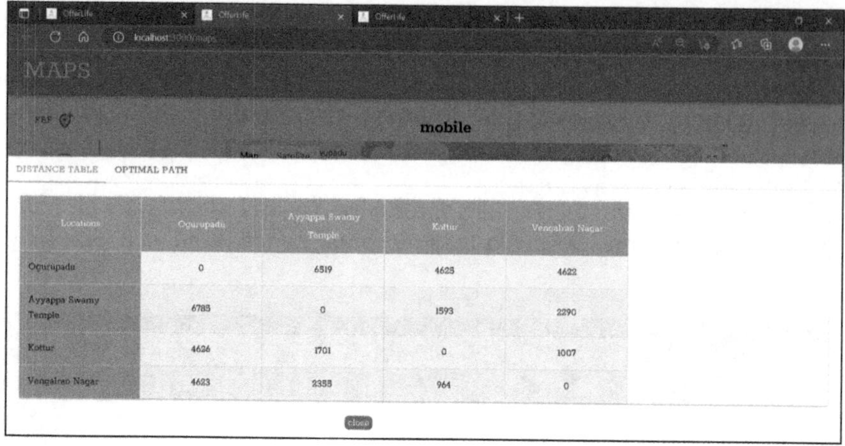

Locations	Ogurupadu	Ayyappa Swamy Temple	Kottur	Vengalrao Nagar
Ogurupadu	0	6519	4625	4622
Ayyappa Swamy Temple	6785	0	1593	2290
Kottur	4626	1701	0	1007
Vengalrao Nagar	4623	2355	964	0

Figure 8.25 MBF distance for various locations.

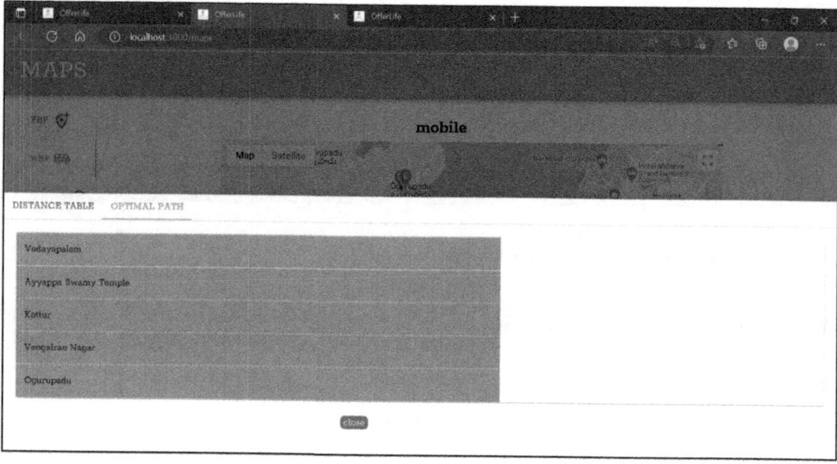

Figure 8.26 MBF optimal path estimation.

the nearest location to B is found and is marked as C, and this process continues until the final location is achieved.

Hence, the optimal path is determined as (Figures 8.26 and 8.27):

Vedayapalem ≥ Ayyappa Swamy Temple ≥ Kottur ≥ Vengalrao Nagar ≥ Ogurupadu

When a hospital registers its demand, its details are stored in table format. Therefore, the registered hospitals are shown in Figure 8.28, and the

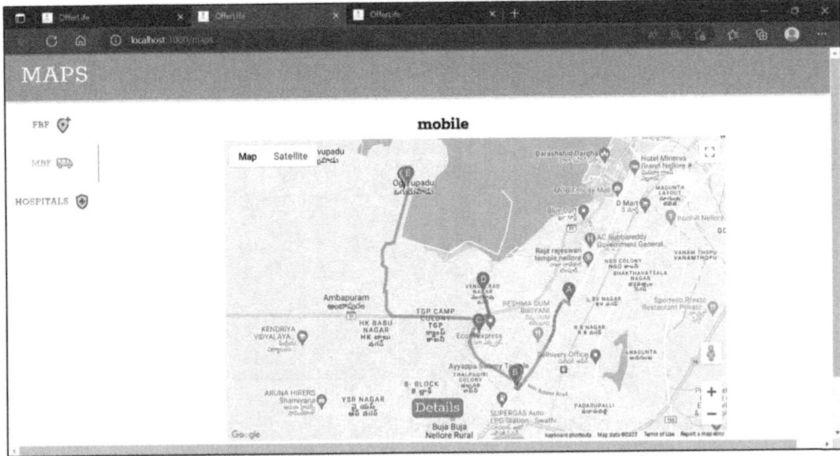

Figure 8.27 MBF optimal path on Google Map.

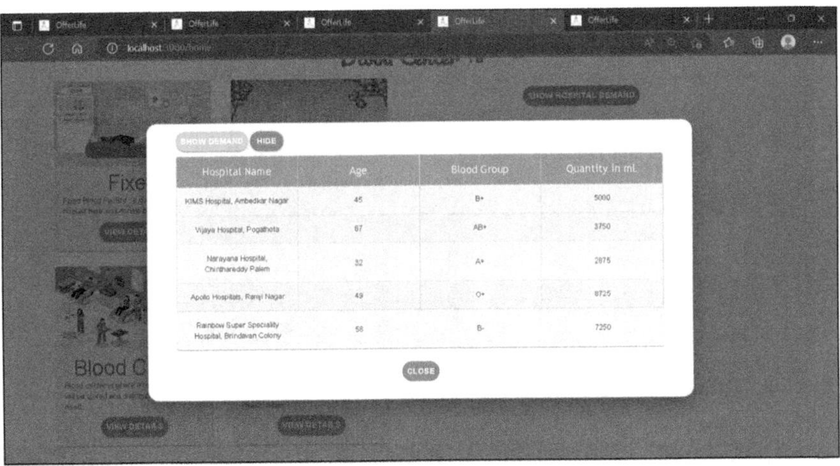

Hospital Name	Age	Blood Group	Quantity in ml
KIMS Hospital, Ambedkar Nagar	45	B+	5000
Vijaya Hospital, Pogathota	67	AB+	3750
Narayana Hospital, Chinthareddy Palem	32	A+	2875
Apollo Hospitals, Ramji Nagar	49	O+	8725
Rainbow Super Speciality Hospital, Brindavan Colony	58	B-	7250

Figure 8.28 Hospital demand details along with registration.

locations will be marked on the map and are shown in Figure 8.29. After marking, the path will be generated between the blood centre and every registered hospital.

The donors who registered under blood centre category will donate their blood at blood centre directly. Hence, the details of donors who register under this category are shown in Figure 8.30. Figure 8.31 shows the details of all the donors irrespective of their category, and from this, the blood centre will know the number of donors on a particular day.

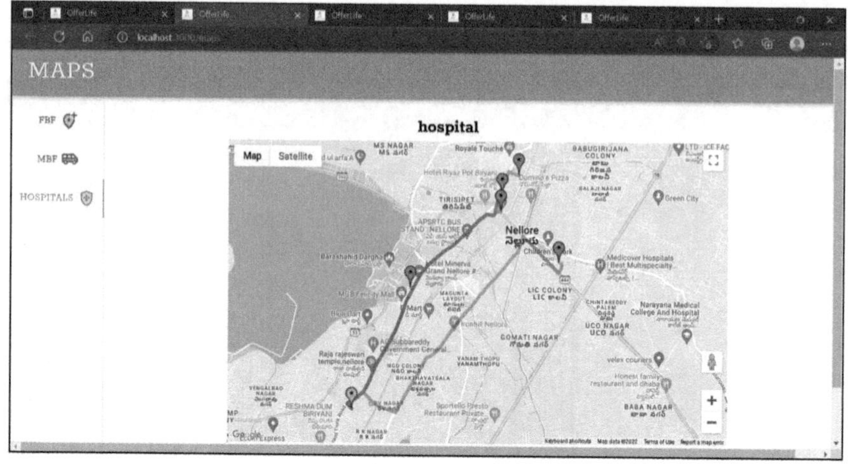

Figure 8.29 Hospital location on Google Map.

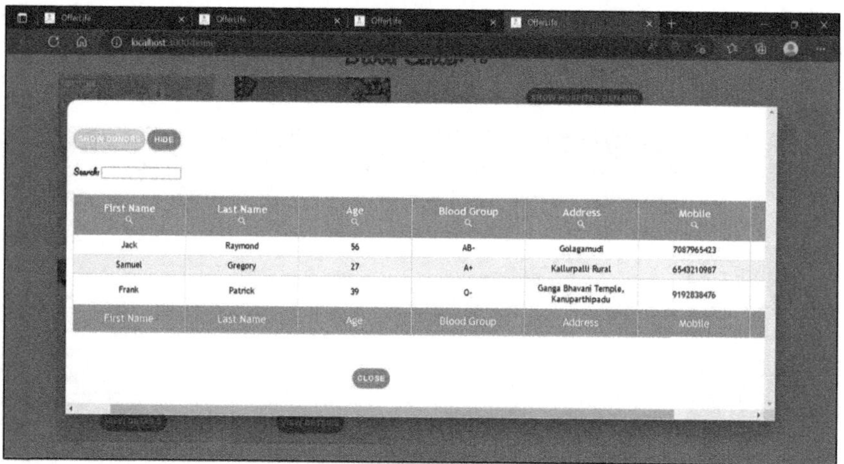

First Name	Last Name	Age	Blood Group	Address	Mobile
Jack	Raymond	56	AB-	Golagamudi	7087965423
Samuel	Gregory	27	A+	Kallurpalli Rural	6543210987
Frank	Patrick	39	O-	Ganga Bhavani Temple, Kanuparthipadu	9192838476
First Name	Last Name	Age	Blood Group	Address	Mobile

Figure 8.30 Blood centre details.

Last Name	Age	Blood Group	Address	Mobile	Facility Choice
Matthew	35	AB-	Ogurupadu	7609358120	mobile
Anthony	28	O+	Ayyappa Swamy Temple	7858643190	mobile
Jason	49	A+	Kottur	8435279076	mobile
Stephen	68	B+	Vengalrao Nagar	6302178923	mobile
Robert	45	A+	Kanuparthipadu	9876543210	fixed
Michael	30	B+	Sportello Presto	4356271929	fixed
Thomas	23	AB+	Ambapuram	7865231409	fixed
Olivia	38	O+	Akkacheruvupadu	9543786455	fixed
Noah	60	B-	Ogurupadu	8926348651	fixed
Raymond	56	AB-	Golagamudi	7087965423	bloodcenter
Gregory	27	A+	Kallurpalli Rural	6543210987	bloodcenter
Patrick	39	O-	Ganga Bhavani Temple, Kanuparthipadu	9192838476	bloodcenter
Last Name	Age	Blood Group	Address	Mobile	Facility Choice

Figure 8.31 Complete details about optimised platelet SCM.

8.6 CONCLUSION AND FUTURE SCOPE

Blood Platelet website is created by utilizing the use cases in Nellore District, Andhra Pradesh. Initially, registration pages are created to get the details of both donors and hospitals and are stored in a table format. Then, Google API locations of donors under FBF, MBF and locations of hospitals are plotted. Further, optimal location is estimated by using the locations of MBF. Hence, optimum time is achieved by using optimal path, which results in low cost with efficient energy consumption.

An acknowledgement can be sent to donors and hospitals on successful registration as a future enhancement. Also, a message regarding optimal location can be sent to the mobile number of FBF donors; appropriate time of blood transportation vehicle arrival can even be sent to the MBF donors. An email regarding the approximate time required to deliver the demanded blood can be sent to the hospitals.

ACKNOWLEDGEMENTS

The work was conducted as a part of the grant financed by the Science and Engineering Research Board (SERB), Department of Science & Technology (DST), India (EEQ/2019/000565). We wish to thank SASTRA Deemed University, India, for its infrastructural support.

- **Data Availability Statement:** We authors confirm that our manuscript has no associated data.
- **Conflict of Interest:** The authors declare that they have no conflict of interest.

REFERENCES

1. Joy John Mammen, Edwin Sam Asirvatham, Jeyaseelan Lakshmanan, Charishma Jones Sarman, Arvind Pandey, Varsha Ranjan, et al., The Clinical Demand and Supply of Blood in India: A National Level Estimation Study, *PLoS One*, Volume 17, Issue 4, 2022.
2. Andrea Pirabán Ramírez, William Javier Guerrero, Nacima Labadie, Survey on Blood Supply Chain Management: Models and Methods, *International Journal of Production Research*, 112, 104756. 2019.
3. B. Zahiri, S. A. Torabi, M. Mousazadeh, S. A. Mansouri, Blood Collection and Management: Methodology and Application, *International Journal of Production Research*, 39(23-24), 7680-7696. 2015.
4. Ali Fallahi, Hadi Mokhtari, Seyed Taghi Akhavan Niaki, Designing a Closed-Loop Blood Supply Chain Network Considering Transportation Flow and Quality Aspects, *International Journal of Production Research*, 2, 170-189. 2021.

5. Mohamadreza Fazli-Khalaf, Soheyl Khalilpourazari, Mohammad Mohammadi, Mixed Robust Possibilistic Flexible Chance Constraint Optimization Model for Emergency Blood Supply Chain Network Design, *International Journal of Production Research*, 283(1), 1079-1109. 2019.
6. Masoud Rabbani, Mohsen Aghabegloo, Hamed Farrokhi-Asl, Solving a Bi-Objective Mathematical Programming Model for Blood Mobiles Location Routing Problem, *International Journal of Production Research*, 8(1), 19-32. 2016.
7. Javid Ghahremani-Nahr, Hamed Nozari, Mehrnaz Bathaee, Robust Box Approach for Blood Supply Chain Network Design under Uncertainty: Hybrid Moth-Flame Optimization and Genetic Algorithm, *International Journal of Production Research*, 1(2), 40-62. 2021.
8. Elmira Farrokhizadeh, Seyed Amin Seyfi-Shishavan, Sule Itir Satoglu, Blood Supply Planning During Natural Disasters under Uncertainty: A Novel Bi-Objective Model and an Application for Red Crescent, *International Journal of Production Research*, 319(1), 73-113. 2021.
9. Peide Liu, Ayad Hendalianpour, Mohamad Sadegh Sangari, A Solution Algorithm for Integrated Production-Inventory-Routing of Perishable Goods with Transshipment and Uncertain Demand, *International Journal of Production Research*, 7, 1349-1365. 2021.
10. Seyyed-Mahdi Hosseini-Motlagh, Mohammad Reza Ghatreh Samani, Shamim Homaei, Blood Supply Chain Management: Robust Optimisation, Distribution Risk, and Blood Group Compatibility (a Real-life Case), *International Journal of Production Research*, 2019.
11. Hamidreza Ensafian, Saeed Yaghoubi, Mohammad Modarres Yazdi, Raising Quality and Safety of Platelet Transfusion Services in a Patient-Based Integrated Supply Chain under Uncertainty, *International Journal of Production Research*, 106, 355-372. 2017.
12. Hadis Derikvand, Seyed Mohammad Hajimolana, Armin Jabbarzadeh, Seyed Esmaeil Najafi, A Robust Stochastic Bi-Objective Model for Inventory-Distribution Management in a Blood Supply Chain, *International Journal of Production Research*, 14(3), 369-403. 2019.
13. Mahsa Rezaei Kallaj, Milad Abolghasemian, Samaneh Moradi Pirbalouti, Majid Sabk Ara, Adel Pourghader Chobar, Vehicle Routing Problem in Relief Supply under a Crisis Condition Considering Blood Types, *International Journal of Production Research*, 2021(1), 7217182.
14. M. Asadpour, Omid Boyer, R. Tavakkoli-Moghaddam, A Blood Supply Chain Network with Backup Facilities Considering Blood Groups and Expiration Date: A Real-World Application, *International Journal of Production Research*, 34(2), 470-479. 2020.
15. Niloofar Gilani Larimi, Saeed Yaghoubi, A Robust Mathematical Model for Platelet Supply Chain Considering Social Announcements and Blood Extraction Technologies, *International Journal of Production Research*, 137, 106014. 2019.
16. Behzad Zahiri, Mir Saman Pishvaee, Blood Supply Chain Network Considering Blood Group Compatibility under Uncertainty, *International Journal of Production Research*, 55(7), 2013-2033. 2016.
17. Mohammad Reza Ghatreh Samani, S. Ali Torabi, Seyyed-Mahdi Hosseini-Motlagh, Integrated Blood Supply Chain Planning for Disaster Relief, *International Journal of Production Research*, 27, 168-188. 2018.

18. Fatemeh Jafarkhan, Saeed Yaghoubi, An Efficient Solution Method for the Flexible and Robust Inventory-Routing of Red Blood Cells, *International Journal of Production Research*, 117, 191-206. 2018.
19. Seyed Mahmood Kazemi, Masoud Rabbani, Reza Tavakkoli-Moghaddam, Farid Abolhassani Shahreza, Blood Inventory-Routing Problem under Uncertainty, *International Journal of Production Research*, 32(1), 467-481.2017.
20. Javad Asl-Najafi, Saeed Yaghoubi, Siamak Noori, Customisation of Incentive Mechanisms Based on Product Life-cycle Phases for an Efficient Product-service Supply Chain Coordination, *Computers in Industry*, Volume 135, 2022, 103582, ISSN: 0166–3615.
21. Shenle Pan, Damien Trentesaux, Duncan McFarlane, Benoit Montreuil, Eric Ballot, George Q. Huang, Digital Interoperability in Logistics and Supply Chain Management: State-of-the-art and Research Avenues towards Physical Internet, *Computers in Industry*, Volume 128, 2021, 103435, ISSN: 0166-3615.
22. Janne M. Denolf, Jacques H. Trienekens, P. M. (Nel) Wognum, Jack G. A. J. van der Vorst, S. W. F. (Onno) Omta, Towards a Framework of Critical Success Factors for Implementing Supply Chain Information Systems, *Computers in Industry*, Volume 68, 2015, Pages 16–26, ISSN: 0166-3615.

Chapter 9

Securing Healthcare

A Comprehensive Examination of Information Security Governance Standards and Frameworks

Abdelkebir Sahid

9.1 INTRODUCTION

In today's healthcare landscape, where the effective management and protection of health information are paramount, the role of information security governance standards cannot be overstated. National Institute of Standards and Technology (NIST) defines Health Information Systems (HIS) as a crucial assembly of information resources meticulously organized to cater to the myriad needs of health information management. A typical HIS encompasses a central hospital information system and ancillary components such as laboratory, pharmacy, and diagnostic imaging systems. Administrative personnel and clinicians, including physicians and nurses, access and utilize these systems through various endpoints like workstations and mobile devices, facilitating the seamless flow of medical and administrative (Maleh et al., 2019). However, with the increasing reliance on digital platforms for managing healthcare data, the vulnerability of these systems to a plethora of security threats has become a pressing concern. Healthcare organizations are at the forefront of combating evolving threats such as cyberattacks, data breaches, and other malicious activities. The stakes are high, considering the sensitive nature of health information and the potential consequences of its unauthorized access or manipulation. Consequently, governments worldwide have enacted stringent regulations mandating healthcare organizations to implement robust security measures to safeguard patient data and ensure compliance with privacy regulations (HealthIT.gov, 2013).

In response to these regulatory demands and the escalating threat landscape, healthcare organizations are turning to information security governance standards for guidance. These standards provide a structured framework for establishing, implementing, and maintaining effective security controls to mitigate risks and protect critical health information assets. By adhering to recognized standards, healthcare entities can ensure a consistent and comprehensive approach to information security, bolstering their defenses against myriad threats.

Moreover, as the complexity and interconnectedness of healthcare IT environments continue to grow, the need for specialized security standards

 DOI: 10.1201/9781003470038-9

tailored to the unique challenges of the healthcare industry becomes apparent. Standards such as COBIT, ISO/IEC 27001:2022, ISO/IEC 27002:2022, and others offer targeted guidance on addressing the specific security concerns inherent in healthcare operations. Understanding the nuances of these standards and their applicability to healthcare settings is crucial for IT management professionals tasked with safeguarding patient information and ensuring compliance with regulatory requirements (Maleh, 2021).

Furthermore, effective IT asset governance is emerging beyond information security as a vital component of healthcare organizational success. With IT assuming a central role in supporting clinical workflows, driving operational efficiencies, and enabling strategic decision-making, the need for robust IT governance structures and mechanisms has never been more pronounced. Organizations can maximize the value derived from their IT initiatives while minimizing risks by aligning IT investments with business objectives, optimizing resource allocation, and fostering transparency and accountability. In light of these imperatives, this chapter explores information security governance standards in healthcare organizations (Yassine et al., 2017). By surveying the landscape of existing standards, analyzing their strengths and limitations, and providing insights into their practical implementation, this study aims to equip healthcare IT professionals with the knowledge and tools needed to navigate the complex terrain of information security governance effectively. Through a nuanced understanding of security standards and governance frameworks, healthcare organizations can enhance their resilience to cyber threats, safeguard patient data, and uphold the trust and confidence of stakeholders in an increasingly digital healthcare ecosystem.

This chapter is organized as follows: Section 9.2 delves into the research methodology employed in this study, outlining the approach taken to gather and analyze data related to IT security governance standards. Section 9.3 provides an in-depth exploration of various IT security governance standards, including their key principles, implementation challenges, and applicability to different organizational contexts. In Section 9.4, a comprehensive comparison and analysis of the identified standards are presented, highlighting their similarities, differences, and effectiveness in addressing IT security challenges. Finally, Section 9.5 offers concluding remarks and insights drawn from the findings, summarizing the key takeaways and implications for future research and practice in the field of IT security governance.

9.2 RESEARCH METHODOLOGY

This section introduces a meta-model designed to evaluate approaches to IT governance (ITG). The meta-model is structured around specific facets inspired by software engineering concepts, providing analytical organization to governance approaches. The meta-model comprises four keywords: subject, use, system, and development, each representing distinct dimensions of IT governance. These words are enriched by supplementary facets, providing detailed insights into governance structures, objectives, informational components, and deployment processes (Maleh et al., 2021a).

9.2.1 Framework Structure

The framework is structured around four keywords, as shown in Table 9.1.

9.2.1.1 Word Subject

The word "subject" delves into the fundamental inquiry of "what constitutes IT governance?" It comprises six facets, as shown in Table 9.2.

9.2.1.2 Word Use

The word "use" addresses the purpose and objectives of IT governance, encompassing four key facets, as shown in Table 9.3.

9.2.1.3 Word System

The "ITG system" word focuses on the informational components essential for IT governance, comprising three facets, as shown in Table 9.4.

9.2.1.4 Word Development

The "development" aspect of IT governance is intricately linked with the other components within the framework, reflecting the deployment characteristics of IT governance. It comprises four facets, as shown in Table 9.5.

This meta-model provides a comprehensive framework for evaluating IT governance approaches, offering structured insights into key dimensions essential for effective governance implementation.

Table 9.1 The Meta-Model Structure

Word	*Description*
Subject	Portrays IT governance as the subject of analysis, focusing on organizational decision-making structures and oversight.
Use	Encapsulates the purpose of ITG, highlighting objectives such as risk mitigation, value generation, and performance attainment.
System	Encompasses all relevant information for ITG activities, serving as the informational foundation for decision-making.
Development	Embodies the processes of ITG, aiming to achieve governance objectives through manipulating information elements.

Table 9.2 Word Subject

Facet	*Description*	*Value*
Governance organization	Organizational structures surrounding decision-making processes include centralized, decentralized, or hybrid models.	Enum{centralized, decentralized, hybrid}
Decision	Typology of decisions related to IS architecture, infrastructure, and project planning.	Enum{IT architecture, IT infrastructure, project planning}
IT process	Essential IT processes for IT management, ranging from control processes to action processes for decision-making.	Enum{documented, piloted, evolutive}
Business process	Classification of business processes based on their contribution to value creation, including primary and supporting processes.	Enum{productive, administrative, ad-hoc, collaborative}
Change	Categorization of organizational change processes, including ad hoc, evolutionary, and corrective changes.	Enum{ad-hoc, evolutive, corrective}
IT project portfolio	Management of IT project portfolios, considering classification and transformation modes.	SET{classification mode: Enum{monocriteria, multi-criteria}; transformation mode: Enum{creation, maintenance, evolution}}

9.3 IT SECURITY GOVERNANCE STANDARDS

We may now go on to discuss the processes that lead to the expected advantages of IT governance, having discovered some of the ideas and issues associated with IT governance, such as the absence of a universally accepted definition of IT governance. According to (De Haes & Van Grembergen, 2009; Weill & Ross, 2004), IT governance is often implemented through a combination of procedures, structures, and relational mechanisms. A conceptual model describing a comprehensive view of the core elements of IT governance was developed by integrating the work of Grant et al. (2007) and Cadete & da Silva (2017). This model is depicted in Figure 9.1. According to Nabiollahi & Sahibuddin (2008), the model has reached a mature state because it accounts for the multi-faceted, ever-changing nature of IT

Table 9.3 Word Use

Facet	*Description*	*Value*
Minimizing risks	Management of risks associated with information requirements, including additional costs, compromised quality, and delays.	Enum{extra cost, non-quality, delay}
Achieving alignment state	Ensuring coherence between the evolution of business and IT strategies and between business and IT services.	Enum{IT evolution, business evolution, co-evolution}
Getting the performance	Enhancing governance performance through ad hoc or mature processes, aligning with objectives outlined in frameworks like COBIT or CMMI.	Enum{ad-hoc, process maturity}
Creating value	Examination of value creation at both IT and organizational levels, encompassing financial and usage value aspects.	Enum{IT asset, business asset, IT usage}

Table 9.4 Word System

Facet	*Description*	*Value*
Content	Management of documents essential for decision-making, including alignment-related, management-related, risk management, performance management, value management, and maturity management documents.	Enum{document name}
Model	Utilization of models for representing various domains relevant to IT governance, such as processes, objects, decisions, and evolutions.	Enum{process, object, decision, evolution}
Metric	Employment of metrics for quantifying and assessing various aspects essential for decision-making and governance oversight, including risk, performance, value, and alignment metrics.	Enum{risk, performance, value, alignment}

Table 9.5 Word Development

Facet	*Description*	*Value*
Nature of processes	Characteristics of processes involved in IT development, categorized as ad hoc or systematic, reflect the flexibility and structure level.	Enum{ad-hoc, systematic}
Process maturity	Level of maturity in IT development processes, influencing the effectiveness of IT governance activities.	SET{level; objective}
Knowledge capitalization	The mechanisms for sharing knowledge during IT governance activities encompass socialization, externalization, internalization, and combination approaches.	Enum{socialization, externalization, internalization, combination}
Software	IT tools dedicated to IT governance activities, categorized as ISI (Information System Intelligence) or CAGE (Computer-aided Governance Engineering).	Enum{ISI, CAGE}

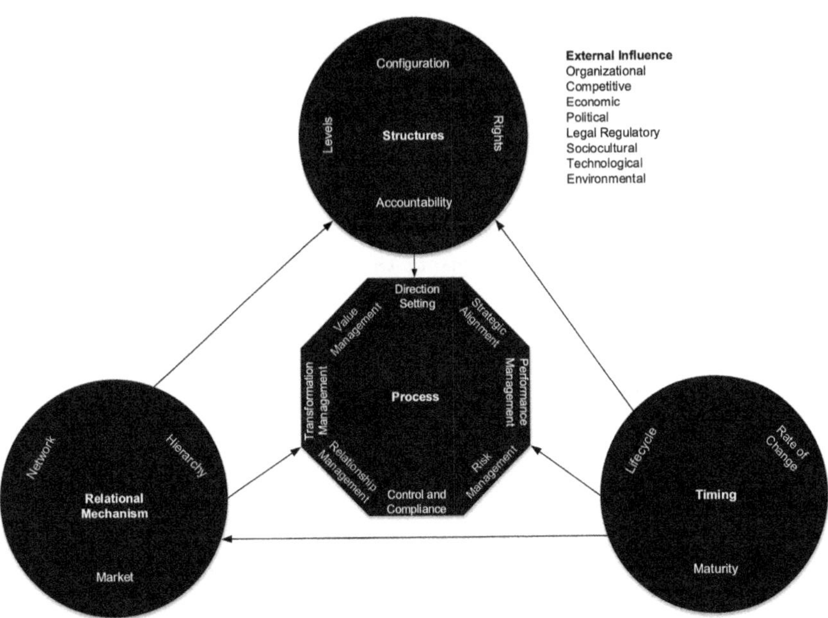

Figure 9.1 Extended IT governance model.

governance, as well as its four driving objectives—IT value delivery and strategic alignment, performance and risk management, and the model's significant components, structure and processes.

Similarly, as shown in Table 9.6 (Van Grembergen & De Haes, 2009), the model's three dimensions—structures, processes, and relational mechanisms—comprise the essential mechanisms for implementing IT governance. This approach has several mechanisms, but ultimately, the organization's context, external factors, and contingencies determine which ones to employ (Nfuka & Rusu, 2011).

Many companies have begun establishing IT governance processes in the last several years, often basing these processes on one or more IT governance frameworks. The Committee of Sponsoring Organizations of the Treadway Commission (COSO) is an example of a business-oriented framework; IT Infrastructure Library (ITIL) is an example of a technology-focused framework; and COBIT is an example of a framework that attempts to align business and technology objectives (Warland & Ridley, 2005). Information technology (IT) governance frameworks provide a uniform approach to decision-making, direction, evaluation, and monitoring of governance-related activities by executives and practitioners. According to Marrone &

Table 9.6 The Dimension of the IT Governance Model

Structures	In this facet, organizations' high-level governance strategies are considered along with planning and organizational components. Rights, accountability, configuration, and levels are the four primary tiers of administration.
Processes	Procedures are how IT governance is managed and assessed. Organizations should implement the eight fundamental aspects shown in Figure 9.1 to provide successful IT governance, which pertain to the procedures dimension. Processes are essential parts of frameworks for IT governance.
Relational mechanisms	For IT governance to be effectively implemented, relational mechanisms are necessary to manage internal and external relationships. The three recognized relational mechanisms are the market, the hierarchy, and the network.
Timing	IT governance implementation is accompanied by temporal characteristics, such as maturity, lifecycle, and pace of change, which are addressed under the timing dimension.
External influences	Organizations' mix of mechanisms is shaped by several external pressures, which should be considered while establishing IT governance. Organizational, competitive, economic, political, legal/regulatory, sociocultural, technical, and environmental are all external influences.

Kolbe (2011), CEOs may better grasp their crucial role in regulating IT by implementing appropriate frameworks. For example, adoption and choice of framework are affected by executives' dedication, strategic goals, and the distribution of resources (Benaroch & Chernobai, 2017; Murphy et al., 2018). From an assessment standpoint, numerous companies enhance their internal control environments and increase their compliance with specific regulations (such as SOX) by using or integrating numerous governance frameworks.

The following frameworks are widely used in information technology governance: COBIT, ISO 38500, ITIL, and COSO (Brown et al., 2005). Concerned with controlling management procedures and decisions, the ISO standard discusses corporate IT governance. In contrast, IT Infrastructure Library (ITIL) is a framework that emphasizes IT service management; it allows IT departments to implement rigorous controls and systematic solid execution of activities (Marrone et al., 2014). According to Dahlberg & Kivijärvi (2006) and De Haes et al. (2013), COBIT is a commonly used framework for IT governance that offers more significant guidance on control over IT than COSO.

Despite their proven utility, IT governance frameworks argue that they are not one-size-fits-all solutions and require customization to fit specific organizational structures, business objectives, and firm sizes. According to (Raghupathi, 2007), there is a pressing need for adaptable IT governance models and frameworks that may be further developed into something more useful for companies and other organizations. Effective adoption and adaptation are crucial for the usefulness of frameworks, best practices, and standards like the COBIT framework. (Dahlberg & Lahdelma, 2007; Simonsson & Johnson, 2006) highlight the lack of academic literature that offers practical advice for implementing IT governance frameworks and structures.

No single framework provides full coverage of IT governance. There are several angles to consider when looking at the information system from a standards perspective. These include production service and management, project development and organization, project management, and the Library for Information Technology Infrastructure (ITIL).

9.3.1 COBIT

After much deliberation, COBIT was established in 1992 by the ITGI and the Information Systems Audit and Control Association (ISACA). The most recent COBIT, version 5, was released in April 2012, with the first edition coming out in 1996. The framework has become a significant player in the IT governance industry worldwide and remains so now (Omari et al., 2012). Developed initially as an IT audit guideline, COBIT now offers auditors a wealth of customizable checklists for different parts of control assessment, detailed guidance on governance practices, and a comprehensive set of standards to improve audit and compliance (ISACA, 2012). Because of these features, COBIT is an ideal framework for achieving control over IT, measuring the effectiveness of IT operations, and helping executives connect control needs, technological challenges, and business risks (Brustbauer, 2016). Furthermore, COBIT is a valuable instrument for establishing a baseline for process maturity, and it offers significant economic value through better compliance, reduced corporate risk, and good accountability. The extensive use of the IT governance framework also contributes to its increasing generalizability.

Enabling value creation via ensuring benefits are realized, risk is reduced, and resources are optimized is the core purpose of COBIT from an IT governance viewpoint. The approach is also said to offer business stakeholders a better way to handle IT risks and to establish good IT governance by using a top-down framework to manage descriptive processes systematically. Organizations of all sizes, from for-profit businesses to public agencies, can use the COBIT framework to gauge the level of maturity in their information technology (IT) processes.

The COBIT framework is becoming the most trusted and efficient method for auditing, implementing IT governance, and evaluating IT capabilities worldwide. It is the gold standard for companies trying to meet US requirements like Sarbanes-Oxley (SOX). According to Cadete & da Silva (2017) and Wood (2010), this standard is widely accepted and trusted because it offers comprehensive sets of predefined processes that can be adjusted and tailored to support various organizational objectives better. This applies to both public and private sectors, as well as to accounting and auditing firms. COBIT provides IT metrics to monitor the attainment of goals and is seen as an all-encompassing framework that covers the whole lifespan of IT investment.

Organizational IT goals, business objectives, and risks may be effectively managed using this paradigm. A goals cascade mechanism is introduced to translate and link stakeholders' needs to specific enterprise, IT-related, and enabler goals (COBIT processes). This is accomplished by utilizing the Balanced Scorecard's Financial, Customer, Internal, and Learning Growth dimensions. The COBIT processes are organized in a sequential fashion and correspond to 17 organizational goals (ISACA, 2012). These goals are also tied to information technology. The COBIT framework offers a collection of IT governance processes and helps with their proper execution and management by outlining who is responsible for what using a detailed RACI matrix. To help achieve various business goals, COBIT offers comprehensive sets of established procedures that may be adjusted and tailored over time.

Stakeholder needs; enterprise end-to-end coverage; single, integrated framework application; enabling a holistic approach; and separation of governance from management are the five cornerstones of the current fifth edition of COBIT. In addition, there are five categories of information technology as outlined in the COBIT 5 PRM:

- Evaluate, Direct, and Monitor (EDM)
- Align, Plan, and Organize (APO)
- Build, Acquire, and Implement (BAI)
- Deliver, Service, and Support (DSS)
- Monitor, Evaluate, and Assess (MEA)

There are 37 broad IT processes and more than 300 specific controls that make up the COBIT 5 domains, all of which address different facets of IT governance and management. Another unique aspect of COBIT is its capacity to classify seven types of enablers, sometimes called factors:

- Principles, policies, and frameworks
- Processes
- Organizational structures
- Culture, ethics, and behavior
- Information
- Services, infrastructure, and applications
- Availability

According to Oliver & Lainhart (2012), it is the best framework for helping business and IT objectives to be aligned.

By unifying its many models into a cohesive framework, COBIT 5 became a framework with a stronger focus on business needs (e.g., Val IT, Risk IT). This consolidation was driven by the need to address all areas of business and functional IT responsibilities, provide a solid foundation for auditors, users, senior managers, and business process owners, and ultimately achieve effective IT governance and management. In addition, the ISO/IEC 15504 Process Capability Model (PCM) is in line with COBIT 5. The transition from SEI's Capability Maturity Model (CMM) and the more recent Capability Maturity Model Integration (CMMI) to the new Process Capability Maturity Model (PCM) has completely transformed COBIT, giving it an advantage in evaluating process capability rather than enterprise maturity. According to Basson et al. (2012), this novel method has several advantages over its predecessors, including greater consistency, repeatability, and verifiability than objective evidence obtained during evaluations. Many European financial organizations have utilized PCM to evaluate their internal controls and see where they may require improvement. The collaboration between the COBIT framework and the PCM provides a measuring scale to objectively assess the presence, sufficiency, efficacy, and compatibility of IT governance procedures, which is an additional benefit organization may anticipate from using COBIT.

9.3.2 COBIT 2019 versus COBIT 5

Recently, COBIT 2019 was published in November 2018. It contains several new, modified, and updated elements (Steuperaert, 2019). A practical governance of information and technologies is essential for the success of any organization's business. This new version confirms the role of COBIT as a key driver of business innovation and transformation.

COBIT 2019 (De Haes et al., 2020)) is an evolution of the previous version of the ISACA governance framework. Building on the foundations of COBIT 5, it incorporates the latest developments affecting information and technology in enterprises. COBIT 2019 offers more flexibility and openness to enhance the relevance of COBIT.

Below are insights into the significant changes brought about by COBIT 2019:

- Introducing new concepts like interest domains and design factors allows businesses to propose best practices for adopting a governance system tailored to their needs.
- Updating alignment with standards, frameworks, and best practices enhances the relevance of COBIT.
- An open-source model will enable the global governance community to contribute to future updates by providing feedback, sharing applications, and suggesting real-time improvements to the framework and derivatives. This approach allows for cyclic releases of new COBIT developments.
- New guidelines and tools support the development of an optimal governance system, making COBIT 2019 more prescriptive.
- COBIT 2019 Reference Model now includes 40 governance management objectives (processes) instead of 37 processes in COBIT 5.
- Enabler Guidance has been removed to streamline COBIT.
- COBIT governance and governance system principles have been renamed and modified.
- IT-related objectives have been renamed alignment objectives.
- The process guide is now structured into "governance/management objectives," with the process guide being only part of it, supplemented by other governance elements.

COBIT 2019 introduces three new governance and management objectives:

- APO14—Managed Data
- BAI11—Managed Projects
- MEA04—Managed Assurance

COBIT 2019 now explicitly incorporates DevOps, which illustrates a component variant and an interesting domain. DevOps encompasses several generic governance and management objectives from the core COBIT model and numerous process and organizational structure variants related to development, operations, and monitoring. DevOps also requires establishing a specific culture and mindset of openness, skill sharing, and pushing teams out of their comfort zones. Similarly, DevOps requires a certain level of automation (services, infrastructure, and applications). DevOps is a priority interest area among the first and is still under development. An interest domain describes a subject, domain, or governance issue addressed by a set of governance and management objectives and their components. Interest domains may contain a combination of generic governance components and variants. The four interest domains currently classified by priority and in the process of being published are:

- Small and medium enterprises
- Cybersecurity
- Risks
- DevOps

The number of interest domains is virtually unlimited, making COBIT open. New interest domains will be added upon request or with the contribution of experts and practitioners. COBIT 5 integrates IT governance best practices, offers tools for process assessment and improvement, and outlines control objectives to enhance IT systems' reliability and security. Differences Between COBIT 2019 and COBIT 5 COBIT 2019 boasts updated content, aligns with other relevant frameworks, emphasizes risk management, and focuses on performance metrics compared to COBIT 5. Transitioning from COBIT 5 to COBIT 2019 requires a thorough understanding of the updated framework, conducting a gap analysis, updating existing processes, and investing in training and education for team members.

9.3.3 Library (ITIL)

ITIL v4 is the fourth and final edition of the ITIL guide. It was published in February 2019 as the official successor to ITIL v3, with the fourth edition primarily seen as an extension or enhancement (Shekhar, 2020). The fundamental principles of the previous edition are still valid today and also play an important role in ITIL v4: indeed, ITIL v3's basic approach to the effective delivery of IT services, the main objective of the ITIL guide, has been carried forward. The basic principle has simply been strengthened in areas such as transparency, collaboration and automation. ITIL v4 is based on a mix of established IT service management practices and modern working methods such as Lean, Agile and DevOps. Two key components characterize ITIL v4: the Service Value System (SVS) and the four-dimensional model.

9.3.4 ITIL v4: What Is the ITIL v4 Service Value System?

The ITIL Service Value System for IT describes the interaction of all the service management components and organizational activities that create value. The system is divided into five key points:

- ITIL Service Value Chain: the combination of the six key activities of Planning, Improving, Engaging, Designing/Transitioning, Maintaining and Delivering/Supporting, to create value for the end-user.
- ITIL Guiding Principles: guiding principles for high-quality IT service management, such as value orientation, transparent collaboration, simplicity or continuous optimization/development.
- Governance: predefined guidelines, directives and rules that IT managers must use as a basis for delivering and managing their services.
- Continual improvement: the quest for constant improvement in the services offered, which also plays a role in other components, such as the value chain.
- ITIL Practices: 34 different best practices provide IT service providers with a set of organizational resources designed to perform a job or achieve an objective.

9.3.5 ITIL v4: What Is the Four-Dimensional Model?

Agile IT Service Management is not just about managing technology. It must also include people, processes and partnerships, as well as the technologies used (Sahid et al., 2018).

Relationships with vendors and suppliers are also essential. ITIL v4 combines these areas for a holistic approach to IT Service Management in the four-dimensional model.

- **Organizations and people**: organizations cover the formal structure and ensure appropriate capability and competence. Everyone involved must always be aware of their role in the service value system.
- **Information and technology**: This dimension concerns the technologies used in IT service management, such as tools or knowledge bases. On the other hand, it concerns processing information that companies generate, store, manage and use while providing an IT service.
- **Partners and suppliers**: depending on various factors such as costs, corporate culture, know-how or strategy, companies integrate third-party organizations into their business processes to a greater or lesser extent.
- **Value streams and processes**: this dimension defines all the activities, workflows and processes required to achieve the company's objectives. It also looks at how the different parts of the business interact and participate in the value-creation process.

9.3.6 ITIL v4 and ITIL v3

In many respects, ITIL v4 can be seen as an extension of the previous edition of ITIL v3, as many of the approaches can already be found in the documents of the third edition of ITIL summarized in 2011. For example, the four-dimensional service management model is an innovation in ITIL v4, but service management is already presented in ITIL v3 as a systems-based approach. In addition, in the third edition, people, information, technology, partners and processes are already important aspects of many processes.

ITIL v4's Service Value System, which describes the interaction of the various components and activities within an organization, is not entirely new either—with its various processes, functions and guidelines, ITIL v3 provides a basic description of the interaction.

With the Service Value System, ITIL v4 provides a more comprehensive approach and a much more flexible one that gives IT managers greater freedom to define customized solutions.

The Service Lifecycle, known since the third edition, is hardly mentioned in ITIL v4. Still, improvement continues to play an important role, for example, in the ITIL Service Value Chain context.

Instead of the 26 processes of ITIL v3, ITIL v4 presents 34 different practices, some of which are new, while the majority are strongly oriented toward the processes of the previous edition.

9.3.7 The Role of Service Desk in Healthcare

In healthcare, an ITIL-aligned service desk is pivotal in supporting hospital IT teams, enabling them to address staff issues and optimize internal processes effectively.

Enhancing Clinical Processes through Incident Management The healthcare industry manages numerous clinical devices and digital applications, including electronic health records (EHR). Prompt resolution of user issues is crucial to ensure uninterrupted operations. Incident management is vital in swiftly addressing infrastructure-related issues, thereby minimizing service interruptions. Given the interconnected nature of medical devices, effective incident management is essential to maintain seamless service delivery.

Efficient Clinical Asset Lifecycle Management Automated asset management facilitates the tracking of device history, encompassing acquisition dates, warranties, costs, contracts, and expiration details. End-to-end asset lifecycle management and tracking interdependencies between assets streamline operations and enhance patient care and experience by safeguarding clinical assets and ensuring optimal performance.

Ensuring System Reliability through Monitoring and Management The clinical service desk leverages its system monitoring capabilities to ensure the uninterrupted functioning of medical systems and infrastructure. Timely alerts and notifications are essential to address any system failures promptly. Given the critical nature of healthcare operations, continuous 24/7 monitoring is imperative to uphold hospital operations.

Proactive IT Management with Problem Management Proactive IT Service Management (ITSM) is essential in healthcare to mitigate potential operational failures and risks. Problem management facilitates root cause analysis (RCA) to identify and implement permanent solutions to recurring issues, enhancing operational efficiency and minimizing disruptions.

Enhancing User Experience with an Intuitive Service Catalog Clinical staff request management is streamlined through an intuitive service catalog, enabling employees to request IT, administrative, and HR-related services seamlessly. The user-friendly interface provides a shopping cart-like experience, allowing end-users to track the availability and status of requested services.

9.3.8 CMMI

A method of process improvement, Capability Maturity Model Integration (CMMI) lays forth the groundwork for successful processes for organizations. When applied to quality management, CMMI has the potential to raise both managerial maturity and service quality. A five-point scale allows for systematically analyzing service operations and improving management quality. In 1987, the Software Engineering Institute at Carnegie Mellon University created CMMI. The primary goal of this approach is to enhance software engineering processes in a systematic and organized way. Many different industries have adopted CMMI in recent years. The CMMI model outlines five stages of process maturity. At the most basic level, we have procedures that have been specified. Several process management activities are put in place, and processes may be controlled with repeatable performance levels on the second level, which is called repeatable. Organizational processes are defined and recorded at the third level. At level four, "managed," the emphasis is on evaluating the current processes' performance and quality. To reach level five, "optimized," an organization must institute continuous improvement programs to boost process performance and quality.

Originating from the need to manage software development processes better, the software process improvement capability determination (SPICE) approach was created. The SPICE approach is another maturity management strategy that helps with the quality and performance of an organization's established services. There are two sides to the SPICE technique, one of which is how development processes are managed. The five-category process dimension comprises the actual processes that are being evaluated. This is the initial dimension. The second dimension is the capability scale, which measures the process's capacity. Every procedure uses an identical capacity scale (Ramírez-Mora et al., 2020). Software process assessment is governed by the international standard ISO/IEC 15504. It specifies a scale for evaluating the efficacy of various software engineering techniques. Five tiers of capacity can be assigned according to ISO/IEC 15504. Each characteristic has its 4-point accomplishment scale in the grading method. Fully Achieved, Largely Achieved, Partially Achieved, and Not Achieved are the four points that make up the scale.

Using the Capability Maturity Model Integration (CMMI) methodology, software development reduces costs and improves timeliness by allocating and managing resources more effectively. The strategy is incorporated into the IS transformation in order to oversee its progress.

9.3.9 ISO/IEC 27002:2005 (Revised by ISO/IEC 27002:2013)

HIS can also benefit from using ISO/IEC 27002:2005 (ISO & Std, 2005), a general standard for information security. It lays out broad ideas and standards for how to start, run, maintain, and enhance information security management. Generally speaking, the aims of information security management are defined in such documents (ISO/IEC, 2013). Therefore, the standard may be utilized by any organization that wishes to implement a thorough program for managing information security or enhance its current information security practices. According to the ISO standard, several different controls may be used to secure information. Functions, rules, processes, organizational structures, and software and hardware controls are all part of this. Developing, implementing, monitoring, evaluating, and improving these security measures is essential for all organizations, including healthcare organizations. According to PRGL (2011), 114 controls covering 14 domains make up ISO/IEC 27001:2013:

1. Information security policies
2. Information security organization
3. Human resources security
4. Asset management
5. Access control
6. Cryptography
7. Physical and environmental security
8. Operations security
9. Communications security
10. Systems acquisition, development, and maintenance
11. Supplier relations
12. Information security incident management
13. Information security aspects of business continuity management
14. Compliance

9.3.10 ISO/IEC 27001:2022

An ISO standard usually remains in effect for five years. Following this time frame, the decision is made as to whether the standard can be maintained, requires revisions, or is withdrawn. Revisions to ISO 27002:2013 were authorized in 2018. The project is anticipated to be released by the end of 2021, since it is now undergoing evaluation. Throughout its 14 chapters, ISO 27002:2013 covers 114 controls. It is going to be reorganized (Malatji, 2023). The 93 controls that will make up ISO 27002:2021 are organized into four chapters: Information security management system (ISMS) certification is open to many different types of businesses as there is no industry-specific global standard. More than 7,300 companies worldwide have already obtained certification that is consistent with ISO/IEC 27001 or its national variants. Although certification is not mandated by law, it is being pursued by certain business partnerships. Business partners can rest easy knowing the organization has their back regarding information security thanks to the certification. This is great for marketing since it means they won't have to worry about doing their security checks. By achieving certification under ISO/IEC 27001, an organization may prove that it has put a system in place to manage information security and is dedicated to maintaining and enhancing that system. ISO/IEC 27001:2022 includes 93 controls with 11 new controls in comparison with 27001:2005.

- People, if they concerned individuals
- Physical, if they concern physical objects
- Technological, if they are concerned technology
- Otherwise, they are classified in the "organization" category

Five attributes only in ISO 27002:2022 (#):

- Control type (preventive, detective, corrective)
- Information security properties (ISC)
- Cybersecurity concepts
- Identify, protect, detect, respond, and recover
- Operational capabilities
- Security domains

9.3.10.1 Series Structure

ISO 27002:2022 is divided into four chapters.

1. Organizational controls (chapter 5)
2. People controls (chapter 6)
3. Physical controls (chapter 7)
4. Technological controls (chapter 8)

9.3.11 Organizational Controls

9.3.11.1 Policies for Information Security (5.1)

The organization's approach to managing information security objectives should be documented. This document must include both high-level and low-level policies, and it must be authorized by management. It is important to examine the policies frequently once they are implemented. The ideal way to handle this is to schedule a meeting regularly and be prepared to call an emergency meeting anytime. The higher-ups must sign off on any alterations. Everyone with a stake, both inside and outside the company, should be privy to the policies.

9.3.11.2 Information Security Roles and Responsibilities (5.2)

Who is accountable for what in terms of information security risk activities, processes, or assets should be specified in the policy. For all tasks, the work must be completed precisely. A small team of five generally doesn't need a full-time security officer, so be sure the duties and responsibilities fit your organization.

9.3.11.3 Segregation of Duties (5.3)

The "power" to completely control a sensitive activity shouldn't be with the same individual to avoid abuse of corporate assets. Logging all actions, dividing critical tasks into doing, verifying, or approving, and starting is the best execution approach. When one person writes and signs all of the company's checks, fraud and mistakes are prevented.

9.3.11.4 Management Responsibilities (5.4)

Upper management is responsible for disseminating and enforcing the company's information security policy to all workers and outside vendors. To set an example and prove the value and need for information security, they should act as an example themselves.

9.3.11.5 Contact with Authorities (5.5)

It must be very apparent in what situations one ought to notify certain authorities (e.g., regulatory bodies, supervisory authorities, or law enforcement) and which authorities (e.g., which region/country) ought to be contacted. A prompt and sufficient reaction to accidents can significantly lessen their impact and could even be required by law.

9.3.11.6 Contact with Special Interest Groups (5.6)

To stay abreast of information security developments and best practices, staff assigned to ISMS duties should maintain excellent communication with specific interest groups. In some situations, you can get professional guidance from these groups, and they can also help you learn more independently.

9.3.11.7 Threat Intelligence (5.7)

In the first instance, responding to threats won't stop them from happening. Gathering and analyzing data on potential dangers to your business might help you determine what safeguards are necessary to ward off those dangers. While large-scale computer chip companies face the risk of targeted IP theft attempts from nation-states, smaller software as a service providers face the much more significant threat of automated phishing emails.

9.3.11.8 Information Security in Project Management (5.8)

Consideration and documentation of information security needs in all projects are essential for a successful organization-wide ISMS deployment. These needs may arise due to meeting legal, commercial, or other regulatory obligations. Including a section on information security in any project management manuals or templates is a must.

9.3.11.9 Inventory of Information and Other Associated Assets (5.9)

The organization should have recognized all assets related to information and information processing. An accurate and up-to-date inventory of all assets is required. Recognizing and anticipating hazards depends on having complete knowledge of all assets, including their nature, location, importance, and handling. For insurance or legal reasons, it could be necessary.

Assuming the inventory is comprehensive, every item must have a designated owner. Asset ownership ensures that assets are monitored and maintained during their entire lifespan. Grouping similar assets and delegating day-to-day monitoring to a so-called custodian keep the owner accountable. Management approval is required for asset ownership.

9.3.11.10 Acceptable Use of Information and Other Associated Assets (5.10)

Rules for accessing information assets should be well-documented. The asset's users must be knowledgeable about and adhere to all applicable information security regulations when using the asset.

Additionally, protocols should be established for the management of assets. Employees must be familiar with asset labeling and able to manage varying degrees of categorization. Since there isn't a single, agreed-upon way to categorize things, it's helpful to be aware of how other parties rank things since their rankings may likely differ from yours.

9.3.11.11 Return of Assets (5.11)

Any time an individual or entity can no longer use an asset—for instance, when their job or agreement ends—they are required to give it back to the organization. Everyone concerned should be aware of the explicit policy on this. It is crucial to document and restore non-tangible assets critical to present operations, such as particular expertise, as soon as possible.

9.3.11.12 Classification of Information (5.12)

While specific details are less important than others, some must stay secret because of their sensitivity (e.g., monetary or legal worth). There has to be a plan for how the company will deal with sensitive data. It is the owner's responsibility to categorize information assets properly. Varied classified assets may need varied degrees of secrecy, ranging from completely nonexistent to devastatingly affecting the organization's capacity to survive.

9.3.11.13 Labeling of Information (5.13)

As said in Section 5.12, not all data is of the same kind. As a result, you should name your data according to its category. Knowing the object's categorization may be crucial for handling, storing, or exchanging information. Unfortunately, this may lead to intriguing things and benefit malicious people. Being aware of this danger is critical.

9.3.11.14 Information Transfer (5.14)

Employees and external parties alike have access to the company's data. Digital papers, physical documents, video, and even word of mouth should all adhere to the same standard when transferring information. Information contamination or leaks can be mitigated by establishing clear guidelines for the secure sharing of data.

An information transfer agreement must be in place before any company data is shared with other parties. In this way, everyone involved in the data transmission is on the same page about its origin, contents, secrecy, transfer medium, and final destination.

The use of electronic messaging has become commonplace in business communication. Companies should keep track of the protected and allowable uses of permitted forms of electronic messages and maintain a list of these forms on hand.

9.3.11.15 Access Control (5.15)

Establishing who has permission to access, what access is, and how access is handled is the job of an access control policy. The onus for determining the regulations governing "their" asset rests squarely on the shoulders of the asset's owners. The words "need-to-know" and "need-to-use" are commonly used in an access control policy. A need-to-know policy limits access to just the information that an employee needs to do their job, while a need-to-use policy limits access to only the processing facilities that are necessary to do their job.

9.3.11.16 Identity Management (5.16)

Users must be registered under an ID to provide access privileges to assets and networks and monitor those gaining access. It is important to deactivate an employee's ID and any associated permissions after they depart an organization. Limiting an employee's access is a simple way to prevent them from doing their job. Using another employee's ID may be more convenient, but management shouldn't usually let this. It becomes tough to ensure that the correct individual is held accountable for their actions when IDs are shared, as this removes the connection between an employee and an access restriction. The process of creating, updating, and finally removing an identity is known as the identity lifecycle.

9.3.11.17 Authentication Information (5.17)

There has to be a system in place for handling secret authentication, such as access cards and passwords. All systems should require a user's secret authentication information (password on PC, swiping access card for doors), prohibit users from sharing secret authentication information, and need new users to change their password upon first use. Other important activities that should be stated in the policy include these points.

Password management solutions should only be used with strong passwords and adhere rigidly to the organization's policy regarding secret authentication information. It is imperative that the password management system securely stores and transmits the passwords themselves.

9.3.11.18 Access Rights (5.18)

Management should establish a mechanism for the granting and revocation of access permissions. It is recommended that certain roles be assigned according to the tasks that particular workers do and that they be granted standard access privileges. There should be consequences for every attempt at unauthorized access as part of any system. Since the asset owner or management may quickly grant or revoke access privileges, employees have no incentive to try to get unauthorized access to restricted areas.

Companies and their workers are dynamic. Employees' roles and responsibilities vary, leading to evolving access requirements. Management should review access rights if a job changes or an employee leaf, and asset owners should do the same regularly. Examining privileged access permissions more often due to their sensitivity is important. It is proper practice to revoke the receiving party's access privileges upon contract or agreement termination.

9.3.11.19 *Information Security in Supplier Relationships (5.19)*

Organizations should adopt a strategy outlining the need for risk reduction as suppliers have access to certain assets. Suppliers must be informed and reach an agreement about this policy. Some examples of such criteria include agreed-upon logistical procedures, incident response duties for all parties involved, non-disclosure agreements, and supply chain documentation.

9.3.11.20 *Addressing Information Security within Supplier Agreements (5.20)*

All vendors dealing with the company's data in any way, shape, or form must adhere to and accept the organization's information security standards. Information categorization standards, permitted usage policies, and audit rights are a few examples. What to do if the provider suddenly stops supplying is an often-overlooked part of any deal. Including a provision for such is crucial.

9.3.11.21 *Managing Information Security in the ICT Supply Chain (5.21)*

The information security requirements, as well as agreements on information and communication technology services and the supply chain, should be included in supplier agreements. The ability to track things as they move through the supply chain and the maintenance of a minimum degree of security at each stage of the "chain" are two examples of needs that are part of this.

9.3.11.22 *Monitoring, Review, and Change Management of Supplier Services (5.22)*

Suppliers are human, too, and inevitably make errors. The outcome remains the same whether the error was intentional: the organization loses out on precisely what was agreed upon, and trust might take a nosedive. Companies should monitor their suppliers and conduct audits as needed because of this. In this manner a company may be alerted if a supplier engages in unusual behavior.

Changes to supplier services require management oversight, just as changes to the system do. They are responsible for maintaining current information security rules and effectively managing service provisioning modifications.

A combination of an out-of-date information security policy and a little tweak to the service could introduce a significant new threat. Changes on the provider's part are common and can take many forms, such as improvements to the service, the introduction of a new app or system, or revisions to the supplier's rules and procedures.

9.3.11.23 Information Security for the Use of Cloud Services (5.23)

When used, the service that cloud providers provide is typically an essential component of the infrastructure that a company relies on. While many SaaS providers deliver their products to clients directly, many others use cloud providers like Amazon Web Services (AWS), Microsoft Azure, or Google Cloud to store Office documents.

Proper measures should be taken to reduce the risks associated with this vital aspect of the business. Every business needs a plan for when to utilize, manage, and eventually leave a used cloud. When you cut connections with one cloud provider, chances are good that you'll soon be working with another. Keeping tabs on the acquisition and transition to the new cloud shouldn't be overlooked.

9.3.11.24 Information Security Incident Management Planning and Preparation (5.24)

Organizations should establish protocols for handling incidents related to information security and clearly define roles and responsibilities. This will allow for the efficient and prompt handling of any information security event. Unexpected security incidents can create a lot of havoc, but a well-established process followed by competent employees can help reduce the impact.

9.3.11.25 Assessment and Decision on Information Security Events (5.25)

Establishing a systematic approach to documenting and evaluating security occurrences is crucial for organizations. The onus is on the accountable party to ascertain whether or not a genuine information security incident occurred by comparing the suspicious event to the criteria. For the sake of future reference, it is important to document the outcomes of this evaluation.

9.3.11.26 Response to Information Security Incidents (5.26)

This may sound like a no-brainer, but it bears mentioning since it can be challenging to implement. Appointed personnel must respond to information security incidents in accordance with established protocols whenever they occur. The steps previously decided upon must be executed, and the entire procedure must be meticulously recorded. By doing so, we can identify any associated security holes and ensure this doesn't happen again.

9.3.11.27 *Learning from Information Security Incidents (5.27)*

Incidents are valuable despite how undesirable they are. The information gathered from resolving an incident may be utilised to avoid future occurrences of the same kind and may even reveal a systemic issue. Always keep an eye on the budget while adding controls; the yearly cost of a new control shouldn't exceed the value of the occurrences it prevents.

9.3.11.28 *Collection of Evidence (5.28)*

It is not always easy to determine what caused an accident once it has happened. Discipline should be met according to the cause's goal and impact, whether an individual or an organization. Evidence must be gathered to connect an occurrence to a cause. This evidence and the methods employed to get it might be used in court in the event of a criminal prosecution. A secure and transparent evidence identification technique is necessary to avoid the negligent or intentional loss of evidence.

9.3.11.29 *Information Security during Disruption (5.29)*

Organizations should assess their needs for information security continuity in the event of a crisis. In a crisis, the best action is to return to normal information security procedures as soon as feasible. To recover with a satisfactory degree of data protection during a disaster, management must first establish and agree upon the necessary procedures, strategies, and controls.

The optimal strategy for handling a crisis also evolves as organizations transform. A different approach than last year would likely be more beneficial for an organization that, for instance, saw a doubling of its size within a year. That is why regularly checking the information security continuity controls is important.

9.3.11.30 *ICT Readiness for Business Continuity (5.30)*

Considerations for potential failures of information technology systems should be given considerable weight in business continuity planning. There has to be a well-defined plan for restoring systems, including who is responsible and how long it could take. Since the core systems alone will probably be sufficient for the first week following a total meltdown, the meaning of "restoring" in a given situation should also be crystal apparent.

9.3.11.31 Identification of Legal, Statutory, Regulatory, and Contractual Requirements (5.31)

Needs are everywhere and must be satisfied. Therefore, businesses should know what information security regulations they must follow and how to comply. Maintaining an up-to-date requirement compliance overview is important since requirements might change or be added. Expanding your organization to a new country on a different continent is one example of a situation that needs change. This nation is likely to have its own set of rules regarding data storage, encryption, and personal privacy.

9.3.11.32 Intellectual Property Rights (5.32)

Legal compliance also includes protecting intellectual property (IP) rights, a crucial subject needing extra care. Because IP may be so valuable, keeping thorough records of one's and others' IP usage is crucial. It is crucial to avoid, at all costs, the (intentional) misuse of someone else's intellectual property, as this might lead to costly litigation.

9.3.11.33 Protection of Records (5.33)

Accounting data and audit logs are no exception; they must be kept secure. Loss, compromise, or unauthorized access to records is a real possibility. Organizational or external factors, such as laws or insurance companies, may impose records preservation obligations. For this, it is necessary to establish and adhere to stringent regulations.

9.3.11.34 Privacy and Protection of Personal Identifiable Information (PII) (5.34)

Legal requirements for securing personally identifiable information may vary between nations or economic regions. The GDPR is in effect for businesses with European Union (EU) locations and/or that handle the personal information of EU residents. Organizations must ensure they are cognizant of and adhere strictly to the standards established by such laws. For example, the General Data Protection Regulation (GDPR) requires openness in data processing, a record of processing activities, and data-processing agreements.

Data-processing register, and data protection impact assessment (DPIA) templates are among the free resources we provide to assist with compliance with GDPR.

9.3.11.35 Independent Review of Information Security (5.35)

A company's information security system can never be reviewed impartially. This is why businesses should schedule frequent or significant change-based information security audits. This ensures that a company's perception of its information security is accurate and open to scrutiny. A full-time internal auditor who is not involved in any other projects or duties and is only responsible for conducting the internal audits would also qualify as an impartial third party.

9.3.11.36 Compliance with Policies and Standards for Information Security (5.36)

Managers should check frequently that the processes and activities within their purview are completely compliant with all applicable security policies, standards, and procedures. To ensure they're following all the laws and regulations, they should use automated reporting technology or be familiar with the specific regulations.

Additionally, information systems should undergo compliance reviews regularly. Automated tooling is the most convenient and economical method for this. With this software, we can swiftly inspect every corner of a system and detail everything that went wrong or may go wrong. While vulnerability testing, like penetration tests, are great for finding security holes, it can damage the system if not executed carefully.

9.3.11.37 Documented Operating Procedures (5.37)

It is important to document and make available to those utilizing equipment the procedures for operating it. No matter how basic, every piece of equipment needs an instruction manual on how to use it properly and safely. This includes everything from turning on a computer to turning it off. Because of their significance, the processes should be handled as formal papers, requiring management approval for any modifications.

9.3.11.38 ISO 27001 vs. COBIT

Table 9.7 shows the security control clauses of ISO/IEC 27001:2013 mapped to the practices of the COBIT 5 process.

9.3.11.39 HITRUST Common Security Framework (CSF)

When it comes to data protection, companies all across the globe rely on HITRUST SF for the structure, transparency, direction, and cross-referencing to authoritative sources that they need to feel assured. For its initial development, HITRUST SF relied on national and international security and privacy frameworks, standards, and regulations such as ISO, NIST, PCI, HIPAA, and COBIT. It continues to incorporate new authoritative sources to ensure a comprehensive set of controls. By standardizing them, the HITRUST SF

Table 9.7 ISO/IEC 27001:2013 Mapped to the Practices of the COBIT 5

	COBIT 5 Process Practice	*ISO/IEC27001:2013 Control Clause*
EDM01.01	Enterprise governance guiding principles	A.5: Information security policies
EDM01.02	Direct the governance system	
AP001.02	Establish roles and responsibilities	A.6: Organization of information security
DSS06.03	Manage roles, responsibilities, and access privileges and levels of authority	
APO07.01	Include background checks in IT recruitment process	A.7: Human resource security (controls that are applied before, during, or after employment)
AP007.03	Maintain the skills and competencies of personnel	
BAI109.01	Identify and record current assets	A.8: Asset management
BAI109.02	Manage critical assets	
BAI109.03	Manage the asset lifecycle	
DSS05.04	Manage user identity and logical access	A.9: Access control
DSS05.05	Manage physical access to IT assets	
DSS01.04	Manage the environment	A.11: Physical and environmental security
DSS01.05	Manage facilities	
DSS01.03	Monitor IT infrastructure	A.12: Operations security
DSS05.01	Protect against malware	A.13: Communications security
DSS01.02	Manage network and connectivity security	
APO13.01	Establish and maintain an information security management system (ISMS)	A.14: System acquisition, development, and maintenance
AP010	Manage suppliers	A.15: Supplier relationships
DSS02.01	Define incident and service request classification schemes and models	A.16: Information security incident management
DSS05.02	Maintain a continuity strategy	A.17: Information security aspects of business continuity management
EDM01.01	Evaluate the governance system	A.18: Compliance (with internal requirements, such as policies, and with external requirements, such as laws)
EDM01.02	Direct the governance system	
EDM01.03	Monitor the governance system	

standard makes compliance easier by making all these standards clear and consistent.

9.3.11.40 Background of CSF

With input from industry heavyweights in healthcare, business, IT, and information security, the Health Information Trust Alliance (HITRUST) developed the Common Security Framework. When released in March 2009, CSF made history as the first IT security architecture tailored to protect healthcare data.

9.3.11.41 Structure of CSF

The two components that comprise CSF are described later.

9.3.11.41.1 Information Security Control Specifications Manual

This standard offers prescriptive implementation guidelines based on best practices. Effective and efficient information security management is ensured using the suggested security governance techniques and security control activities. A total of 13 groups of security controls, 42 goals, and 135 details are included in the handbook. Here are the control categories:

1. Information Security Management Program
2. Access Control
3. Human Resources Security
4. Risk Management
5. Security Policy
6. Organization of Information Security
7. Compliance
8. Asset Management
9. Physical and Environmental Security
10. Communications and Operations Management
11. Information Systems Acquisition, Development, and Maintenance
12. Information Security Incident Management
13. Business Continuity Management

Under circumstances where CSF requirements are difficult or impractical to implement, CSF supports "a concept of approved Alternate Controls as a risk mitigation or compensation strategy for a system control failure."

9.3.11.41.2 Standards and Regulations Mapping

This component reconciles the framework with common, diverse parts of generally accepted standards and regulations. Above, we saw that CSF uses and references healthcare-related legislation and standards.

You can see how HITRUST CSF fits in with other standards by looking at the mapping between control specifications and implementation requirements. This makes the organization's compliance activities easier. Other criteria do not fill up all of the gaps, that much is certain. These holes are filled by CSF when they are identified in the mapping phase (HITRUST, 2012).

If you are a healthcare information security expert, you must subscribe to HITRUST Central, a controlled online community, to access CSF. Individuals from qualifying organizations as specified by HITRUST are eligible to get standard subscriptions at no cost. A subscription is required to access the CSF Assurance Kit, reliable sources, and the online, interactive version of the CSF (HITRUST, 2012).

9.3.12 NIST CSF 2.0

To assist businesses in comprehending, reducing, and conveying cybersecurity threats, the NIST has published a preliminary version of the Cybersecurity Framework (CSF) 2.0, an updated tool in February 2024 (Pascoe, 2023), that was initially introduced in 2014 (Sedgewick, 2014). To accommodate evolving cybersecurity threats and facilitate the CSF implementation across all types of organizations, NIST has released a draft update for public review and discussion.

Compared to the 2015 original and 2018 version 1.1, 2.0 is more of a collection of resources meant to support the framework's implementation rather than a static resource in and of itself. "The CSF has been a vital tool for many entities, helping them anticipate and address cybersecurity threats," said Laurie E. Locascio, Under Secretary of Commerce for Standards and Technology and Director of NIST. "CSF 2.0" is more than a document; it expands upon earlier editions. The cybersecurity demands and capacities of public and commercial organizations might vary over time, so can this set of resources, which can be utilised alone or in combination.

"Governance" is the most significant structural alteration to the CSF; the five preceding functions—identify, protect, detect, respond, and restore—are based on it. Organizations can use the "outcomes," or desirable states, presented by this function to guide and prioritize actions that will bring about the outcomes of the other five functions, which are all part of enterprise risk management programs that include cybersecurity. Figure 9.2 shows NIST Cybersecurity Framework 2.0 functions.

Creating a governance category is intended to elevate all cybersecurity risk management activities to the level of organizations' management and board of directors. "The main objective of this version 2.0 is to make governance a function," explained Padraic O'Reilly, founder and chief innovation officer of CyberSaint. "What we understand today, and this is quite common in the cybersecurity field, is that if governance is not actively involved, we're just going in circles."

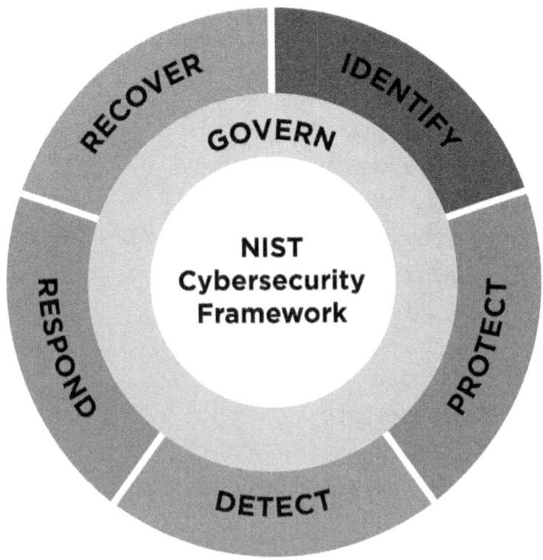

Figure 9.2 NIST Cybersecurity Framework 2.0 functions.

The Cybersecurity Framework 2.0 also integrates and expands on the supply chain risk management findings contained in CSF 1.1, grouping most of them under the governance function. Framework 2.0 believes that, given "the complex and interconnected relationships in this ecosystem, supply chain risk management (SCRM) is essential for organizations." Cybersecurity SCRM (C-SCRM) is a systematic process for addressing this risk and developing appropriate response strategies, policies, and procedures. The subcategories of the CSF's C-SCRM category [GV.SC] bridge the gap between purely cybersecurity and C-SCRM-oriented outcomes.""

Integrating supply chain risk management into the governance function is just one step toward solving one of the thorniest cybersecurity issues. "The supply chain is a mess," Padraic O'Reilly enthuses, "It's a mess because it's complex. Part of this subject has been placed under the umbrella of governance because it has to be managed more and more at the management level. Certain practices are halfway satisfactory, but they only cover half the problem. Table 9.8 shows the CSF 2.0 Function and Category Mapping.

9.3.12.1 NIST Special Publication 800–53

Special Publications (SP) are publications that the NIST creates and releases to the public as guidelines and recommendations. The stated goal of SP 800–53 is "to offer recommendations for choosing and outlining security measures for data systems that back up the federal government's executive agencies." That was in 2009, according to NIST. The text says that commercial organizations and state, regional, and tribal governments can all utilize the principles when needed. As a result, healthcare organizations

Table 9.8 NIST CSF 2.0 Function and Category Mapping

CSF 2.0 Function	*CSF 2.0 Category*	*CSF 2.0 Category Identifier*
Govern (GV)	Organizational context	GV.OC
	Risk management strategy	GV.RM
	Roles and responsibilities	GV.RR
	Policies and procedures	GV.PO
	Asset management	ID.AM
Identify (ID)	Risk assessment	ID.RA
	Supply chain risk management	ID.SC
	Improvement	ID.IM
	Identity management, authentication, and access control	PR.AA
	Awareness and training	PR.AT
Protect (PR)	Data security	PR.DS
	Platform security	PR.PS
	Technology infrastructure resilience	PR.IR
Detect (DE)	Adverse event analysis	DE.AE
	Continuous monitoring	DE.CM
	Incident management	RS.MA
Respond (RS)	Incident analysis	RS.AN
	Incident response reporting and communication	RS.CO
	Incident mitigation	RS.MI
Recover (RC)	Incident recovery plan execution	RC.RP
	Incident recovery communication	RC.CO

may safeguard their sensitive data by following the instructions (Bodeau & Graubart, 2013).

9.3.12.2 Background of NIST SP 800–53

Protecting the Integrity of Government Information Systems and Organisations is the title of NIST Special Publication 800–53. It was in 1990 when NIST developed the Special Publication 800 series. Publications in this series are aimed at the computer security community as a whole. They detail the IT Lab's partnerships with businesses, universities, and government agencies and its computer security research, recommendations, and outreach initiatives.

9.3.12.3 Structure of NIST SP 800–53

In response to information systems' growing complexity and interconnectedness, national attention on security and privacy is paramount. A 2017 report by the Task Force on Cyber Deterrence underscores the vulnerabilities in US critical infrastructure and essential information systems. Over the next decade, urgent action is needed to fortify these systems against cyber threats, particularly from capable adversaries. NIST Special Publication 800–53 Revision 5 (Amiruddin et al., 2021) addresses this imperative by proactively developing comprehensive safeguarding measures for all computing platforms, including those in critical sectors like cyber-physical systems and IoT devices. These measures aim to enhance system resilience, limit attack damage, and protect individual privacy. This update represents a multi-year effort to refine security and privacy controls, making them more usable across diverse consumer groups. Significant changes include making controls outcome-based, integrating security and privacy controls, introducing a supply chain risk management control family, and separating control selection processes. By incorporating new controls based on the latest threat intelligence, this revision ensures the systems we rely on are better equipped to withstand cyber threats. Additionally, separating control selection from controls and removing control baselines streamline the publication, with additional guidance being relocated to other NIST publications. In the future, NIST plans to provide interactive online access to all control information through a web-based portal, enhancing user accessibility.

Enhancing the foundational information systems, products, and services vital to the nation's critical infrastructure is urgent. This involves ensuring their trustworthiness and resilience to support the economic and national security interests of the United States. In response to a call by the DSB, NIST Special Publication (SP) 800–53 Revision 5 takes a proactive approach to developing comprehensive safeguarding measures for various computing platforms. These measures encompass security and privacy controls to safeguard critical operations, assets, and individual privacy. The objectives include enhancing the resilience of information systems, limiting damage from attacks, and protecting privacy.

Revision 5 of NIST SP 800–53 represents a multi-year effort to develop the next generation of security and privacy controls. Significant changes include making controls outcome-based, integrating security and privacy controls into a consolidated catalog, and establishing a new supply chain risk management control family. Control selection processes are separated from controls to cater to diverse user groups. Additionally, new controls based on the latest threat intelligence have been incorporated. While some guidance has been removed from SP 800–53, it will be relocated to other NIST publications. NIST also plans to provide interactive online access to control information.

9.3.12.4 NIST Special Publication 1800–1

This item, NIST SP 1800–1, is part of NIST's Special Publications (SP) series, much like the one listed before (NIST SP 800–53). "Provides users with information they need to replicate this approach to securing electronic health records transferred among mobile devices" is the stated goal of the paper, which aims to serve as a "standards-based reference design" (O'Reilly & Rigopoulos, 2020). Given the breadth of both the target audience and the topics addressed, NIST SP 1800–1 is a useful reference for many people who are responsible for putting IT security principles into practice. For example, the publication shows how to configure networks in a way that makes healthcare systems or EHR less vulnerable to exploitation, and it also brings attention to the vulnerabilities of mobile computing within these systems when it comes to processing and transmitting patient data. To rephrase, the guide's utility is conditional on the user's level of technical competence in healthcare settings.

9.3.12.5 Background of NIST SP 1800–1

NIST Special Publication 1800–1 entitled *Securing Electronic Health Records on Mobile Devices* was released in July 2018.

The NIST Cybersecurity Practice Guide, titled "Securing Electronic Records on Mobile Devices," illustrates how existing technologies can fulfill the need for enhanced information protection in EHR systems. The guide demonstrates how security professionals, leveraging commercially available and open-source tools consistent with cybersecurity standards, can assist healthcare organizations in securely sharing patients' health records using mobile devices. The guide outlines steps to achieve this objective by employing a layered security approach. Organizations can consider adopting a similar approach outlined in the guide. Commercial and open-source products, aligned with standards, are readily accessible and compatible with common IT infrastructure and investments.

Key features of the guide include:

- Mapping security characteristics to standards and best practices from NIST, other standards organizations, and the HIPAA Security Rule.
- Providing a comprehensive architecture and capabilities addressing security controls.
- Streamlining ease of use through automated configuration of security controls.
- Addressing various implementation options, whether in-house or outsourced.
- Offering implementation guidance for security engineers and implementers to replicate the reference design wholly or partially.

While the guide references a suite of commercial products, it does not endorse specific products. Information security experts should identify products that integrate seamlessly with existing tools and IT system infrastructure. Organizations can choose to adopt the provided solution or one that is entirely aligned with the guidelines or use the guide as a foundation for customizing and implementing components of a solution.

9.3.12.6 Structure of NIST SP 1800–1

NIST SP 1800–1 is divided into five volumes (lettered a–e). The following is a list of the volumes and a cursory summary of the content (O'Reilly & Rigopoulos, 2020).

(1) NIST SP 1800–1a: Executive Summary
- Describes the difficulties healthcare organizations encounter when using mobile computing to manage patient records.
- Calls attention to the need for a standards-based cybersecurity strategy to safeguard an organization's network and its patients' personal information.
- Principally useful for heads of healthcare organizations' information security and healthcare IT departments.

(2) NIST SP 1800–1b
- Establishes a relationship between security features and guidelines established by several organizations, including NIST, HIPAA, and others.
- Offers a thorough framework with an emphasis on security rules.
- Aids usability by use of automatic security control configuration.
- Brings to light the necessity of various implementation methods (in-house vs. outsourcing).
- Considers the following risks while conducting risk assessments: disclosure, compromise, and unavailability
- Serves primarily as a reference for security engineers and implementers.

(3) NIST SP 1800–1c: How-To Guides
- Presents a made-up situation in which primary care physicians utilize mobile devices.
- Describes every product used for construction reference.
- Highlights the impact of the items on the given solution.
- Target audience: IT experts

(4) NIST SP 1800–1d
- Gives a comprehensive rundown of all security standards utilized in architectural development.
- Details recommended methods
- Target audience: IT experts

(5) **NIST SP 1800–1e**
- Describes in detail the process that occurs during an attempt to obtain EHR through cyberattack.
- Describes many approaches to risk evaluation:
  - Approach based on tables
  - Attack/fault tree evaluation technique
- Reports the findings of an impartial evaluation of the guide's reference blueprint.
- Target audience: IT experts

9.3.12.7 NIST Special Publication 1800–8

This entry, NIST SP 1800–8 (O'Brien et al., 2018), is part of NIST's Special Publications (SP) series, much as the ones stated before (NIST SP 800–53 and NIST SP 1800–1). Healthcare delivery organizations (HDOs) rely on external infusion pumps, and this guide aims to educate IT professionals and engineers on the many security vulnerabilities in these pumps and offer them guidelines to protect themselves.

Historically, infusion pumps have not been integrated into complex systems or wireless networks; instead, they have operated as "standalone instruments". However, as medical technology progressed, these devices could be wirelessly linked to other sources in healthcare networks and systems, adding to the IoT. Specifically, medical devices are becoming more capable of communicating with other devices and networks through the Internet, a phenomenon NIST calls the Internet of Medical Things (IoMT) (NIST, 2017). Although infusion pumps are becoming more interconnected and improving patient care, there are also risks associated with them. These include unauthorized access from malicious attacks, which can lead to the loss of patient data and healthcare services, health information breaches, and substantial financial consequences from the public's lack of trust in the security of patient data. Consequently, according to NIST (2017), the following are among the primary objectives of NIST SP 1800–8:

- To prepare for the deployment of wireless infusion pumps and reduce the risk of cyberattacks.
- Steer clear of operational risks and their repercussions, including device interference and patient data loss.
- To prevent a breach due to a weak link and build a multi-level security plan.
- Educate HDOs on the practical use of cybersecurity best practices and standards.

9.3.12.8 Background of NIST SP 1800–8

Securing Wireless Infusion Pumps in Healthcare Delivery Organisations is the August 2018 NIST Special Publication 1800–8 title. The fast development of technology has resulted in the broad implementation of the IoT, enabling tangible objects to link and exchange data. Consequently, the IoMT has emerged in the healthcare industry, allowing for integrating equipment such as wireless infusion pumps into healthcare delivery organizations (HDOs). Cybersecurity threats, such as eavesdropping and malfunctioning medical devices, are introduced by this integration. A solution to these problems has been devised by the National Cybersecurity Centre of Excellence (NCCoE) at NIST. It shows how HDOs can secure the wireless infusion pump ecosystem, which includes patient data and medication library dosage limits, by utilizing commercially available cybersecurity technologies. Due to this effort, the NIST Cybersecurity Practice Guide, *Securing Wireless Infusion Pumps in Healthcare Delivery Organisations*, was created. This guide provides a reference design and an example implementation for effectively handling this problem in clinical settings.

9.3.12.9 Structure of NIST SP 1800–8

Volume A provides an executive summary, Volume B details the approach, architecture, and security characteristics, and Volume C provides how-to guides; these three volumes make up NIST Special Publication 1800–8A-C. An overview of the key points covered in each book is provided below (NIST, 2017).

- *Volume A: Executive Summary*
  - Introduces HDO challenges in securing the wireless infusion pumps.
  - Presents the example solution created at the NCCoE.
  - Discusses the advantages of implementing NCCoE's solution.
- *Volume B: Approach, Architecture, and Security Characteristics:* this volume is divided into nine sections.
  - Section 1, Summary, delves into the challenges the NCCoE project addresses, detailing our approach, architecture, security characteristics, the solution demonstrated, its benefits, and the technology partners involved. It also guides how to offer feedback on this guide.
  - Section 2, How to Use This Guide, outlines how various readers, including business decision-makers, program managers, IT professionals, and biomedical engineers, can effectively utilize each part of the guide.
  - Section 3, Approach, provides an extensive overview of the project's scope, discussing the assumptions underlying security platform

development, the risk assessment driving platform development, and the technologies provided by industry collaborators to enable platform development.
- Section 4, Risk Assessment and Mitigation, focuses on identifying risks, proposing potential responses, and suggesting mitigation efforts to reduce risks for HDOs.
- Section 5, Architecture, elucidates the supported usage scenarios of project security platforms, detailing the NIST Cybersecurity Framework Functions facilitated by each component contributed by our collaborators.
- Section 6, Life Cycle Cybersecurity Issues, examines cybersecurity considerations across product lifecycles, encompassing procurement, maintenance, and end-of-life aspects.
- Section 7, Security Characteristics Analysis, provides insight into the tools and techniques used to conduct wireless infusion pump risk assessments.
- Section 8, Functional Evaluation, summarizes the test sequences employed to showcase security platform services, linking each test sequence to relevant NIST Cybersecurity Framework Functions and applicable controls from NIST Special Publication (SP) 800–53 Revision 4.
- Section 9, Future Considerations, briefly explores potential applications that NIST may explore to enhance support for wireless infusion pump cybersecurity.

- *Volume C: How-to Guides*
  - Information technology experts can use this paper as a blueprint to replicate the solution it contains.
  - An instruction manual for recreating the build from the NCCoE lab, including steps for installation, setup, and integration.
  - Related subjects: tools for risk assessment, core network security, identity services, Symantec endpoint security, and intrusion detection

9.3.12.10 Center for Internet Security (CIS)

The CIS Controls® initiative originated from a grassroots effort to identify prevalent cyberattacks affecting enterprises, translate this knowledge into actionable steps for defenders, and share it with a broader audience. Initially modest in scope, the goal was to assist individuals and enterprises in focusing their efforts on critical defense measures against significant cyber threats (Groš, 2021).

Under the guidance of the Center for Internet Security® (CIS®), CIS Controls have evolved into an international community comprising volunteer individuals and organizations. This community:

- Collaborates to analyze attacks and their root causes, translating findings into defensive strategies.

- Develops and shares tools, resources, and success stories to facilitate adoption and problem-solving.
- Aligns the CIS Controls with regulatory and compliance frameworks to prioritize and focus collective efforts.
- Addresses common challenges and obstacles, such as assessment and implementation roadmaps, through collaborative solutions.

The CIS Controls draw upon the expertise of diverse stakeholders from various sectors and roles, including threat responders, technologists, IT operators, policymakers, and auditors. Together, they contribute to the development, adoption, and support of CIS Controls, reflecting a collective commitment to enhancing cybersecurity practices.

9.3.12.11 *Critical Security Controls*

The most recent version of the CIS Controls, released in 2021, is version eight, which retains prioritization based on importance but introduces notable changes in organization and content. Tasks and activities now group controls, and what were previously termed subcontrols are now referred to as main controls, as shown in Figure 9.3.

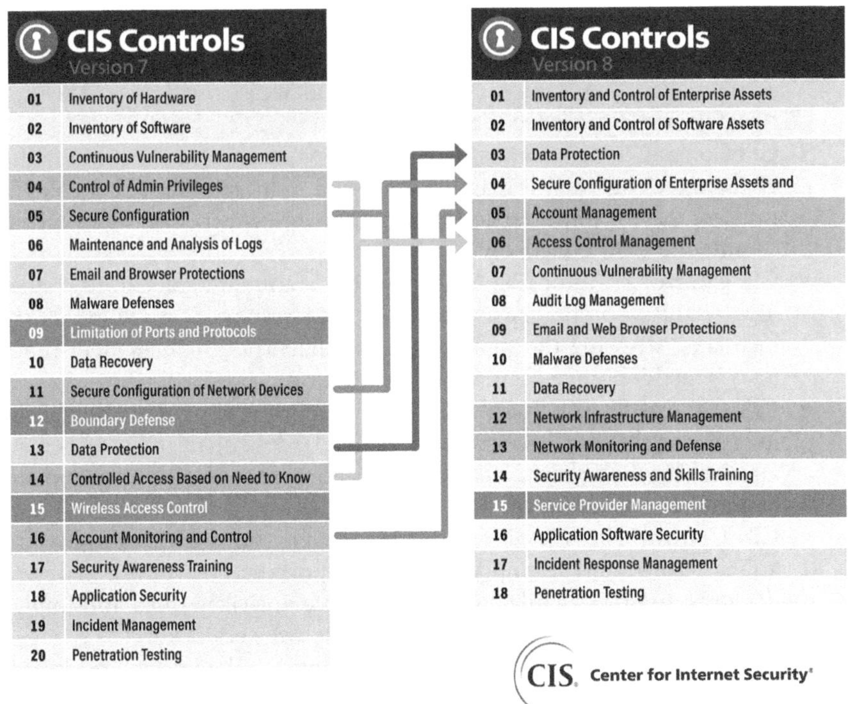

Figure 9.3 CIS Controls mapping between version 7 and version 8.

- **CIS Control 1:** Inventory and Control of Enterprise Assets. Initiating a comprehensive view of network devices is pivotal to reducing an organization's attack surface. Continuous employment of active and passive asset discovery solutions ensures ongoing monitoring and accountability for all hardware.
- **CIS Control 2:** Inventory and Control of Software Assets. Similarly focused on asset discovery, this control underscores the importance of network inventorying as the fundamental step in strengthening system defenses, emphasizing that effective asset management hinges on awareness and tracking.
- **CIS Control 3:** Data Protection. Formulating a robust data management strategy entail understanding and classifying enterprise data and implementing policies and response procedures. This control is particularly complex due to the ongoing process of managing sensitive information.
- **CIS Control 4:** Secure Configuration of Enterprise Assets and Software. This control highlights the necessity of file integrity monitoring to uphold configuration standards, emphasizing the need for automated monitoring to detect deviations from established baselines across various systems.
- **CIS Control 5:** Account Management. Protecting authentication mechanisms and administrative credentials is paramount to thwarting unauthorized access. Rigorous monitoring and control of accounts fortify defenses against malicious activities and asset compromise.
- **CIS Control 6:** Access Control Management. Beginning with inventorying wireless access points, this control delves into mitigating wireless access risks, advocating for encryption and access restriction measures to safeguard against security breaches.
- **CIS Control 7:** Continuous Vulnerability Management. Addressing the challenge of staying abreast of emerging vulnerabilities, this control underscores the importance of continuous assessment and remediation to mitigate risks effectively.
- **CIS Control 8:** Audit Log Management. Maintaining accurate system logs enables comprehensive analysis and response to cybersecurity incidents, stressing the significance of diligent log management practices in incident investigation and resolution.
- **CIS Control 9:** Email and Web Browser Protections. Beyond phishing threats, this control emphasizes safeguarding against various email and web browser-based attacks, advocating for robust protections to counteract potential exploits.
- **CIS Control 10:** Malware Defenses. Given the rise in ransomware attacks, this control emphasizes the importance of robust malware defenses, urging organizations to integrate antivirus tools and implement regular updates to mitigate malware risks effectively.
- **CIS Control 11:** Data Recovery. Preparing for data recovery during preventive control failures is critical, necessitating regular backups and comprehensive testing to ensure swift and effective data restoration capabilities.

- **CIS Control 12:** Network Infrastructure Management. By implementing automated port scanning and application firewalls, organizations can minimize their attack surface, reinforcing network security through proper configuration and administration of network devices.
- **CIS Control 13:** Network Monitoring and Defense. Centralized security event alerting and robust intrusion detection systems are crucial components of effective network monitoring and defense, underlining the importance of ongoing attention to network security measures.
- **CIS Control 14:** Security Awareness and Skills Training. Recognizing the importance of cybersecurity training, this control advocates for ongoing employee education to cultivate a culture of cyber hygiene and resilience against social engineering attacks.
- **CIS Control 15:** Service Provider Management. Managing third-party service providers' security is essential, given their access to sensitive data, emphasizing the need for stringent security measures and compliance standards.
- **CIS Control 16:** Application Software Security. This control underscores the importance of rigorous security assessments for in-house developed code, advocating for comprehensive application security controls to mitigate vulnerabilities effectively.
- **CIS Control 17:** Incident Response Management. Establishing strategies for incident response planning and testing is critical for effective incident mitigation, emphasizing the importance of post-incident reviews to refine response procedures.
- **CIS Control 18:** Penetration Testing. Regular penetration testing is essential for identifying vulnerabilities and attack vectors, providing crucial insights into potential critical vulnerabilities within an organization's networks, applications, and systems.

9.3.12.12 HIPAA

To clarify the responsibilities of organizations regarding particular rules outlined in the Health Insurance Portability and Accountability Act, a framework known as HIPAA was established in 1996 (Ihs.gov, 1996). Important parts of health data management, such as patients' right to privacy and the necessity of suitable security measures to safeguard health data, are outlined in these rules (HIPAA, 1999).

Private data, and healthcare companies' requirements can be at risk if a malevolent third party hacks such data. Data protection is a key component of this architecture. Important parts of HIPAA and its regulations include data physical security, data encryption standards, and data documentation, transmission, and storage protocols. There are rules in place to protect the privacy of patients' medical records in this age of EHR, data transmission over the internet, and (more lately) cloud computing, and these rules are overseen by the HHS and the OCLR.

Businesses must follow HIPAA regulations to protect patients' private health information from disclosure to unapproved parties. Additional safeguards provided by HIPAA prohibit the disclosure or use of protected health information for purposes other than those for which it was initially collected. Companies that are required to follow HIPAA regulations are:

- Insurance providers for medical coverage
- Medical information hubs
- Medical facilities, doctors, dentists, and other dental and medical professionals
- Partners of covered entities (including billing and document storage services)
- Health food stores
- Nursing homes for the elderly
- Establishments engaged in research
- Authorities in public health
- Company owners
- Academic institutions

9.3.12.13 The HIPAA Privacy Rule

Regarding patients' right to privacy and secrecy, the HIPAA Privacy Rule establishes a nationwide norm. Furthermore, it sets the standard for electronic protected health information (ePHI), including its definition, required security measures, permitted and prohibited uses, transmission, and storage (HIPAA, 1999). The administrative procedures and exemptions that companies handling ePHI must follow are another aspect of the confidentiality requirement. Any personally identifiable information (PHI) that the covered entity or any affiliated company is required to keep secret is referred to as "ePHI" in this regulation. The following types of data are considered "protected health information":

- Any past, present, or future documentation of physical or mental conditions.
- Any information relating to the patient's care.
- And information referring to past, present, or future payments for healthcare.

According to the regulation, very few circumstances involving healthcare, research, or legal matters are permitted for covered entities to divulge private health information. In and of themselves, these scenarios are quite narrow and open to judicial interpretation.

The golden rule is that the responsibility for protecting the privacy of electronic protected health information (ePHI) lies with the covered company and its business associates.

9.3.12.14 HIPAA Privacy Rule Checklist

To ensure that healthcare organizations and their business associates comply with the HIPAA Privacy Rule, we have put together this checklist comprising 10 critical elements. Everything that has to be done to safeguard sensitive patient health information is included in this checklist, from choosing a Chief Privacy Officer to creating policies for sharing PHI with outside parties (Kafali et al., 2017). Organizations may save money and avoid legal trouble by following these rules, and patients will have more faith in the healthcare system. Among them are:

- Designating a privacy officer
- Developing and implementing written policies and procedures
- Providing training for staff
- Obtaining patient consent for certain disclosures
- Maintaining appropriate safeguards for protected health information (PHI)
- Implementing a system to review and verify PHI requests
- Responding to patient requests for access to PHI
- Informing patients in the event of a breach of unsecured PHI
- Assigning unique identifiers to individuals and groups
- Establishing protocols for disclosing PHI to business associates and other third parties

9.4 COMPARISON AND ANALYSIS

Here, we look at six different governance models, each focusing on a different set of IS characteristics. Prior evaluation is essential for the large-scale IT governance project to avoid implementation failure.

IT governance is a major worry for large and medium-sized businesses. Starting and finishing governance work takes a lot of effort, time, and money. The establishment of committed teams and the ongoing participation of stakeholders are prerequisites for successfully executing the governance project. Costs associated with training in-house staff, bringing in an outside consultant, and certifying the standard can quickly increase during implementation. Governance is not a silver bullet as each approach addresses a unique set of problems. The implementation expenditure makes the return on investment even less guaranteed.

Governance and the study of management information systems go hand in hand. This work examines the potential interplay between software architectures and transactions. Our concern may be addressed by the fact that governance deals with the concept of alignment. Table 9.9 compares several IT governance standards (COBIT, ISO 27001, NIST, HIPAA, HITRUST) using the four keywords mentioned in Section 9.2.

Table 9.9 Comparison of IT Governance Standards and Models across Four Words Framework

The Frame of the Four Words	*Facet*	*IT Governance Standards and Models*				
		COBIT	*ISO 27001*	*NIST*	*HIPAA*	*HITRUST*
Subject	Governance organization	*	*	—	—	*
	Decision	—	—	Infrastructure	—	Plan, project
	IT process	*	*	*	*	*
	Business process	—	*	*	—	*
	Change	*	—	Evolutive	*	*
	IT project portfolio	—	—	*	Class.: Multi-criteria Transform.: *	Clas.: Multi-criteria Transfo.: *
Usage	Minimize risks	*	*	—	—	*
	Reach alignment status	—	—	—	—	—
	Getting performance	*	—	—	—	—
	Create value	—	—	—	—	—
System	Content	*	*	*	*	*
	Model	*	*	*	*	*
	Metrics	*	*	*	*	*
Development	Nature of processes	*	*	*	*	*
	Process maturity	*	—	—	*	*
	Knowledge capitalization	*	*	*	*	*
	Software	*	*	*	*	*

Fully covered facet,—Uncovered facet

The following concepts—cost, supply, services, standardization, project management, and quality—and their roles in IT governance have been clarified by this overview of the main approaches. The operational aspects of IT transformation may be better managed and regulated with the help of good governance principles. Since both the IT governance function and the corporate architecture deal with IT, it is important to be knowledgeable about the former to avoid confusion between the two.

The primary goals of most IT governance frameworks are to provide insight into the general health of your IT department, the KPIs that are most important to management, and the ROI your IT expenditures are producing for your company.

Unlike COBIT, which is primarily applied to risk management, ITIL is useful for improving service and operations efficiency. The Capability Maturity Model Integration (CMMI) has expanded beyond its original software engineering focus to encompass hardware development, service delivery, and procurement processes. It has already been stated that FAIR's primary purpose is to evaluate cybersecurity and operational risks.

The goal of COBIT is IT management and compliance, even though it is one of the most prominent frameworks used by the publicly listed corporations of the United States to comply with the Sarbanes-Oxley Act. While improving healthcare system security is a significant side effect of COBIT, it is not the primary objective. If smaller healthcare organizations are looking to strengthen their system's security, this standard might not be the best fit.

Organizations of any size that care about the safety of their systems' data can use ISO/IEC 27002:2005. Organizations can utilize this standard to manage their information security program. A company can have its information security management system certified to meet the requirements of ISO/IEC 270001: 2005.

The CSF developed by HITRUST is not a brand-new standard but rather an amalgam of preexisting standards and practical industry knowledge. Only HITRUST members have access to the standard. Healthcare organizations who can do so financially can take advantage of HITRUST's healthcare information security education and certification programs.

When it comes to the administrative side of information security, healthcare organizations might utilize the standards above. On the other hand, ISO/TS 25237:2008 and ISO 17090:2008 deal with more narrowly focused technological concerns in healthcare IT. The International Organisation for Standardisation (ISO) has published two sets of guidelines: ISO 17090:2008 addresses the safe transfer of healthcare information using digital certificates and ISO/TS 25237:2008 addresses the pseudonymization of sensitive patient data.

Commonly used security standards or frameworks are covered in this document. Further standards in this area are available. One way to ensure all the bases are covered regarding risk is to use the standard ISO 31000:2009. To meet the specific needs of EHR communications, ISO/TS 13606–4:2009 offers a methodology that details the rights needed to access EHR data. To make an access decision, it also reflects and conveys information special to EHRs. There is a reference to "points at technical solutions and standards that specify details on services meeting these security needs" (ISO, 2013) that outline the general security requirements that apply to EHR communications. Also, ISO/TS 21547:2010 lays out the fundamentals for the safe storage of EHR for the long haul, regardless of their format. Remote maintenance services (RMS) for HIS are addressed in ISO/TR 11633–1:2009, which also guides how to conduct a risk analysis to ensure the security of the system and individual health records. Part 2 of the standard, ISO/TR 11633–2:2009, demonstrates how measures for RMS security can be chosen and implemented. ISO/PRF TS 14441 is currently being developed, a new standard pertaining to health informatics and the security and privacy requirements of systems for use in conformity assessment. As the name indicates, EHR security and privacy is its primary focus.

Successfully applying the security measures required requires a coordinated effort from upper management down to end users, regardless of the standard(s) used. The recommendations' applicability, relevance, and practicability to healthcare business and operational operations can only be guaranteed by extensive risk analysis. Before implementing any selected Standards, organizations should do "a 'gap analyses to identify the current security controls within the organisation, the potential problems and issues, the costs and benefits, the operational impact, and the proposed recommendations." After a gap analysis has been completed with the backing of management, implementation may proceed. Considerations such as the organization's risk acceptance criteria, available risk treatments, and overall risk management strategy should inform the selection of security measures. Ensuring the chosen decision complies with all applicable national and international laws and regulations is of utmost importance.

Programs for user awareness and training should also be implemented. This is done to ensure that before new security rules and procedures are implemented, all workers know the pros and cons. When this fails, users frequently complain after the installation. A balance of functional, security, and user demands demonstrates that the information security standard(s) have been successfully implemented.

Finally, successfully establishing security standards requires buy-in from employees at all company levels. Truthfully, everyone should be involved with security. Neither the IT department nor upper management should be considered exclusive responsibility for it. On the contrary, "senior management, information security practitioners, IT professionals and users all have a role to play in securing an organisation's assets." With everyone pitching in, we can make sure everyone is protected.

Managing and safeguarding health information against evolving cyber threats and regulatory requirements is paramount in the complex healthcare landscape. Different IT governance standards and models, such as COBIT, ISO 27001, NIST, HIPAA, and HITRUST, offer varying approaches to address the multifaceted challenges faced by healthcare organizations. While COBIT and ISO 27001 prioritize governance and risk management, HITRUST's focus on project management and planning aligns well with the dynamic nature of healthcare IT environments. Additionally, ISO 27001 and NIST emphasize risk minimization, which is crucial for ensuring robust data protection measures within healthcare systems. These standards and systematic processes, maturity models, and knowledge capitalization provide a comprehensive framework for healthcare organizations to enhance security and compliance. By involving stakeholders at all levels and conducting thorough risk assessments, healthcare organizations can effectively implement security measures that safeguard patient data, mitigate cybersecurity risks, and ensure compliance with regulatory requirements.

9.5 CONCLUSION

This chapter has offered a comprehensive framework for analyzing IT governance, considering four key perspectives: the subject, use, system, and development of ITG. This framework has elucidated various facets and their corresponding values, providing a nuanced understanding of IT governance. Applying this framework to five established IT governance standards revealed a notable observation: none of the existing approaches fully encompass all facets of the framework. Instead, these approaches focus on discrete collections of best practices, lacking a holistic vision of ITG. The emphasis often lies on regularly updated compilations of good practices rather than a unified and overarching perspective. This analysis underscores the need for further research into the holistic nature of ITG, aiming to develop a more integrated and comprehensive approach. The overriding goal of this chapter has been to provide healthcare IT professionals with a deep understanding of IT governance standards and frameworks, enabling them to navigate the intricate landscape of information security governance effectively. By embracing a multifaceted perspective and leveraging insights from diverse standards, healthcare organizations can fortify their resilience against cyber threats, safeguard patient data, and instill trust among stakeholders in an increasingly digital healthcare ecosystem.

REFERENCES

Amiruddin, A., Afiansyah, H. G., & Nugroho, H. A. (2021). Cyber-risk management planning using NIST CSF v1. 1, NIST Sp 800–53 rev. 5, and CIS controls v8. *2021 International Conference on Informatics, Multimedia, Cyber and Information System (ICIMCIS)*, 19–24.

Basson, G., Walker, A., McBride, T., & Oakley, R. (2012). ISO/IEC 15504 measurement applied to COBIT process maturity. *Benchmarking: An International Journal*, *19*(2), 159–176. https://doi.org/10.1108/14635771211224518

Benaroch, M., & Chernobai, A. (2017). Operational IT failures, IT value destruction, and board-level IT governance changes. *MIS Quarterly*, *41*(3), 729–762. https://doi.org/10.25300/MISQ/2017/41.3.04

Bodeau, D., & Graubart, R. (2013). Cyber resiliency and NIST special publication 800–53 rev. 4 controls. *MITRE*, Technical Report.

Brown, A. E., Grant, G. G., & Sprott, E. (2005). Framing the frameworks: A review of it governance research. *Communications of the Association for Information Systems*, *15*, 696–712. https://doi.org/Article

Brustbauer, J. (2016). Enterprise risk management in SMEs: Towards a structural model. *International Small Business Journal*, *34*(1), 70–85. https://doi.org/10.1177/0266242614542853

Cadete, G. R., & da Silva, M. M. (2017). *Assessing IT governance processes using a COBIT5 model BT—information systems* (M. Themistocleous & V. Morabito, Eds.; pp. 447–460). Springer International Publishing.

Dahlberg, T., & Kivijärvi, H. (2006). An integrated framework for IT governance and the development and validation of an assessment instrument. *39th Hawaii International Conference on System Sciences*, *00*(C), 1–10. https://doi.org/10.1109/HICSS.2006.57

Dahlberg, T., & Lahdelma, P. (2007). IT governance maturity and IT outsourcing degree: An exploratory study. *Proceedings of the Annual Hawaii International Conference on System Sciences*, 1–10. https://doi.org/10.1109/HICSS.2007.306

De Haes, S., Van Grembergen, W., & Debreceny, R. S. (2013). COBIT 5 and enterprise governance of information technology: Building blocks and research opportunities. *Journal of Information Systems*, *27*(1), 307–324. https://doi.org/10.2308/isys-50422

De Haes, S., Van Grembergen, W., Joshi, A., Huygh, T., De Haes, S., Van Grembergen, W., Joshi, A., & Huygh, T. (2020). COBIT as a framework for enterprise governance of IT. *Enterprise Governance of Information Technology: Achieving Alignment and Value in Digital Organizations*, 125–162.

De Haes, S., & Van Grembergen, W. (2009). An exploratory study into IT governance implementations and its impact on business/IT alignment. Information Systems Management, 26(2), 123-137.

Grant, G., Brown, A., Uruthirapathy, A., Mcknight, S., & Grant, G. G. (2007). Association for information systems AIS electronic library (AISeL) an extended model of IT governance: A conceptual proposal an extended model of IT governance: A conceptual proposal. *AMCIS 2007 Proceedings*, 215.

Groš, S. (2021). A critical view on CIS controls. *2021 16th International Conference on Telecommunications (ConTEL)*, 122–128.

HealthIT.gov. (2013). *Guide to privacy and security of health information. April*, 27–40.

HIPAA. (1999). *HIPAA health insurance portability and accountability act of 1999.* CRC Press. http://www.hhs.gov/ocr/privacy/hipaa/administrative/privacyrule.

Ihs.gov. (1996). IHS HIPAA security checklist. *HIPAA Security*, *308*(5), 308–311. http://www.ihs.gov/hipaa/documents/ihs_hipaa_security_checklist.pdf

ISACA. (2012). *COBIT 5: A business framework for the governance and management of enterprise IT*. Information Systems Audit and Control Association.

ISO, I., & Std, I. E. C. (2005). *Information technology-security techniques-code of practice for information security management*. ISO 27002: 2005.

ISO/IEC. (2013). ISO/IEC 27002:2013. Retrieved March 24, 2014 from http://www.iso.org/iso/home/storecatalogue_ics/catalogue_detail_ics.htm?csnumber=54533.

Kafali, O., Jones, J., Petruso, M., Williams, L., & Singh, M. P. (2017). How good is a security policy against real breaches? A HIPAA case study. *Proceedings—2017 IEEE/ACM 39th International Conference on Software Engineering, ICSE 2017*, 530–540. https://doi.org/10.1109/ICSE.2017.55

Malatji, M. (2023). Management of enterprise cyber security: A review of ISO/IEC 27001: 2022. *2023 International Conference on Cyber Management and Engineering (CyMaEn)*, 117–122.

Maleh, Y. (2021). Digital transformation and cybersecurity in the context of COVID-19 proliferation. *IEEE Technology Policy and Ethics*, *6*(5).

Maleh, Y., Sahid, A., Alazab, M., & Belaissaoui, M. (2021a). *IT governance and information security: Guides, standards, and frameworks*. CRC Press. https://doi.org/10.1201/9781003161998

Maleh, Y., Sahid, A., & Belaissaoui, M. (2019). *Strategic IT governance and performance frameworks in large organizations*. IGI Global. https://doi.org/10.4018/978-1-5225-7826-0

Marrone, M., Gacenga, F., Cater-Steel, A., & Kolbe, L. (2014). IT service management: A cross-national study of ITIL adoption. *Communications of the Association for Information Systems*, *34*(1), 865–892.

Marrone, M., & Kolbe, L. M. (2011). Uncovering ITIL claims: IT executives' perception on benefits and Business-IT alignment. *Information Systems and E-Business Management*, *9*(3), 363–380. https://doi.org/10.1007/s10257-010-0131-7

Murphy, K., Lyytinen, K., & Somers, T. (2018). A socio-technical model for project-based executive IT governance. *Proceedings of the 51st Hawaii International Conference on System Sciences | 2018 A*, *9*, 4825–4834.

Nabiollahi, A., & Sahibuddin, S. bin. (2008). Considering service strategy in ITIL V3 as a framework for IT Governance. *2008 International Symposium on Information Technology*, *1*, 1–6. https://doi.org/10.1109/ITSIM.2008.4631631

Nfuka, E. N., & Rusu, L. (2011). The effect of critical success factors on IT governance performance. *Industrial Management & Data Systems*, *111*(9), 1418–1448. https://doi.org/10.1108/02635571111182773

O'Brien, G., Edwards, S., Littlefield, K., McNab, N., Wang, S., & Zheng, K. (2018). Securing wireless infusion pumps. *NIST Special Publication 1800–8*, 8B.

Oliver, D., & Lainhart, J. (2012). COBIT 5: Adding value through effective geit. *EDPACS*, *46*(3), 1–12. https://doi.org/10.1080/07366981.2012.706472

Omari, L. Al, Barnes, P. H., & Pitman, G. (2012). An exploratory study into audit challenges in IT governance: A Delphi approach. *Symposium on IT Governance, Management and Audit*. https://eprints.qut.edu.au/53110/

O'Reilly, P., & Rigopoulos, K. (2020). *NIST/ITL cybersecurity program*. NIST Special Publication, 800, 206.

Pascoe, C. E. (2023). *Public draft: The NIST cybersecurity framework 2.0*.

Raghupathi, W. (2007). NIST. Corporate governance of IT: A framework for development. *Communications of the ACM*, *50*(8), 94–99. https://doi.org/10.1145/1278201.1278212

Ramírez-Mora, S. L., Oktaba, H., & Patlán Pérez, J. (2020). Group maturity, team efficiency, and team effectiveness in software development: A case study in a CMMI-DEV Level 5 organization. *Journal of Software: Evolution and Process*, *32*(4), e2232. https://doi.org/10.1002/smr.2232

Sahid, A., Maleh, Y., & Belaissaoui, M. (2018). A practical agile framework for IT service and asset management ITSM/ITAM through a case study. *Journal of Cases on Information Technology*, *20*(4), 71–92.

Sedgewick, A. (2014). *Framework for improving critical infrastructure cybersecurity, version 1.0*. CSWP, 4162018, 7.

Shekhar, G. (2020). Instructor led training and certification—ITIL V4 foundation. *Proceedings of the 21st Annual Conference on Information Technology Education*, 355. https://doi.org/10.1145/3368308.3415453

Simonsson, M., & Johnson, P. (2006). Defining IT governance-a consolidation of literature. *The 18th Conference on Advanced Information Systems Engineering*, 6.

Steuperaert, D. (2019). Cobit 2019: A significant update. *EDPACS*, *59*(1), 14–18. https://doi.org/10.1080/07366981.2019.1578474

Warland, C., & Ridley, G. (2005). Awareness of IT control frameworks in an Australian state government: A qualitative case study. *Proceedings of the 38th Annual Hawaii International Conference on System Sciences*, *00*(C), 236b–236b. https://doi.org/10.1109/HICSS.2005.116

Weill, P., & Ross, J. W. (2004). How top performers manage IT decisions rights for superior results. *IT Governance, Harvard Business School Press Boston, Massachusetts*, 1–10. https://doi.org/10.2139/ssrn.664612

Wood, D. J. (2010). *Assessing IT governance maturity: The case of San Marcos, Texas* (Master's thesis), Texas State University, San Marcos, TX.

Yassine, M., Abdelkebir, S., & Abdellah, E. (2017). A capability maturity framework for IT security governance in organizations. *In Innovations in Bio-Inspired Computing and Applications: Proceedings of the 8th International Conference on Innovations in Bio-Inspired Computing and Applications (IBICA 2017)* held in Marrakech, Morocco, December 11-13, 2017 (pp. 221-233). Springer International Publishing.

For Product Safety Concerns and Information please contact our EU representative GPSR@taylorandfrancis.com Taylor & Francis Verlag GmbH, Kaufingerstraße 24, 80331 München, Germany

Batch number: 10397790

Printed by Printforce, the Netherlands